The Psychology of
B.F. Skinner

D0147301

William O'Donohue

Kyle E. Ferguson

Sage Publications
International Educational and Professional Publisher
Thousand Oaks ▪ London ▪ New Delhi

For information:

Sage Publications, Inc.
2455 Teller Road
Thousand Oaks, California 91320
E-mail: order@sagepub.com

Sage Publications Ltd.
6 Bonhill Street
London EC2A 4PU
United Kingdom

Sage Publications India Pvt. Ltd.
M-32 Market
Greater Kailash I
New Delhi 110 048 India

Printed in the United States of America

Library of Congress Cataloging-in-Publication Data

O'Donohue, William T.
    The psychology of B.F. Skinner / by William T. O'Donohue and Kyle E. Ferguson.
        p.   cm.
    Includes bibliographical references and index.
    ISBN 0-7619-1758-6 (hardcover) — ISBN 0-7619-1759-4 (pbk.)
    1. Behaviorism (Psychology) 2. Skinner, B. F. (Burrhus Frederic), 1904-
    I. Title: Psychology of Burrhus Frederic Skinner.   II. Ferguson, Kyle E.
    III. Title.
    BF199 .O39 2001
    150.19′434′092—dc21   00-011616

01 02 03 10 9 8 7 6 5 4 3 2 1

Acquiring Editor:	Jim Brace-Thompson
Editorial Assistant:	Anna Howland
Production Editor:	Diana E. Axelsen
Editorial Assistant:	Cindy Bear
Copy Editor:	Linda Gray
Typesetter:	Doreen Barnes
Indexer:	Rachel Rice
Cover Designer:	Jane M. Quaney

Contents

❖

We would like to dedicate this book
with loving appreciation to our parents:
Marge O'Donohue
and
Ann and Ed Ferguson.

Foreword

❖

Six major publications about B. F. Skinner and his work have appeared since his death in 1990, surpassing the number in any previous decade. Why all of this increasing interest? Clearly Skinner has something to say to the 21st century.

Perhaps renewed interest in Skinner's work stems from the realization that the major problems facing mankind are all problems of behavior. Overpopulation is a behavioral problem. Procreation beyond replacement levels inevitably depletes the riches of the earth upon which all animal and plant life depends. Pollution is a behavioral problem. It produces health problems and death. Conflict and war are behavioral problems. They cause immense human suffering and destruction. Only by improving what people do can we provide a better life for our world now and in the future.

That is exactly where Skinner can help. For what he discovered, outlined in this book, was the basic mechanism by which the behavior of every creature on earth adjusts according to the cumulative effect of moment to moment interactions with its environment. Backed by decades of research on relationships called "contingencies," the science that Skinner began tells us where to look to understand behavior and what to do to improve it. Skinner challenged the idea that behavior is "free" in the sense of being without cause. Ironically, Skinner's recommendations promoted what most people think of as freedom; that is, he stressed positive over punitive methods of control in every facet of human interaction—in teaching, in therapy, in everyday relationships, and in the design of cultures.

Unfortunately, misconceptions about the man and his science have prevented many who could most benefit from learning Skinnerian science from taking it seriously. Many of my colleagues and students have told me how they dismissed Skinner altogether because of completely inaccurate statements made about him or his science. Just last week I received an e-mail saying, "I am looking for information on the experiment that B. F. Skinner did with his daughter. It's the one where he kept her in the house until she was 21. He used his house as a Skinner Box.

Any suggestions on where to find this information?" That such entirely false rumors still exist shows an extraordinary extent of ignorance about both Skinner and the science he began.

This book should help overcome both the lack of knowledge and some of the prejudices about Skinner. It summarizes Skinner's science and philosophy in simple language. With many everyday examples, it clears up some common misconceptions. For example, one often hears Skinner classified as a logical positivist, then dismissed when flaws in logical positivism are pointed out. But Skinner was not a logical positivist, as Chapter 4 shows. Often misunderstood is Skinner's position on covert actions. Chapter 6, "Skinner on Cognition" clarifies Skinner's acceptance of thinking as behavior subject to the same laws as overt behaviors others can observe. Skinner's analysis of the factors determining what we say, write, or think (our verbal behavior) was misrepresented by Noam Chomsky, a widely read linguist, at the end of the last century. Chomsky conflated Skinner's position with Watson's, then criticized Watson's Stimulus-Response (S-R) approach. But, as Chapter 11 shows, Skinner, from his earliest writings, stressed the futility of an S-R framework for explaining verbal behavior. Skinner's main contribution, begun while he was still a graduate student, was the discovery of how behavior changes through selection by *postcedents,* not antecedents. Watson's emphasis on a preceding event continued a tradition that Skinner's research showed to be faulty for most of our behavior. Another common misrepresentation of Skinner's ideas implies that he dealt only with simple, rote, or repetitive behaviors. The full discussion in Chapter 7 of his approach to "understanding" and his suggestions for variables to consider to produce "inspiration" for creative writing, presented at the end of Chapter 9, should dispel these notions.

Skinner's book *Verbal Behavior* is not an easy book to read. The difficulty lies in shifting attention away from what is said (the words) to controlling variables (why the person talks, writes, or gestures as he or she does). Skinner gives an example of how one word, "Fire," could be primarily a tact (if said because of the presence of a fire), an echoic (if said because of hearing "Fire,"), a mand (if said in order to get someone to pull a trigger on a gun), or a number of other types of verbal utterances, all depending on the controls over the speaker. In fact, Skinner would argue, all verbal behavior is multiply controlled; that is, many factors act together to determine what a person says, writes, or gestures at any particular moment. Chapter 7 helps clarify Skinner's overall framework of analysis of verbal behavior with definitions and well-chosen quotes from Skinner himself.

Many professionals differ on subtle points about Skinner's work, and he himself changed a few aspects of his analysis as the science evolved. Thus any book about Skinner necessarily interprets what he said. I do not agree with many of the interpretations made in the last three chapters. The list of "valid criticisms" in Chapter 11 even contradicts other parts of the book. It seems odd that, after a whole chapter on verbal behavior—which is, after all, the most complex human activity known—the authors propose "Valid criticism # 5: Skinner's experimental analysis of behavior has limited relevance to complex human behavior." It is an especially odd criticism given the increasing number of direct applications of Skinner's work in regular and special education classrooms, in business and industry, and in the home. Of course, no science stays static. Skinner expected his science to evolve like any other cultural practice, so he would not have minded criticisms that are data based. But none of these sections presents any evidence against selection by consequences as the main process through which behavior changes over the lifetime of all animals, including human beings. Nor do any of the criticisms invalidate Skinner's insistence that appeal to inner agencies such as "mind" diverts inquiry away from actual causes of behavior.

In spite of the shortcomings in the later chapters, this book provides a needed introduction to the full range of topics addressed by Skinner. The authors have read widely from and about Skinner, as the diversity of sources shows. The wealth of short quotations from Skinner himself provides a flavor of Skinner's style as well as giving ample examples of what he himself said. Even where the book differs from my understanding of what Skinner said, it should stimulate discussion in classes, and it will therefore contribute to a better understanding of the issues involved in the explanation of behavior.

Julie S. Vargas
West Virginia University

Preface

❖

We have written this book partly to express our appreciation for a psychologist whose work we admire. We admire B. F. Skinner's work for a variety of reasons: We believe it hangs together logically; it is simple and elegant; it is consistent with important work in other sciences (e.g., evolutionary biology); it is experimental and data oriented; it has been successful in uncovering powerful regularities; and, most important, its applications have helped relieve suffering. We have seen this in many ways, but one of the most profound experiences we have had is to witness the remarkable changes in the lives of children with autism (a condition associated with severe developmental delays and communication problems) or mental retardation. We have seen many instances of these children going from near "vegetables" in institutions to living independent and happy lives in their own homes. Most important, we have seen these "miracles" conducted in rigorously controlled environments so that the cause of their changes can be validly attributed to the behavior therapy that they received.

Bertrand Russell, the eminent 20th-century philosopher, said,

> Three passions, simple but overwhelmingly strong, have governed my life: the longing for love, the search for knowledge, and unbearable pity for the suffering of mankind. These passions, like great winds, have blown me hither and thither, in a wayward course, over a deep ocean of anguish, reaching to the very verge of despair.
>
> I have sought love, first, because it brings ecstasy—so great that I would often have sacrificed all the rest of life for a few hours of this joy. I have sought it, next, because it relieves loneliness—that terrible loneliness in which one shivering consciousness looks over the rim of the world into the cold unfathomable lifeless abyss. I have sought it, finally, because in the union of love I have seen, in a mystic miniature, the prefiguring vision of the heaven that saints and poets have imagined. This is what I sought, and though it might seem too good for human life, this is what—at last—I have found.

With equal passion I have sought knowledge. I have wished to understand the hearts of men. I have wished to know why the stars shine. And I have tried to apprehend the Pythagorean power by which number holds sway above the flux. A little of this, but not much, I have achieved.

Love and knowledge, so far as they were possible, led upward toward the heavens. But always pity brought me back to earth. Echoes of cries of pain reverberate in my heart. Children in famine, victims tortured by oppressors, helpless old people a hated burden to their sons, and the whole world of loneliness, poverty, and pain make a mockery of what human life should be. I long to alleviate the evil, but I cannot, and I too suffer.

This has been my life. I have found it worth living, and would gladly live it again if the chance were offered me. (Russell, 1951, pp. 3-4)

We think that Skinner's psychology exemplifies the spirit contained in this inspiring quote.

We do not mean to imply that other psychologists' work is not valuable. There are many other psychologists who also deserve to have their work summarized and explored in the way that we do in this book with Skinner's. We may even do this someday. However, our purpose in writing this was to more thoroughly explore the work of one psychologist.

Science is inevitably competitive, and we do believe that in many ways Skinner's work does stand above that of his competitors. We know that this is a controversial claim, and we ask the reader to reserve judgment on this issue until the end of the book. Prejudice (literally "pre-judgment") is a bad thing. There are prejudices regarding intellectual matters as well as prejudices regarding races and religions. We believe that there has been a lot of prejudice against B. F. Skinner. Like most prejudices, these are based on misinformation and overly quick and superficial judgments. We hope that upon concluding this book, the reader will see the value of Skinner's work. We do not worship at the altar of Skinner's psychology. We don't believe that he was some sort of god who was infallible. At times, some of Skinner's followers have been dogmatic and have taken Skinner as some sort of demigod. People are flawed, and interesting studies need to be done on the variety of factors that motivate people to become scientists—some of these might not be the "coldly rational" reasons often given but might instead reflect more prosaic factors, such as the need to feel "right" or " part of a group" or other reasons. But let's not go too far with this sort of speculation.

We believe that Skinner developed an experimental paradigm that has revealed a lot of order. This is a goal of science. His system, as we will argue in this book, allows more accurate prediction and control than other systems do. It may not be as "sexy" at times as other systems. Skinner might not talk about how our dreams reflect our sexual and aggressive motives, for example. But his relatively "banal" system works, and when parents come to you suffering because of the developmental delays of their autistic child, or when an eight-year-old is embarrassed and cannot go to camp because of his bedwetting, you want something that works, not something that is sexy.

A few words about our title. *The Psychology of B. F. Skinner* will be a strange title to some insiders, because they will make the following claims: (a) First, *psyche* has something to do with spirit or mind, and Skinner would reject these entities and therefore would certainly not support an "ology" (study) of them. (b) Skinner himself rarely used this word for his system, preferring instead words and phrases such as *the science of human behavior, behavior analysis*, and *the experimental analysis of behavior.* We do not disagree with either of these points. However, Skinner did concern himself with much of the same phenomena that many psychologists address—the behavior of organisms. Although these psychologists sometimes use different explanatory mechanisms to understand behavior and at times have questions that, from Skinner's point of view, are problematically posed (How does self-esteem cause neurosis?), ultimately all are concerned with questions that are basic to psychology: How do we understand, describe, explain, and predict behavior?

There are many people we would like to thank for their help with this book. Particularly, we'd like to thank Julie Vargas, Sid Bijou, and Ernie Vargas for their critical comments on earlier drafts. Their comments have vastly improved the manuscript, although weaknesses are still the fault of our less-than-optimal learning histories. We'd also like to thank Claudia Avina and Michele Pasquale for their editorial assistance. To our copy editor, Rachel Hile Bassett, we are indebted for many useful suggestions as to how the text could be improved, and we are grateful for the great care and attention she brought to her immense task. We have made use of a paper by the senior author, "Skinner on Cognition," which appeared in the *Journal of Behavioral Education,* Vol. 6, 1996, and are grateful for permission to do so. Finally, we'd like to thank our families—Jane, Katie, Anna, and Robin—for their support and encouragement.

Reference

Russell, B. (1951). *The autobiography of Bertrand Russell.* Boston: Little, Brown.

CHAPTER 1

Introduction

❖

O ne of the most influential psychologists of the 20th century was B. F. Skinner. One gauge of Skinner's influence is the number of times his work is mentioned in the writings of other psychologists. For the past several decades, he has been one of the 10 most frequently cited figures in psychology—at times competing with Freud for the title. It appears that many of his fellow psychologists were either relying on or reacting to his writings. A measure that suggests that Skinner had some impact on the popular culture is a survey of the general public conducted in 1975 (Guttman, 1977). The results of this survey indicated that Skinner was the best-known scientist in the United States.

Another index of a psychologist's value and influence is the number of awards won. B. F. Skinner was awarded honorary degrees from Hamilton College (his alma mater), McGill University, University of Chicago, University of Exeter (England), Western Michigan University, Tufts University, and Ohio Wesleyan University. He won the Distinguished Scientific Contribution Award of the American Psychological Association in 1958; the National Medal of Science in 1968, which was presented to him by President Johnson; the International Award of the Joseph P. Kennedy, Jr., Foundation for Mental Retardation in 1971; the Humanist of the Year Award of the American Humanist Society in 1972; the Gold Medal Award of the American Psychological Foundation; the Award for Distinguished Contributions to Educational Research and Development of the American Educational Research Association in 1978; the first Distinguished Scientist Award by the National Association of Retarded Citizens; and the first American Psychological Association citation for

1

Outstanding Lifetime Contributions to Psychology, given to him just eight days before his death. Skinner was clearly an influential and distinguished researcher, scholar, and humanitarian.

Psychologists are often interested in the practical problems of everyday life. For example, psychologists are interested in how to assist people who are experiencing a psychological problem (clinical psychology), and they are also interested in how to help teachers teach better (educational psychology). Skinner's work has been influential in the development of effective strategies for a number of applied problems. For example, in a recent and influential report, a theoretically eclectic committee organized by the American Psychological Association identified for which interventions there was good evidence that they "worked." Of the 27 techniques, over 20 behavior therapy techniques were listed as "empirically validated" (Task Force on Promotion and Dissemination of Psychological Procedures, 1995). Many of these therapies are heavily influenced by Skinner's work. As a case in point, the application of Skinner's work to the behavioral deficits of children and adults with mental retardation has resulted in such a significant increase in skills for these individuals that many who were once institutionalized are now living independently. Certainly, other psychologists, such as Freud, have also been influential in developing therapy techniques. However, the difference between Freud and Skinner is that the work of Skinner and his students has resulted in interventions that have been clearly shown to actually help people regarding a significant number of their problems. Freud's work, unfortunately, has not. Skinner's influence in developing and implementing effective therapies will clearly extend into the 21st century, whereas Freud's influence has been steadily declining, and there is little reason to believe that this trend will end. We will discuss how Skinner's work has been helpful in improving practical problems in Chapter 8.

Skinner is an interesting psychologist to study because, although his work was quite conceptually focused, he did important work on a number of topics. He is best known for his work in human and animal learning. He coined the term *operant conditioning* and discovered many important principles of operant learning. In brief, operant conditioning occurs when the frequency of behavior changes based on the behavior's consequences. In this sense, Skinner is a colleague of other great learning researchers such as Pavlov, Thorndike, Hull, Guthrie, Tolman, and Mowrer. However, again, it can be argued that he was a more successful researcher than many of these in that his conditioning research was more fruitful—he discovered more principles. We will discuss operant conditioning and the experimental analysis of behavior in Chapter 5.

Skinner was an important philosopher of psychology. Every scientist, particularly in a field in which there has not been much progress, needs to develop general principles for understanding how to study the field and how to define and approach problems in the field. Skinner developed what he termed *radical behaviorism,* which was his philosophy for studying psychological matters. We will discuss radical behaviorism in Chapter 4. Pragmatically, one can argue that Skinner's philosophy of science has been vindicated by the success of this science. Whatever one's ultimate evaluation of the quality of Skinner's science, we will argue that Skinner has presented a coherent, interesting, and reasonable philosophy of psychology.

Generally, philosophies of science say something about research methodologies. That is, they propose an answer to the question "How do we best go about producing new information about the problems in which we are interested?" Skinner was an innovative research methodologist. He suggested something that was fairly unorthodox—that psychology would not make optimal progress by studying the average behavior of groups of subjects, but rather that the best progress would be made by experimentally analyzing the behavior of *single* organisms. Moreover, he strongly argued for using the rate of behavior as the dependent variable. That is, he was interested in discovering the conditions under which the frequency of some response either increases or decreases. Thus, in Skinner's work, one will seldom see him presenting group averages; rather, he presents recordings of the frequency of behavior of one organism at a time. We will discuss Skinner's methodological innovations more in Chapters 4 and 5.

Moreover, it is clear that Skinner, at the minimum, was an important historical figure in psychology. He had an enormous influence in many branches of psychology for a good portion of the 20th century. Certain disciplines have a tradition of studying their important historical figures in great detail. For example, philosophers study important philosophers of the past such as Plato, Aristotle, Descartes, and Kant. The reasoning is not necessarily that the scholar agrees with everything or even with most of what the historical figure has said. Rather, the rationale is that the historical figure has had a large influence upon the discipline, at least at one point in time, and that it is therefore worthy to try to accurately understand what the figure has said. Another part of the rationale is that even if there are mistakes, there are in all likelihood some "gems" in the work as well. Thus, even if you view Skinner's work as wrongheaded, we would still suggest that this book is worth reading, because it is important to understand as accurately as possible what this important historical figure said.

One argument that we will pursue in this book is that to really understand and evaluate the work of B. F. Skinner, one needs to understand the interrelationships between his philosophy of science—called *radical behaviorism*—his arguments and practices regarding research methodologies and the regularities that have been discovered when using these methodologies—called *operant conditioning* or, alternatively, *the experimental analysis of behavior*—and his practical extensions of this philosophy, research methodology, and principles to applied problems—called *applied behavior analysis*. These form a web of relationships that show important continuities. Moreover, these interrelationships also function to allow the worth of each to feed back and support the merit of the others. This book will contain chapters on each of these facets of Skinner's work and will discuss their interrelationships and networks of mutual support. In this regard, this book is different from some other books on Skinner's work—that is, this book attempts to elucidate each of the major parts of Skinner's work in the context of seeing it as a coherent, interdependent whole.

Thus, if one is interested in (a) the history of psychology, (b) the future of psychology, (c) effective interventions for various practical problems, (d) animal and human learning, (e) research methodology, or (f) the philosophy of psychology, one should have knowledge of the life and work of B. F. Skinner.

The reader might be wondering why we have been so positive about the work of B. F. Skinner. Our bet is that many of you have heard that Skinner's philosophy of science has been shown to be false, that his research has been shown to be wrong or has been superseded by more recent research, and that the practical extrapolations from this work are ineffective or cruel. Our contention is that these claims, as well as other similar allegations, are all false. However, in the end, we want you to judge this issue for yourself. You may ultimately come to the conclusion that Skinner and his students were wrong about a number of matters. That's fine with us. All we ask is that you accurately understand what Skinner said. If he said something, portray this accurately. If he didn't say something, don't say that he did. If scholars in the past had followed these two simple rules, a large number of paper-producing trees could have been saved.

Our task in this book is to fairly and accurately present the work of B. F. Skinner, so that, ultimately, you can judge its strengths and weaknesses. However, let us reveal our judgment at the outset: We think that Skinner's work has often been unfairly criticized and that it has much more quality than is often attributed to it. Most of Skinner's critics have not accurately understood his work. They have instead criticized a caricature—a straw man. This violates one of the major principles of fair scholarly criticism. It is a waste of time as well as misleading to criticize someone for saying x, when in fact that person never said x. This is, unfortunately, an all-too-common experience in argumentation. How many times have you yourself said in some argument, "That's not what I said!" or "That's not what I meant!"? You feel that the person has treated you unfairly by mischaracterizing what you really did say, or you feel that the argument is off track and a waste of time because your opponent is focusing on something irrelevant—something that you did not say or mean. Far too many of the negative judgments about Skinner are based on things Skinner never said. An important principle of scholarship that should be applied to anyone, including Skinner, is that one should make sure to first accurately understand what the scholar has said before beginning to criticize the scholar's work.

Here's just one concrete example of this problem: J. L. Gould (1982) criticized Skinner's behaviorism because of what he saw as a "fatal mistake" made by Skinner. Gould alleged,

> It is now widely accepted that behaviorism is on the decline, its loss of vigor the result of its inability to come to grips even with the existence of innate behaviors, much less with their mechanisms and evolutionary origins. (p. 8)

This is a fairly typical example of the kind of criticism that is leveled at Skinner, claims that Skinner's behaviorism is dead or dying because something that Skinner asserted is actually wrong.

Now, it is important that you realize that the truth of Gould's (1982) claim depends on two factors: (a) Did Skinner actually have "problems coming to grips with innate behaviors" and their evolutionary origins? That is, did Skinner claim that innate behavior does not exist? (b) If Skinner actually did say these things (i.e., that there are no innate behaviors, that evolution has not played a role in species differences in behavior), are these claims, in fact, wrong? That is, are there innate behaviors that have evolutionary origins?

In this particular example, the second issue is not a problem, although we will not have space to review the relevant research. However, suffice it to say that we agree with Gould (1982) that research has shown that there are innate behaviors that have evolutionary origins. Now what is at issue is the first claim; that is, did Skinner fail to see that there are innate behaviors that have evolutionary origins? We will deal with this general topic in more detail in Chapter 4. However, consider two quotes: first, Skinner (1974) stated, "The human species, like all other species, is the product of natural selection" (p. 33). Second, Skinner (1974) also wrote,

> A person is first of all an organism, a member of a species and a subspecies, possessing a genetic endowment of anatomical and physiological characteristics, which are the product of the contingencies of survival to which the species has been exposed in the process of evolution. The organism becomes a person as it acquires a repertoire of behavior under the contingencies of reinforcement to which it is exposed during its lifetime. The behavior it exhibits at any moment is under the control of a current setting. It is able to acquire such a repertoire under such control because of the processes of conditioning which are part of its genetic endowment. (p. 207)

And regarding whether he realized that there are innate behaviors, Skinner stated, "No reputable student of animal behavior has ever taken the position that the animal comes to the laboratory as a virtual tabula rasa, that species differences are insignificant, and that all responses are about equally conditionable to all stimuli" (Skinner, 1966, p. 1205).

What should be quite evident is that Gould's (1982) criticism is simply off the mark. Skinner clearly did believe (as we shall discuss in more detail later) that evolution has played (and continues to play) a large role in forming human behavior and that there are clearly innate behavioral differences between species. Because Gould does not read Skinner accurately, his criticisms are misdirected and therefore wrong. However, the problem is that those who are not sufficiently well acquainted with what Skinner actually said may believe the aspersions of critics like Gould and come to wrong conclusions about what Skinner actually claimed and the value of these claims.

Remember, there can be two problems with saying that someone is wrong because this person said x. In this example, the problem was that the person did not actually say x. However, the other problem with such a criticism can be that the person did say x and that x is actually correct. In other examples, we will see that critics have criticized Skinner for saying something, when it is quite reasonable to have said it.

This is not an isolated example. Todd and Morris (1992) have done a nice job of identifying many misreadings of Skinner that have occurred in psychology textbooks and the popular media. Later in this book, in Chapter 11, we will have occasion to examine an example of this in some detail—Chomsky's (1959) famous (or infamous) critique of Skinner's (1957) book *Verbal Behavior*.

Scholars call the production of an accurate, full reading of someone's writing *exegesis*. This book is an attempt to provide an exegesis of the major work of Skinner. Because of space limitations, we cannot deal with all his work, and we cannot go into a lot of detail about all aspects of his work. However, our goal is that after reading this book you will have an accurate understanding of the major work of Skinner and some of his students. We will use a lot of direct quotations from Skinner so you can see that he actually said the things that we will attribute to him. But beware, we can still take quotations out of context. However, this is a good general rule about how to react to secondary sources: Be cautious when someone says another individual has asserted some claim. If you don't see a quote, the commentator is asking you to take his or her word that this is what the person actually said. If you do see a quote, still be cautious that it may be taken out of context.

The reader may also wonder to what extent we will be "objective" about the work of Skinner. To what extent is this book a fair, balanced presentation of Skinner's work? Or, alternately, to what extent is this a biased presentation influenced by the authors' prejudices and lack of appreciation of legitimate criticisms of Skinner? These are reasonable concerns. To answer these, we need to clarify one important misconception about objectivity. Objectivity does not mean that the writer must describe an equal number of assets and deficits about his or her subject matter. That is, if we were writing about Hitler and Nazism and desired to be objective, we would not need to write equally about positive and negative aspects of this subject matter. If it is actually the case that there are only negative aspects about this subject matter, or that the positive aspects are inconsequential, our treatment of him could still be objective, although entirely negative. The opposite situation might apply if we were writing about the work of Mother Teresa. Thus, one cannot judge the objectivity of a piece of writing by its general evaluation or tone. Our evaluation of Skinner's work is largely quite positive, because we believe that the quality of his work, properly understood, merits this evaluation. Throughout this book, we will try to explicate our reasons for this positive evaluation by discussing its assets and by considering possible objections. Thus, we believe that our positive evaluation is not based on irrational, antecedent biases but instead comes only after a rather dispassionate analysis.

Accuracy and completeness have much to do with what people mean by *objectivity*. As we see it, our task is to accurately depict what Skinner said and to accurately point out his work's strengths and weaknesses. Again, ultimately, you will need to be the judge of how well we have accomplished these tasks.

We also want to clear up another important misconception at the outset. Some people have claimed that operant psychology, behavior modification, and radical behaviorism are dead, mostly because of the criticisms that have been leveled against them. We fear that you might be preparing yourself to read about topics that you view as holding no relevance for the present or future. However, these are clearly not dead. Although their death would make Skinner's detractors happy, it would leave stranded many thousands of retarded children and adults, autistic children and their families, hyperactive children, schizophrenic inpatients, and many other individuals in need of assistance. The lives of these individuals, among others, are improved daily because of the vitality of operant psychology, behavior modification, and radical behaviorism. For, as we shall see in Chapter 8, therapies based on Skinner's research have helped many individuals in many ways.

Calling something "dead" is an interesting and sometimes effective rhetorical move in scholarly debate. However, to paraphrase Mark Twain, the rumors of the death of Skinner's work are greatly exaggerated. For evidence, consider that a scholarly association of people working in Skinner's tradition (the Association for Behavior Analysis) currently has 4,600 members in 34 affiliate organizations, half in the United States and half in other countries worldwide. Furthermore, consider that there are approximately two dozen scholarly journals that publish either basic operant research (e.g., *Journal of the Experimental Analysis of Behavior*), clinically relevant research based on Skinner's work (e.g., *Journal of Applied Behavior Analysis*), or conceptual papers relating to radical behaviorism (e.g., *Behavior Analyst* and *Behavior and Philosophy*) that continue to be well read and well cited and, most importantly, that continue to publish new findings. Wyatt, Hawkins, and Davis (1986) found that these journals publish over 500 articles annually and have over 20,000 subscribers. These represent but a few examples, because there are other organizations and other ways that Skinner's work is continuing to have an influence. Thus, the legacy of B. F. Skinner is currently alive and well and will be discussed in the final chapter. However, the concern is that these rumors and false attributions may be hurting its future. Why should students entering the field of psychology who have heard so much about the death of Skinner's work spend time with a corpse?

We will argue in this book that there is something quite interesting but also problematic about how a large portion of psychologists currently view the work and legacy of B. F. Skinner. Our claim is that the numerous misrepresentations and misunderstandings of Skinner's claims have taken a large toll on most psychologists' evaluations of the worth of this work. However, because these critiques are themselves quite problematic, the current fairly negative evaluation of Skinner's work by the field is also problematic.

In the history of science, some approaches are legitimately criticized and supplanted by superior approaches. A clear example is the replacement of Newtonian physics by Einsteinian physics or the replacement of Lamarckian evolutionary theory by Darwinian. Philosophers of science say that a new theory or paradigm should replace an old one when the old one cannot explain some critical findings and the new one can explain all of what the old one can explain and some of the anomalies. Is this what happened in the "cognitive revolution" in psychology in the 1960s?

Our claim is that in the so-called cognitive revolution, we do not have a similar situation to the Einsteinian revolution. We do not have the superseding of a theory that is "drowning in a sea of anomalies" by one that can better explain the phenomena under study. Our claim, which will be explained more fully in Chapters 11 and 12, is that the popularity and fate of Skinner's work were influenced more by poor exegesis than by accurate criticism and replacement by a theory that could better account for the same phenomena. This should be quite interesting to historians of psychology: Psychology in this instance changed more by misrepresentation than by substantive reasons. In attempting to provide an accurate exegesis of Skinner's work in this book, we will attempt to show that, although it is not without flaws, it is still a viable and even one of the strongest approaches to the study of human behavior.

This is not to say that Skinner's assertions are not controversial. Many of them clearly are, because a significant portion of what he claimed directly contradicts many prevailing beliefs. We all come to psychology with our prejudices—what some call "folk psychology" (O'Donohue, Callaghan, & Ruckstuhl, 1998). That is, when we approach certain academic subjects, we entertain few or no preconceptions regarding what the answers should look like. When we learned calculus, for example, we had no preconceptions about how one would go about figuring out the area under a curve. When we took our first chemistry course, we had few preconceptions about what kinds of chemical bonds there are or how many elements there are. However, when we approach psychology, we generally have a number of preconceived ideas. For example, we often believe that it is what we think that determines our behavior (How many of us as children have heard about the little train that said, "I think I can, I think I can"?). Many of us also believe that we have free will—that we are free to make our choices to do almost anything we want. Moreover, Nye (1979) has suggested that Skinner is also controversial because:

1. Skinner's radical determinism contradicts the American ideal of self-determination. It opposes concepts of free choice, personal responsibility, and rugged individualism. Also, it follows that if our behavior is fully determined by past and present conditions, we can't "take credit for" our accomplishments.

2. He emphasizes that by controlling the environment we can control behavior and advocates that we should do this to improve our society and our lives. This disturbs those who don't like the connotations of the word "control" or the implications of "being controlled."

3. He originally based his suggestions for improving human behavior on findings from research with lower animals. There are critics who feel that such findings are not relevant to human activities and/or that it is insulting to apply them to humans.

4. His behavioral concepts have often been interpreted simplistically. This has resulted in criticism from those who feel that he either ignores or negates the richness of human life. (p. 66)

Thus, when we hear Skinner denying these and other chestnuts, it is understandable that at first his positions strike us as strange. However, it is important to realize that science often causes us to change our original beliefs (otherwise, if we knew everything before doing science, we really wouldn't need to do science). For example, the physicist tells us that the table is actually mostly empty space, the astronomer tells us that we are on a planet that is spinning and moving rapidly, and the physiologist tells us that there are millions of electrical firings occurring in our bodies at any instant. Thus, although you may well feel that some things you read initially sound strange, give them a chance. No one has said that a good science of psychology needs to be consistent with what you learned at your mother's knee. Other sciences have contradicted these things. After all, if what we learned at our mother's knee was complete and accurate, we wouldn't be left with unanswered questions or puzzling situations!

We also want to caution against the view that this book presents a restricted view of a specialized, narrow subject. Skinner's work is directly involved with many exciting streams of learning. In this book, the student will learn something about logic, argumentation and critical thinking, philosophy of science, research methodology, conditioning principles, Darwinian evolution, behavior therapy, political philosophy, the history of psychology, cognitive psychology, and the work of Francis Bacon and Ernst Mach.

Finally, we would like to warn the reader of two problems. First, Skinner wrote over a period of more than 50 years. Although he was remarkably consistent in some matters, over this span of time, his views did evolve. Something we will say about Skinner may not be true of his earliest writings. From a historical point of view, accurately capturing Skinner is somewhat like trying to hit a moving target. We will concentrate on Skinner's most recent views, those from 1960 onwards. Thus, this book is not written for the historian who is primarily interested in the early writings of Skinner. Second, Skinner trained a number of students, who, in turn, trained a number of students. Skinner also convinced a number of people without face-to-face training. Thus, there are a number of Skinnerians and neo-Skinnerians. Most of these individuals agree with a lot of what Skinner said but disagree on some points. Thus, what we say should not be taken to be true about all Skinnerians. There is a "family resemblance" (to use Wittgenstein's, 1953, felicitous phrase) among these points of view, but there are a number of important divergences. There are prominent scholars, such as Murray Sidman, Sidney Bijou, Richard Herrnstein, Howard Rachlin, John Staddon, William Timberlake, and Steven Hayes, who to greater or lesser degrees agree with a lot of what Skinner had to say but who also disagree with him on a number of key issues. The first author has coedited a book titled *Handbook of Behaviorism* (O'Donohue & Kitchener, 1998) and edited a book, *Learning and Behavior Therapy* (O'Donohue, 1998), in which these scholars discuss their philosophical and empirical agreements and disagreements more fully.

Some students who read an earlier draft of this book suggested that it might be useful to provide some information about us. We think this suggestion was meant in the spirit that this would allow readers to better understand our perspective.

FIRST AUTHOR: WILLIAM T. O'DONOHUE

I am a clinical psychologist trained in a behavioral program (State University of New York at Stony Brook). One of my mentors was a well-known behaviorist (Len Krasner) and the other a well-known cognitive behavior therapist (Jim Geer). I "grew up" intellectually respecting the point of view of each, although arguing more with Jim Geer. After I received a doctorate in clinical psychology, I decided I wanted to know more about philosophy and the philosophy of science, so I studied these for four years at the graduate level at Indiana University. My mentor there, Noretta Koertge, was a Popperian. Popperians typically think that Skinner was generally wrong (see, e.g., Popper, 1963). I received a master's degree in philosophy from Indiana University. One of the important things

I learned during my years studying philosophy is that, counter to the rumors that contemporary philosophy has shown that behaviorism is false, behavioral philosophy is quite alive, and I learned that one of the most prominent analytic philosophers of the 20th century, Wilford Van Orman Quine, regarded himself as a behaviorist (see Gibson, 1996).

As I write this book, I am currently a professor in a doctoral clinical program that is behavioral, although I believe that I am seen as one of the more "cognitive" members of the program. I think that it is also important to point out that I met Skinner and spent a day with him in 1980 and found him to be a generous, charming gentleman. Thus, I have had some, although limited, direct experience with the man.

SECOND AUTHOR: KYLE E. FERGUSON

I am a graduate student in behavioral psychology at the doctoral level (University of Nevada, Reno). My first exposure to Skinner's work was through the teachings of David Pierce and the late Frank Epling while completing a bachelor's degree in psychology (University of Alberta). They introduced me to a philosophical orientation called radical behaviorism (see Chapter 4).

I worked several years in a brain injury hospital before returning to the academy. There I was provided with ample opportunities to employ Skinnerian principles to improve the lives of survivors of acquired brain injury. From work at the hospital I moved to Carbondale, Illinois, to obtain a master's degree in behavior analysis (Southern Illinois University). There I took classes from Brandon Greene, Tony Cuvo, and Roger Poppen. Brandon taught me that clients' problem behaviors were often a symptom of poor staff training. Tony taught me about the rigors of science. And Roger, my mentor, helped me appreciate the complexities of human behavior. As far as applied work is concerned, I worked as an intern under the auspices of Roger in his behavioral medicine lab. Since then, I have worked primarily with Linda Hayes at the University of Nevada, Reno. She has taught me much about the philosophy of science and about Skinner's analysis of verbal behavior in particular. In light of the above list, readers familiar with their work will see their "legacy" in mine.

References

Chomsky, N. (1959). Review of B. F. Skinner's *Verbal behavior. Language, 35,* 26-58.

Gibson, R. (1996). Quine's behaviorism. In W. O'Donohue & R. Kitchener (Eds.), *The philosophy of psychology* (pp. 96-107). London: Sage.

Gould, J. L. (1982). Why do honey bees have dialects? *Behavioral Ecology and Sociobiology, 10,* 6-15.

Guttman, N. (1977). On Skinner and Hull: A reminiscence and projection. *American Psychologist, 32,* 321-328.

Nye, R. (1979). *What is B. F. Skinner really saying?* New York: Prentice Hall.

O'Donohue, W. T. (Ed.). (1998). *Learning and behavior therapy.* Boston: Allyn & Bacon.

O'Donohue, W. T., Callaghan, G. M., & Ruckstuhl, L. E. (1998). Epistemological barriers to radical behaviorism. *Behavior Analyst, 21,* 307-320.

O'Donohue, W. T., & Kitchener, R. (Eds.). (1998). *Handbook of behaviorism.* San Diego, CA: Academic Press.

Popper, K. R. (1963). *Conjectures and refutations: The growth of scientific knowledge.* New York: Harper & Row.

Skinner, B. F. (1957). *Verbal behavior.* New York: Appleton-Century-Crofts.

Skinner, B. F. (1966). The phylogeny and ontogeny of behavior. *Science, 153,* 1205-1213.

Skinner, B. F. (1974). *About behaviorism.* New York: Knopf.

Task Force on Promotion and Dissemination of Psychological Procedures. (1995). Training in and dissemination of empirically-validated psychological treatments: Report and recommendations. *Clinical Psychologist, 48,* 3-23.

Todd, J. T., & Morris, E. K. (1992). Case histories in the great power of steady misrepresentations. *American Psychologist, 47,* 1441-1453.

Wittgenstein, L. (1953). *Philosophical investigations.* New York: Macmillan.

Wyatt, W. J., Hawkins, R. P., & Davis, P. (1986). Behaviorism: Are reports of its death exaggerated? *Behavior Analyst, 9,* 101-105.

CHAPTER 2

B. F. Skinner—The Man

❖

In this chapter we will provide a brief biographical sketch of B. F. Skinner. We will do this for two major reasons: (a) Most of us are curious about the personal lives of the great scholars whose works we read. We want to understand something of the person behind the ideas. We can be interested in the question of whether there is something in their personal lives that explains why they held certain views. What follows will give the reader a general idea of the life of Fred Skinner. (b) Unfortunately, not only have Skinner's writings been attacked through misinterpretations, but also he himself has been personally attacked. There have been numerous false reports that he hurt his children, that his children have been committed to mental institutions, and other such nonsense. The record needs to be clear on these issues. Some have even argued that these alleged biographical facts somehow invalidate Skinner's assertions.

However, we wish to point out an important logical point. That is, even if Skinner had engaged in these actions (and he did not!) or in other problematic behaviors, this would not reflect one bit on the truth or falsity of his arguments or assertions. Trying to discredit someone's argument based on a personal attack is an informal logical fallacy called an ad hominem (literally, "at the man") argument. If, for example, you claim that $2 + 2 = 4$, and we say (and perhaps can even prove) that you are a baby seal clobberer, robber, murderer, kidnapper, liar, cheater, and child abuser and that you never ate your vegetables, still, your moral depravity has no relevance to the truth of your assertion. What you are asserting is simply true, and your character (or lack of it) is simply not relevant. Biographical details are not generally relevant to the truth, falsity, or effectiveness of someone's arguments or claims. Facts about you are relevant only in one special case, that is, if you assert something about yourself or your character. So, if you claim that you are the best person in the world; that you have never hurt anyone; that you "feel my pain"; or that you prefer to kick, rather than club, baby seals, then it is relevant for us to marshal evidence that you are a murderer or cruel to animals. In this special case, your claims have made your life and your character relevant. But when you are not asserting claims about yourself or your character, that is, when you are talking about philosophical or methodological issues in psychology, your character is simply irrelevant.

As another example, suppose you knew that two people were having a disagreement about some point. Furthermore, suppose you knew that person A was a low-down and immoral character and that person B was a forthright, honest soul. Now, can you tell by virtue of this biographical information whose claim is in fact correct? Of course not! You need to know what the point being argued is, not biographical information about the disputants. If A is saying that $2 + 2 = 4$ and B is arguing that it does not, then like it or not, A is right and B is wrong.

We are not mentioning this important point because there is something to hide about Skinner. He led a fairly typical life of an academic. He remained married to his first wife until his death (admittedly, this might not be so typical!). He retired with honors from the same university that granted him his doctorate (Harvard). He raised two daughters who state that they had happy childhoods, who remained very close to their father until his death, and who still speak about him quite fondly. In short, he led a life such that, even if one were inclined to construct an ad hominem argument, one would have no real material to get the argument off the ground.

SKINNER'S LIFE

B. F. Skinner was born on March 20, 1904, in Susquehanna, Pennsylvania. Susquehanna was a small railroad town in a beautiful river valley in northeastern Pennsylvania. He died at the age of 86 on August 18, 1990, in Cambridge, Massachusetts, as a retired professor of psychology at Harvard University; his death was caused by complications associated with leukemia. He was working on manuscripts the day before he died and gave a speech to a standing-room-only audience at the annual meeting of the American Psychological Association eight days before he died.

B. F. Skinner's childhood was, on all accounts, a reasonably happy one. He described his home life as "warm and stable" (Skinner, 1970, p. 1). His parents named him Burrhus Frederic Skinner (Burrhus was his mother's maiden name), but for all his life he was known as Fred to his friends. His father was a lawyer who worked for the Erie Railroad and was in private legal practice. Skinner described his mother as "bright and beautiful," although somewhat rigid in what she regarded as "right." His parents were moderately religious Presbyterians. They led a respectable, stable, small-town, middle-class life. Skinner graduated from the same small school that his parents had attended. The school housed 12 grades in one room, and there were only eight students in his graduating class.

During his childhood, Skinner read a lot. He described his father as "a sucker for book salesmen" (Skinner, 1976, p. 59). However, Skinner was also a physically active boy and enjoyed typical activities that rural life provided: swimming, fishing, canoeing, hiking, and the like, although he had little talent for organized sports. Beyond his penchant for reading, the other childhood hobby that Skinner regarded as predictive of his future career was his extraordinarily mechanical inclination. He built roller skate scooters, steerable wagons, sleds, merry-go-rounds, rafts, sleds, wagons, model airplanes, makeshift musical instruments, and even a full-scale glider on which he tried to fly. Skinner was clearly precocious in his mechanical abilities. He reported that when he was 10, his mother would repeatedly scold him for his failure to hang up his pajamas:

> I solved it by building a little gadget. It was a hook on a string in that little closet where I would hang the pajamas and the string passed over a nail and . . . came down in the doorway and there's a sign saying "hang up your pajamas." Now if the pajamas were on the hook the sign went up out of the way, but when I took them off at night the sign came down on the door and in the morning I got up, got dressed, I started to go out, there would be this sign there. I'd go back, get the pajamas, hang them up and the sign would get out of the way. (quoted in Bjork, 1993, p. 13)

Skinner liked school. He graduated second in his high school class (as, somewhat uncannily, did both his parents) and attended Hamilton College, a small liberal arts college in Clinton, New York, where he majored in English. During his early years there, his brother, his only sibling, died at the age of 16 of a cerebral hemorrhage. Interestingly, Skinner stated that his brother's death did not emotionally affect him a great deal, and later he felt somewhat puzzled and guilty about this. In later life, Skinner was regarded by some of his colleagues as being a bit "cold."

During college, Skinner's goal was to become a writer. In his last years in college he met the poet Robert Frost, who asked Skinner to send him some of his writings. Skinner sent him three short stories, and Frost wrote back stating that he was favorably impressed. While in college, Skinner also had a reputation for being somewhat rebellious. For example, one prank he engaged in with classmates involved printing posters claiming that the famous actor Charles Chaplin was giving a lecture at Hamilton. The local press fell for this, giving the event a lot of publicity. A crowd formed for the announced event, although, of course, they were quite disappointed when Chaplin did not show.

After graduating in 1926, Skinner moved back home and attempted to write. He was not successful at writing short stories, but his father secured a job for him writing a digest of decisions regarding grievances brought by coal companies and unions. Skinner wrote his first book, *A Digest of Decisions of the Anthracite Board of Conciliation,* which, of course, did not rocket to the best-seller list. However, when he realized that he shouldn't pursue a career as a writer because he had "nothing to say," he decided to attend Harvard Graduate School to study psychology. He (1970) stated,

> I had failed as a writer, because I had nothing important to say, but I could not accept that explanation. It was literature which must be at fault. A girl I had played tennis with in high school—a devout Catholic who later became a nun—had once quoted Chesterton's remark about a character of Thackeray's: "Thackeray didn't know it but she drank." I generalize the principle to all literature. A writer might portray human behavior accurately, but he did not therefore understand it. I was to remain interested in human behavior, but the literary method had failed me; I would turn to the scientific. Alf Evers, the artist, had eased

the transition. "Science," he once told me, "is the art of the twentieth century." The relevant science appeared to be psychology, though I had only the vaguest idea of what that meant. (p. 7)

Skinner became interested in psychology when reading Bertrand Russell's book *Philosophy*. In this book, Russell described Watson's behaviorism. Skinner then decided to read Watson's book *Behaviorism,* which furthered his interest in philosophical issues in psychology. He had also read Ivan Pavlov's *Conditioned Reflexes* and thus became acquainted with classical conditioning and the experimental techniques used in the study of learning. He stated, "Russell and Watson had given me no glimpse of experimental method, but Pavlov had: control the environment and you will see order in behavior" (Skinner, 1970, p. 10).

Skinner began Harvard as a committed behaviorist. However, the psychology department at Harvard at that time was not at all behavioral. The department was chaired by Edwin Boring, who was a clear opponent of Watson's. Skinner did most of his research as a graduate student under the direction of William Crozier, who provided a good haven for Skinner because: (a) he was in the physiology rather than the psychology department; and (b) Crozier was a student of Jacques Loeb, who did original research in tropisms. A *tropism* is a reflex in which a stimulus causes an organism to orient in a certain way. For example, a phototropism occurs when a planarian moves toward a light. A tropism is a type of reflex, and reflexes were Skinner's major interest as a graduate student.

At Harvard, Skinner met a fellow graduate student, Fred Keller, and they became lifelong friends, partly because of their mutual affinity for behaviorism. For many years, Fred Keller taught at Columbia University and trained many prominent Skinnerians. Keller himself engaged in important research, developing and investigating the application of behavioral principles to education.

In 1931 Skinner received a doctorate from Harvard. His dissertation was an examination of the "concept of the reflex." That is, he conceptually and experimentally examined the notion of the relationship between environmental stimuli and the responses they elicit. After graduating, he spent five additional years at Harvard as a postgraduate fellow.

In 1936 he accepted his first academic job, at the University of Minnesota, and married Yvonne Blue, who was an English major at the

University of Chicago. The Skinners had two children: Julie, who is a professor of behaviorology at West Virginia University, and Deborah, who studied art in London and is now a successful etcher living in London. Julie once called him a "storybook father" (Vargas, 1993).

The ever-inventive Skinner, in response to his wife's complaints of the drudgery of some of the tasks involved in child care, designed and built an "air crib" for Deborah. The air crib, or "baby tender" as Skinner preferred to call it (one wag once called it an "heir conditioner"), provided a better sleeping environment by maintaining a constant temperature and provided a stretched-woven plastic sheet that felt like linen. However, many misunderstood the air crib and suggested that it was a cage in which the child was isolated.

Skinner (1983) stated,

> Deborah had survived the rumors about her. When a distinguished English critic told Harry Levin that he was sorry to hear that she had committed suicide, Harry replied, "Well, when did she do that? I was swimming with her yesterday." A well-known psychiatrist told Eunice Shriver that the child we "raised in a box" became psychotic: he apologized abjectly when I wrote to ask where he had heard the story. Later it was said that Deborah was suing me. These rumors were sometimes fostered by clinical psychologists who found it useful in criticizing behavior therapy. One night, just as I was falling asleep, the phone rang and a young man said, "Professor Skinner, is it true that you kept one of your children in a cage?" Possibly because of the baby-tender and the rumors about it I had been solicitous." (pp. 385-386)

In 1938, Skinner published his first book, *The Behavior of Organisms,* which was based on his doctoral dissertation. In 1942, in order to help the military effort in World War II, he conceived and worked on Project Pigeon. The goal of this project was to place trained pigeons in bombs. The pigeons would previously have been conditioned to peck keys that would home the bomb toward its target.

In 1945 he became the Chair of Psychology at Indiana University. Three years later, Skinner returned to Harvard as a professor of psychology and published *Walden Two.*

The following statement (Skinner, 1970) gives an interesting glimpse into some of his values:

I have been powerfully reinforced by many things: food, sex, music, art, and literature—and my scientific results. I have built apparatuses as I have painted pictures or modeled figures in clay. I have conducted experiments as I have played the piano. I have written scientific papers and books as I have written stories and poems. I have never designed and conducted an experiment because I felt I ought to do so, or to meet a deadline, or to pass a course, or to "publish rather than perish." I dislike experimental designs which call for the compulsive collection of data, and particularly, data which will not be reinforcing until they have been exhaustively analyzed. I freely change my plans when richer reinforcement beckons. My thesis was written before I knew it was a thesis. *Walden Two* was not planned at all. I may practice self-management for Protestant reasons, but I do so in such a way as to maximize non-Protestant reinforcements. I emphasize positive contingencies. For example, I induce myself to write by making production as conspicuous as possible (actually, in a cumulative record). In short I arrange an environment in which what would otherwise be hard work is actually effortless. (p. 17)

Earlier we described Skinner's exceptional ability to build things. Skinner once said to me (the first author) that he thought that his ability for, and attraction to, building things contributed greatly to his success. He stated that if he had not been able to design "the Skinner box" (the operant chamber in which animals were run) and the cumulative recorder (the device that measured the rate of response), he would not have discovered the orderly relations that he did. Skinner also built teaching machines, which allowed students a more active role in learning and more immediate feedback.

For those who want to learn more about Skinner's life, we would recommend the following. If you want a very full account, read the three volumes of Skinner's autobiography: *Particulars of My Life* (1976), *The Shaping of a Behaviorist* (1979), and *A Matter of Consequences* (1983). If you want a shorter autobiography, read Skinner (1970). Finally, if you want to read a midlength and very good biography, we would highly recommend Bjork's (1993) *B. F. Skinner: A Life.*

Skinner was quite prolific throughout his life, publishing approximately 200 items. Because his greatest influence was through the books he wrote, we here provide a list of these books, the years they were published, and the chapters in which they are discussed in this book (an asterisk indicates a collection of reprinted work, rather than new work):

> *The Behavior of Organisms: An Experimental Analysis* (1938), Chapter 5
>
> *Walden Two* (1948), Chapter 10
>
> *Science and Human Behavior* (1953), Chapters 4 through 10
>
> *Schedules of Reinforcement* (Ferster & Skinner, 1957), Chapter 5
>
> **Cumulative Record* (1972), Chapters 4 through 10
>
> *The Analysis of Behavior: A Program for Self-Instruction* (Holland & Skinner, 1961), Chapter 5
>
> *The Technology of Teaching* (1968), Chapter 4
>
> **Contingencies of Reinforcement: A Theoretical Analysis* (1969), Chapter 4
>
> *About Behaviorism* (1974), Chapter 4
>
> *Particulars of My Life* (1976), Chapter 2
>
> **Reflections on Behaviorism and Society* (1978), Chapter 10
>
> *The Shaping of a Behaviorist: Part Two of an Autobiography* (1979), Chapter 2
>
> *Notebooks* (1980), all chapters
>
> **Skinner for the Classroom* (1982), all chapters
>
> *Enjoy Old Age* (Skinner & Vaughan, 1983), Chapter 9
>
> *A Matter of Consequences* (1983), Chapter 2
>
> **Upon Further Reflection* (1987), Chapter 2
>
> **Recent Issues in the Analysis of Behavior* (1989), Chapters 4 and 5

CONCLUSION

No doubt Skinner, like all humans, was a flawed man. Our goal is not to try to argue that his personal life was so exceptional that he should be canonized. Sometimes followers of Skinner have been accused of idolizing the man, and there is some truth to this claim. However, as we discussed in the beginning of the chapter, what is relevant is a person's assertions and work, not the person him- or herself.

Because some of Skinner's critics have spread various rumors about him, we argue that his life was a decent one that should not be vilified and that certainly should not be used in any way to cast doubt on the truth or quality of his work.

Skinner's early life by all accounts contained no developmental trauma. We want to be clear that we do not buy into a psychology that involves uncovering early childhood trauma to explain adult behavior. However, we anticipate that some critics of Skinner will buy into this kind of psychology. But the facts of Skinner's life provide them with little grist for their mills.

Skinner was an incredibly well-rounded person. Although he had little athletic talent, he knew a lot about music and was accomplished at many instruments. From his early interest in becoming a writer, and from his wife's lifelong interest in literature, he was well-read in fictional literature. He also continued to design and make many items with his hands. He kept up with current events and was a lively conversationalist regarding most of the pressing issues of the day. Finally, he was an active scholar who could discuss major trends in philosophy and science. His daughter said of him,

> When I think of how I would characterize my father, I have to agree with those who call him a Renaissance man. He was well-read in a variety of fields, skilled in music and in oil-painting, and a true gentleman. I never heard him raise his voice in anger. But my father also carried his Pennsylvania small town origins in his love of tinkering and his practical do-it-yourself approach to solving problems. Characteristic, too, was his special affection for children, and his predilection to check the truth of an idea by observing directly rather than by appealing to authority. Most characteristic of all, however, was his devotion to improving the world and his enthusiasm for living life to the fullest. (Vargas, 1993, pp. 59-60)

Skinner was a very hard worker who was quite dedicated to developing and advancing a science of human behavior. His long list of publications and students are a testimony to his productivity. But in an important sense, Skinner saw his science of human behavior as a means to an end—the end of helping people and improving the human condition. As mentioned in Chapter 1, Skinner won an award for being a humanist. In Chapter 8, we will see in more detail how his science and its application have helped people.

Skinner had a very interesting combination of strengths that go a long way toward explaining his success. First, he was hard working, organized, and focused. Second, he was good with his hands, and thus he could invent and build experimental apparatuses that were critically important innovations that allowed new regularities to be discovered. Third, he was an original, critical thinker. He did not passively acquiesce in accepted ways of doing things, including things in science. Rather, he questioned nearly everything and used science and reason to allow him to argue for better ways of doing things. Finally, because of the importance he placed on writing, he was a good, clear writer. Some scholars may have something interesting to say, but their awkward, jargon-filled prose greatly detracts from their ability to communicate. Skinner was a clear and forceful writer, and this no doubt contributed to his fame and influence.

References

Bjork, D. (1993). *B. F. Skinner: A life*. New York: Basic Books.

Ferster, C. B., & Skinner, B. F. (1957). *Schedules of reinforcement*. New York: Appleton-Century-Crofts.

Holland, J. G., & Skinner, B. F. (1961). *The analysis of behavior: A program for self-instruction*. New York: McGraw-Hill.

Pavlov, I. P. (1927). *Conditioned reflexes: An investigation of the physiological activity of the cerebral cortex*. (G. V. Anrep, Trans.) Oxford, England: Oxford University Press.

Russell, B. (1927). *Philosophy*. New York: Norton.

Skinner, B. F. (1938). *The behavior of organisms: An experimental analysis*. New York: Appleton-Century.

Skinner, B. F. (1948). *Walden two*. New York: Macmillan.

Skinner, B. F. (1953). *Science and human behavior*. New York: Macmillan.

Skinner, B. F. (1968). The technology of teaching. *Proceedings of the Royal Society, Series B, 162*, 427-443.

Skinner, B. F. (1969). *Contingencies of reinforcement: A theoretical analysis*. New York: Appleton-Century-Crofts.

Skinner, B. F. (1970). B. F. Skinner, an autobiography. In P. B. Dews (Ed.), *Festschrift for B. F. Skinner* (pp. 1-21). New York: Appleton-Century-Crofts.

Skinner, B. F. (1959). *Cumulative record: A selection of papers* (Enlarged ed., 1961; 3rd ed., 1972). New York: Appleton-Century-Crofts.

Skinner, B. F. (1974). *About behaviorism.* New York: Knopf.

Skinner, B. F. (1976). *Particulars of my life.* New York: New York University Press.

Skinner, B. F. (1978). *Reflections on behaviorism and society.* Englewood Cliffs, NJ: Prentice Hall.

Skinner, B. F. (1979). *The shaping of a behaviorist.* New York: New York University Press.

Skinner, B. F. (1980). *Notebooks* (R. Epstein, Ed.). Englewood Cliffs, NJ: Prentice Hall.

Skinner, B. F. (1982). *Skinner for the classroom* (R. Epstein, Ed.). Champaign, IL: Research Press.

Skinner, B. F. (1983). *A matter of consequences.* New York: New York University Press.

Skinner, B. F. (1987). *Upon further reflection.* Englewood Cliffs, NJ: Prentice Hall.

Skinner, B. F. (1989). *Recent issues in the analysis of behavior.* Columbus, OH: Merrill.

Skinner, B. F., & Vaughan, M. E. (1983). *Enjoy old age: A program of self-management.* New York: Norton.

Vargas, J. (1993). B. F. Skinner: A glimpse of the scientist as a father. *Behaviorology, 1,* 55-60.

CHAPTER 3

Skinner's Intellectual Background

❖

Psychologists date the beginning of scientific psychology to 1879, when Wilhelm Wundt founded the first psychological laboratory, in Liepzig, Germany. Skinner began his scholarly career in psychology about 50 years later. Although, during these first 50 years of psychology, a number of psychologists had tried a variety of different ways of defining and studying psychological phenomena, none had been particularly successful. Few scientific problems had been solved, and many dead ends had been encountered. Wundt (1862), for example, tried to use *introspection* (which involved training subjects to accurately report the details of their conscious experience) to discover "the elements of the mind." However, few orderly relations were found, and there was little agreement on what were the basic elements of consciousness. Franz Joseph Gall created *phrenology* and argued that psychology should study the specific locations of brain functioning by examining the bumps and indentations on the skull. However, his claims and methods in assessing the relationships between the structure of a person's skull and his or her personality were found to be unreliable and invalid (Hergenhahn, 1992). William James (1890) argued against Wundt, stating that consciousness cannot be divided into elements but should be studied as a continuous stream. However, he failed to develop a scientific method for studying "the stream of consciousness." Although James said some very interesting things about a wide variety of human experience, such as religious experience, he mainly approached psychology from a philosophical, rather than a scientific, perspective. There were many other attempts at establishing a successful approach to studying human behavior. A good textbook on the history of psychology (e.g., Hergenhahn, 1992; Leahey, 1987) will provide the interested reader more information regarding these and other approaches.

Notice that each of these predecessors of Skinner defined the proper subject matter of psychology (e.g., elemental sensations, personality, or the stream of consciousness) and the proper ways of studying this subject matter (e.g., introspection, measuring the skull, or philosophical analysis) in his own unique way. Wundt (1862), for example, suggested that the proper subject matter was the elements of consciousness and that the proper method was introspection. Notice also that there was not a consensus about what the subject matter of psychology was and about how to properly study any such subject matter. The young Skinner was confronted with a field in which there was much controversy, little consensus, and very few examples of successful puzzle solving.

Skinner, we shall see, initially added to the controversy, because he did the same sort of thing as his predecessors. Each of these prominent psychologists felt free to define psychology in novel ways, because each thought that whatever was the then-standard way of doing psychology was either unsuccessful, overly limited, or, more strongly, entirely off track. This kind of situation is not unusual in the history of science. The philosopher of science Thomas Kuhn (1970) has suggested that an examination of the history of physics reveals that there are often a number of false starts in the development of a science. Scientists define problems and methodologies in certain ways, argue for the legitimacy and even the supremacy of these ways, and then go about trying them. Many of these attempts simply fail. They do not solve any important puzzles or problems. For example, early chemists (known as *alchemists*) attempted to turn base metals into gold through a combination of reasonable chemical techniques and some fairly far-out magic. Early chemists also attempted to understand combustion by invoking an explanation that referred to the release of an element called *phlogiston* (which turned out not to exist) from the combusting substance (instead of the absorption of oxygen). This approach was not a successful solution to any problem. Most contemporary psychologists would argue that Wundt, Gall, and James also failed to solve any significant problem.

However, sometimes someone successfully defines the proper subject matter and methods and solves an important problem. Kuhn (1970) called this a *scientific revolution*. Kuhn suggested that when this happens, other scientists adopt the successful definition of the field and its problems and the puzzle-solving methodology. They use the puzzle-solving methods and concepts as a paradigm for solving other scientific problems. Kuhn called science using the paradigm to attempt to solve other scientific problems *normal science*. In Chapter 5, we will argue that Skinner, in his research into operant conditioning, did solve a problem and developed a paradigm.

All this is to say that when the young Skinner looked at what was then contemporary psychology, he found that a successful approach to defining the proper domain and methods had not been discovered. Thus, one of the important influences on Skinner was the relative lack of a successful problem-solving tradition (i.e., a paradigm) in what was then contemporary psychology. He quite reasonably decided to define his own approach to these issues. In defining his new approach, he was influenced by some earlier scientists and philosophers, notably a 16th-century philosopher of science named Francis Bacon and a 20th-century physicist named Ernst Mach. He was also influenced by the great evolutionary theorist Charles Darwin, although this influence is more clear and direct in Skinner's later writings. Finally, he was influenced by early conditioning researchers Ivan Pavlov, Edward Thorndike, and John Watson, although he had important disagreements with each of these. Pavlov's discovery of classical conditioning, Thorndike's discovery of the law of effect, and Watson's and his students' application of classical conditioning to some human problems might be regarded as some of the most clear examples of problem solving that had occurred in psychology up to that point. We will discuss these influences in the following sections.

It is important to note that although Skinner was influenced by these scholars, he added new elements of his own, and thus in no way did Skinner simply extrapolate the views of these scholars. He picked and chose some of the ideas from each, combined these with his own ideas, and came up with a wholly unique philosophy of science and experimental approach.

FRANCIS BACON

Because of his literary interests, Skinner became interested in Bacon while he was still in junior high and high school. Little is known about William Shakespeare, and some scholars have speculated that Francis Bacon actually wrote what is commonly attributed to William Shakespeare. Skinner, while reading Shakespeare, became interested in this theory and therefore read the works of Bacon.

Francis Bacon was an English statesman and philosopher who lived at the end of the 16th and the beginning of the 17th century. At that time, scholars were very interested in ancient Greek philosophy, particularly in Aristotle and Plato. Many scholars would base their arguments on the writings of these authorities. This is an argument form called "argument from an appeal to authority." Thus, many scholars in Bacon's day would argue that to settle a question, one needed to consult the works of Aristotle to see what he said about the subject. Whatever Aristotle said was to be regarded as correct.

Bacon strongly criticized ancient Greek philosophy, stating that Aristotle failed to properly argue for the use of observation in discovering new information. Bacon (as quoted in Urbach, 1987) stated that Aristotle's use of observation

> comes too late, after his mind was made up. His practice was not to seek information from unfettered experiment but to exhibit experience captive and bound. He did not introduce a wide impartial survey of experience to assist his investigation of truth; he brought in a carefully schooled and selected experience to justify his pronouncements. (p. 96)

In addition, Bacon argued that this philosophy "has the characteristic property of boys: it can talk, but it cannot generate; for it is fruitful of controversies but barren of works" (as quoted in Urbach, 1987, p. 13). Francis Bacon is often regarded as one of the founders of modern science because of his criticisms of arguments appealing to authority and tradition and because of his emphasis upon observation and induction.

Bacon was not interested in scholarship producing verbal agreement, but rather in what he called *works,* that is, practical inventions and innovations that would improve people's quality of life. One has to remember that the material conditions of humankind in the 16th and 17th centuries were quite poor. There were few labor-saving devices, little effective medicine, poor water and sewer systems, no efficient farming methods, and few creature comforts. Life was nasty, brutish, and short. (Life is much better now—it is now nasty, brutish, and long.) Bacon wanted scholars to focus not on abstract metaphysical matters with few or no implications for improving the human condition, but rather on science and its implications for practical problems.

Bacon attributed the lack of progress of philosophy and its empirical inquiries to problematic methods of investigation. Bacon argued that hypotheses should not be tested by verbal argument (what he called the "giddy whirl of argument") or by informal observations. He argued that the best method for making discoveries about nature was by systematic and controlled observation.

Bacon argued that *induction* would lead to the most efficient growth of knowledge. Induction proceeded from "the senses and particulars" and ended with "the highest generalities" (as quoted in Urbach, 1987, p. 25). Induction is a form of logic in which one observes many of individual instances of the same general type (e.g., swans) and uses these particular observations to support a more general conclusion ("All swans are white"). Bacon argued that induction, properly practiced, requires that the scientist gather observations with a completely open, unbiased mind. Hypotheses formulated before data are collected can only interfere with accurate observation, as they will bias the observer. Bacon further argued that antecedent hypotheses will tend to be similar to "conventional wisdom" and therefore will not free the observer from the error contained in conventional wisdom. "The discoveries which have hitherto been made in the sciences are such as lie close to vulgar notions, scarcely beneath the surface" (as quoted in Urbach, 1987, p. 28).

Thus, Bacon thought that the way to gain information about nature was to study nature directly, rather than to study what others had written about nature. He often referred to his empirical studies as "reading the book of nature."

Bacon suggested that before scientists can accurately observe nature, they must become aware of and rid themselves of certain biases, superstitions, and dogmas. He proposed that there were four major types of prejudices: (a) idols of the tribe, (b) idols of the cave, (c) idols of the marketplace, and (d) idols of the theater.

Idols of the tribe come from human nature and the way the senses and intellect receive impressions from objects. Bacon named this type of bias *idols of the tribe* because these mistakes are thought to be made by all humans, perhaps because they are inherent in human nature. Bacon was concerned that, although the senses are crucial in scientific investigation, they have significant limitations. Bacon argued that humans have a bias toward believing that there is more order and regularity in the world than is actually justifiable to believe. Moreover, once some simple relation is claimed, humans tend to pay selective attention to confirming instances and ignore criticisms or counterexamples. As one instance of this *confirmation bias,* Bacon recounted a story about a church in which sailors, before their journeys, would pray for their safe return. When they returned safely they would hang a picture of themselves in gratitude for the effectiveness of their prayers. Some took all these pictures as indications that prayers do work. However, Bacon (as quoted in Urbach, 1987) stated,

> And therefore it was a good answer that was made by one who when they showed him hanging in a temple a picture of those who had paid their vows as having escaped shipwreck, and would have him say whether he did not now acknowledge the power of the gods,—"Aye," asked he again, "but where are they painted that were drowned after their vows?" (p. 88)

Whereas idols of the tribe affect nearly all humans, the *idols of the cave* "take their rise in the peculiar constitution, mental or bodily, of each individual; and also in education, habit and accident" (as quoted in Urbach, 1987, pp. 87-88). Bacon stated that each person has his or her own private cave from which he or she intercepts and "distorts the light of nature." This type of error may be due to an overly strong admiration of tradition or, conversely, to an extreme interest in novelty. Moreover, Bacon stated that this idol involves interpreting things in light of one's own dispositions or favorite theories.

Bacon (as quoted in Urbach, 1987) stated,

> Men become attached to certain particular sciences and speculations, either because they fancy themselves the authors and inventors thereof, or because they have bestowed the greatest pains upon them and become most habituated to them. But men of this kind, if they betake themselves to philosophy and contemplations of a general character, distort and colour them in obedience to their former fancies. (p. 88)

The *idols of the marketplace* concern problems encountered when we use certain words and expressions. This error receives its name from the prominent role words play in the intercourse and commerce between individuals. Bacon thought that by employing certain words and phrases, we can perhaps with no great awareness become committed to implicit theories contained in the words. Bacon (as quoted in Urbach, 1987) argued that often we learn our words in the vernacular, and these words,

> being commonly framed and applied according to the capacity of the vulgar, follow those lines of division which are most obvious to the vulgar understanding. And whenever an understanding of greater acuteness or a more diligent observation would alter those lines to suit the true divisions of nature, words stand in the way and resist the change. (p. 92)

Another mistake that falls under idols of the marketplace is that two people can use the same word, but the word may have different meanings for each of them. When someone who is against abortion uses the word *baby,* it usually means something different than the same word when used by someone who is pro-choice.

Finally, the *idols of the theater* refer to biases that are created by various abstract or philosophical dogmas. These are called idols of the theater because they are really inventions, like a stage play, that do not give a true picture of reality. Problematic philosophies that are based on poor methodologies, and empirical methodologies that are not sufficiently rigorous because of "the narrowness and darkness of a few experiments" (as quoted in Urbach, 1987, p. 96) are examples of this type of dogma.

Bacon thought that the fortune of humankind could be improved by the application of his inductive method, because this method would produce rules for manipulating nature to the ends of humankind. Bacon stated, "Nature to be commanded must be obeyed" (Bacon, 1620/1960, p. 39).

WAS SKINNER INFLUENCED BY BACON?

This is what Skinner said about himself:

> Whether my early and quite accidental contact with Bacon is responsible or not, I have followed his principles closely. I reject verbal authority. I have "studied nature not books," asking questions of the organism rather than of those who have studied the organism. I think it

can be said, as it was said of Bacon, that I get my books out of life, not out of other books. . . . I also follow Bacon in distinguishing between observation and experimentation. Bacon no doubt underestimated the importance of extending the range of human sense organs with instruments, but he did so in emphasizing that knowledge is more than sensory contact. I would put it this way: *observation* overemphasizes stimuli; *experimentation* includes the rest of the contingencies which generate effective repertories. (Skinner, 1970, p. 18)

Skinner was influenced by Bacon in five major ways: (a) Skinner emphasized empirical observation and experiment as the best way to gain knowledge; (b) Skinner saw scientific method as inductive, not as the testing of antecedently conceived hypotheses; (c) Skinner wanted science to produce technologies that could help people; (d) Skinner did not read "the literature" but instead read "the book of nature"; and (e) Skinner took seriously the kind of errors that Bacon enumerated in his "idols." Skinner also agreed with the following ideas:

1. One should not just assume or assert something to be the case, but rather, that one needs to look carefully and systematically to see if it is so. That is, often one needs to conduct scientific experiments to discover what orderly relationships actually exist.

2. One should be aware of confirmatory biases, that is, of paying selective attention to instances that seem to fit one's beliefs.

3. One needs to be cautious in accepting "what everyone believes." It is an informal fallacy (called *argument from the crowd*) to take as evidence for a proposition the fact that everyone (or nearly everyone) believes it. Skinner was sometimes quite iconoclastic in his rejection of "what everyone believes" when he saw insufficient warrant for these common beliefs.

4. Skinner often analyzed the denotations and connotations of words and suggested how these can involve us in problematic theories. Skinner thought that words mattered and was quite circumspect in his word choice. He (1974) stated,

> The English language is heavy-laden with mentalism. Feelings and states of mind have enjoyed a commanding lead in the

explanation of human behavior; and literature, preoccupied as it is with how and what people feel, offers continuing support. As a result, it is impossible to engage in casual discourse without raising the ghosts of mentalistic theories. The role of the environment was discovered very late, and no popular vocabulary has yet emerged. (pp. 19-20)

ERNST MACH

Ernst Mach agreed with Francis Bacon on a number of important issues. Thus, although Skinner certainly picked up some new ideas from Mach, particularly Mach's notion of cause as a functional relationship and the notion of the great value of an indigenous, scientific (rather than philosophical) epistemology, to a great degree Mach served to reinforce and extend the influence of Bacon on Skinner.

Ernst Mach was an Austrian physicist and philosopher who lived in the last half of the 19th and the beginning of the 20th century. Mach agreed with Bacon that the only way to discover information about the world is through sense experience. He also agreed that induction—observing many particulars and generalizing to more universal claims—was the proper logic of science. He also agreed with Bacon that words often contain excess meanings that the scientist must clarify. He stated that the scientist must "clear up ideas, expose the real significance of the matter, and get rid of metaphysical obscurities" (Mach, 1883/1942, p. xiii).

Mach also agreed with Bacon that science should be practical—it should help people survive and prosper. Mach (1886/1959) stated that "the task of science is to provide the fully developed human individual with as perfect a means of orienting himself as possible. No other scientific ideal can be realized, and any other must be meaningless" (p. 36). However, Mach often expressed this sentiment in Darwinian terms. He stated that the purpose of science was to help satisfy humans' biological needs, that is, to aid in the survival and welfare of the species. We will see this theme strongly in Chapter 10, when Skinner talks about the role of science in saving the species.

According to Mach, the aim of science is to provide concise, economical descriptions of phenomena. Mach argued for a descriptive

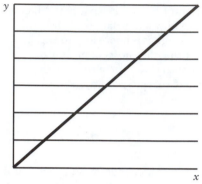

Figure 3.1. $y = f(x)$.

approach to science: Scientists should aim to provide the most economical descriptions of facts.

In the 19th century, the British philosopher David Hume said something quite startling. He said that we don't ever really see causation. If you were to ask yourself what causation looks like, all you could say is (a) it is a constant conjunction between two events, and (b) the event that comes first is called the "cause" and the event that follows is called the "effect." Causation is nothing more than this orderly relationship, this "constant conjunction."

Mach essentially agreed with Hume, stating that when scientists search for causes they are really looking for *functional relationships* between variables. In mathematics, a functional relationship can be shown on a graph such as the one above. In this we can say $y = f(x)$. That is, the value of y is a function of the value of x. Another way of saying this is to state that y depends on x (see Figure 3.1).

Here's a concrete example. We can say that if you are being paid based on the number of hours that you work, your income is a function of total hours worked. We can also say that increasing the number of hours that you work *causes* your income to rise.

Smith (1995) said,

Most thinkers, according to Mach, conceive of a cause as pushing or pulling to produce its effects; but such a notion of cause is metaphorical, superfluous, and to be rejected in scientific formulations. Instead Mach advocated a purely descriptive notion of cause and effect as correlated changes in two classes of phenomena, a correlation that could be represented concisely as the functional relation between two variables in a mathematical equation. (p. 42)

Mach also argued against science as hypothesis testing. Mach believed that we err when we expect to gain more understanding from a hypothesis than from the facts themselves. Mach would largely agree with Bacon that the scientist should rid him- or herself of any biases or preconceptions and view nature in a neutral and open manner.

Finally, Mach argued that philosophy provides poorer answers to the questions of *epistemology* than does science. Mach attempted to situate the study of knowledge and the growth of knowledge within science, particularly within evolutionary biology. This is a type of *naturalized epistemology*. Thus, Mach asserted that the organism has been shaped by evolution to perceive, know, and learn things about its environment, and an understanding of these historical environmental influences can better provide answers to epistemological questions than any purely philosophical analysis. However, Mach also argued that all we can know are the ideas and sensations that we immediately experience. In this regard, Mach is known as an *epistemological phenomenalist*. Skinner strongly disagreed with this aspect of Mach's epistemology and attempted to ground his epistemology in behavioral terms.

Skinner was influenced by Mach in four main ways: (a) Skinner thought science should search for causal relations but argued along Machian lines that causal relations could best be conceived as functional relationships between variables. In fact, in applied behavior analysis, an important part of understanding what causes an organism's behavior is conducting a *functional analysis*. This term is derived from the Machian concept. (b) Skinner constantly sought the most economical description of the facts. His arguments against physiological and cognitive explanations of molar behavior were often Machian, in that he argued that these were not the most economical descriptions of these behavioral facts. (The terms *molar* and *molecular* refer to the level of detail of an analysis [Catania, 1992]. Molar analyses examine behavior broadly, such as average rates of responding over sessions. Molecular analyses break down these overall measures, e.g., into the interval of time between responses.) Physiological and cognitive explanations are problematic because they are an "explanation of an observed fact which appeals to events taking place somewhere else, at some other level of observation, described in different terms, and measured, if at all, in different dimension" (Skinner, 1950, p. 193). Appealing to these physiological or cognitive events makes the explanation less economical. (c) Mach argued that science, not philosophy, provides the best analysis of knowledge and of how knowledge grows. Thus, Skinner never tried to import a philosophical epistemology into psychology but rather attempted to develop an indigenous, behaviorally based epistemology. We will further discuss this epistemology in the next chapter. (d) Mach showed how a fundamental reliance on Darwinian biology could provide a useful foundation for answering major questions about human behavior and human knowing.

Although Bacon and Mach were the strongest influences on Skinner's general views about the proper ways to proceed scientifically, it was the learning researchers Pavlov, Thorndike, and Watson who influenced him on the specifics of how to study the behavior of organisms. We turn now to brief descriptions of these researchers.

IVAN PAVLOV

Ivan Pavlov (1849-1946) was a Russian physiologist who studied the digestive system and earned a Nobel Prize for this work. Sometimes scientists, when studying one thing, discover something very important about another thing. This is called *serendipity*. If you will excuse the sexism, one definition of serendipity is looking for the needle in the haystack and discovering the farmer's daughter.

Pavlov made an important serendipitous discovery. He was studying how gastric juices such as saliva work in digestion. He was using dogs as experimental animals. He noticed that dogs would salivate a lot when food was present and much less so when food was absent. In his laboratory, Pavlov had a routine in which he would reliably enter the lab and feed the dogs at a fixed time of day. However, what was important is that he noticed that his dogs would begin salivating not when they saw or smelled the food, but when they heard the noises of his assistants entering the lab with the food. These noises were paired with the imminent arrival of food.

Pavlov studied this phenomenon experimentally, and this learning process has come to be known as *Pavlovian* or *classical conditioning*. Pavlov paired a neutral stimulus (one that does not evoke the target response) with a stimulus that does evoke the response. The neutral stimulus is called the *conditioned stimulus*. The stimulus that without learning can evoke the response is called an *unconditioned stimulus*. After repeated pairings (a pairing is said to occur when the two events are correlated or occur in close temporal proximity), the animal begins to respond to the neutral stimulus. In Pavlov's experiments, the neutral stimulus was a tone (dogs do not initially salivate to tones). The unconditioned stimulus was food. The *unconditioned response* was salivation, and the *conditioned response* (i.e., the response that is learned) was also salivation. Pavlov also demonstrated other learning phenomena associated with classical conditioning, such as extinction, generalization, and discrimination. We will discuss these phenomena in Chapter 5.

Because of Pavlov's interest in physiology, he tried to explain classical conditioning by suggesting brain processes that could be involved. Although Skinner was quite impressed with the general phenomenon of classical conditioning, he strongly disagreed with Pavlov's attempt to explain molar behavior-environmental relationships in physiological terms. Remember Skinner's (1950) criticism of an "explanation of an observed fact which appeals to events taking place somewhere else, at some other level of observation, described in different terms, and measured, if at all, in different dimension" (p. 193): Skinner wanted to remain at one level, and he eschewed scientific accounts that involve an explanation beyond "observed facts," which appeal to events taking place elsewhere at some "other level of observation." Such accounts are not economical.

EDWARD THORNDIKE

In 1898, Edward Thorndike (1874-1949), then at Harvard, published a paper on what he called *the law of effect*. According to Thorndike (1911),

> The law of effect is that: Of several responses made to the same situation, those which are accompanied or closely followed by *satisfaction* to the animal, will, other things being equal, be more firmly connected

with the situation, so that when it recurs, they will be more likely to
recur, those which are accompanied or closely followed by *discomfort*
to the animal, will other things being equal, have their connections
with that situation weakened, so that, when it recurs, they will be less
likely to occur. The greater the *satisfaction* or *discomfort*, the greater
the strengthening or weakening of the bond. (p. 244 [italics added])

Thorndike had studied how cats escaped from puzzle boxes. Puzzle
boxes were cages that had a variety of things in them, some of which, if
the cat manipulated them in the right way, would open a door so that the
cat could escape. Thorndike observed that cats would try many ways of
manipulating the objects in the box, eventually hitting upon the means
of opening the door. When placed in the box again, they would more
quickly engage in this behavior. Thorndike asserted that the *pleasure* of
escaping from the box strengthened the behavior that led to the escape,
and that this behavior would occur more frequently in the future.
Thorndike (1911) stated,

The behavior of all but 11 and 13 [the identification numbers of the
cats] was practically the same. When put into the box the cat would
show evident signs of *discomfort* and of an *impulse* to escape from
confinement. It tries to squeeze through any opening; it claws and bites
at the bars or wire; it thrusts its paws out through any opening and
claws at everything it reaches; it continues its efforts when it strikes
anything loose and shaky; it may claw at things within the box. It does
not pay very much attention to the food outside, but seems simply to
strive *instinctively* to escape confinement. The vigor with which it
struggles is extraordinary. For eight or ten minutes it will claw and bite
and squeeze incessantly. With 13, an old cat, and 11, an uncommonly
sluggish cat, the behavior was different. They did not struggle vigorously or continually. On some occasions they did not even struggle at
all. It was therefore necessary to let them out of the box a few times,
feeding them each time. After they thus associate climbing out of the
box with getting food, they will try to get out whenever put in. They do
not, even then, struggle so vigorously or get so excited as the rest. In
either case, whether the impulse of struggle be due to *instinctive* reaction to confinement or to an association, it is likely to succeed in letting

the cat out of the box. The cat that is clawing all over the box in her impulsive struggle will probably claw the string or loop or button so as to open the door. And gradually all the other nonsuccessful *impulses* will be *stamped out* and the particular *impulse* leading to the successful act will be *stamped in* by the resulting *pleasure,* until after many trials, the cat will, when put in the box, immediately claw the button or loop in a definite way. (pp. 35-40 [italics added])

This sounds similar to a modern conception of the law of effect. However, Thorndike's concept is different in a variety of ways. First, Thorndike talked about internal states of pleasure and pain as being re-sponsible for the law of effect. There are two problems with this: (a) as we shall see in Chapter 5, research has shown that reinforcers and pun-ishers do not need to be pleasurable or painful; and (b) appealing to internal, emotional states is an unnecessary complication that can reduce the reliability of the account, because it requires the use of the subject's self-report of his pleasure or pain. Another problem with Thorndike's conceptualization is that he failed to round out his account by providing more information about the law of effect. He did not answer questions such as what antecedent conditions are related to it, what is the effect of intermittent consequences, and what happens when the consequences are withdrawn.

Thus, although Skinner was influenced by Thorndike's work, Skin-ner, following Mach, did not believe that Thorndike provided the most economical description of the phenomena; he also thought that Thorndike did not provide a full account of the associated features of the law of effect. In addition, Thorndike's research was based on informal observa-tions. Skinner wanted a more rigorous, experimental study of operant conditioning.

JOHN WATSON—B. F. SKINNER WAS NOT JOHN WATSON

John Watson was more of a polemicist—someone who produces a lot of arguments and tries to persuade—for behaviorism than a learning researcher. Watson, for example, discovered no new learning principles. However, his research was important because it showed that human behavior could be classically conditioned and that some human problems (e.g., fear) could be established and cured through the use of conditioning procedures. Watson (1913) stated,

> Psychology as the Behaviorist views it is a purely objective experimental branch of natural science. Its theoretical goal is the prediction and control of behavior. Introspection forms no essential part of its methods, nor is the scientific value of its data dependent upon the readiness with which they lend themselves to interpretation in terms of consciousness. The Behaviorist, in his efforts to get a unitary scheme of animal response, recognizes no dividing line between man and brute. The behavior of man, with all of its refinement and complexity, forms only a part of the Behaviorist's total scheme of investigation. (p. 158)

In addition, Watson (1919) stated,

> The goal of psychological study is the ascertaining of such data and laws that, given the stimulus, psychology can predict what the response will be; or, on the other hand, given the response, it can specify the nature of the effective stimulus. (p. 10)

Watson is famous (or infamous) for his experiments showing that a young infant named Albert could be classically conditioned to fear something the infant started out not fearing—a white rat. He also showed that once the fear was conditioned to the white rat, it was generalized to other similar stimuli, such as a white rabbit and additional furry white objects.

Skinner (1974) said the following about John Watson:

> The first explicit behaviorist was John B. Watson, who in 1913 issued a kind of manifesto called *Psychology as the Behaviorist Views It*. As the title shows, he was not proposing a new science but arguing that psychology should be redefined as the study of behavior. This may have been a strategic mistake. Most of the psychologists at the time believed they were studying mental processes in a mental world of consciousness, and they were naturally not inclined to agree with Watson. Early behaviorists wasted a good deal of time, and confused an important issue, by attacking the introspective study of mental life. (p. 3)

Skinner believed that Watson made other mistakes, including the following:

1. Watson made exaggerated claims about the role of learning over the role of nature.

2. Watson tried to explain too much with too few psychological principles. Watson knew about Pavlovian classical conditioning, but he did not know about operant conditioning. Because operant conditioning explains so much, Watson was attempting to explain many phenomena without all the right tools.

3. Watson emphasized reflexes (or behavior that is elicited by some stimulus) as opposed to more properly emphasizing emitted behavior that is not reflexively elicited by previous stimuli. Skinner stated that Watson was a Stimulus-Response psychologist, whereas he himself was not.

4. Watson seemed to imply that humans have few or no distinguishing characteristics. Humans clearly do.

5. Most important, Watson, according to Skinner, was arguing for a certain type of behaviorism, *methodological behaviorism*. According to methodological behaviorism, only items that can be *intersubjectively verified* can be allowed into science. *Intersubjective* (literally, "between people") *verification* (literally, "seeing what is the case") means that only public information, that is, only information that two or more people can perceive, can play a role in science. Cognition, thinking, believing, feeling pain, and so forth are not intersubjectively verifiable, and therefore, according to Watson, they should not play a role in the science of psychology. Skinner disagreed with this and rejected the "psychology of the other one" (meaning that someone else also needs to perceive what you perceive in order for it to be a legitimate piece of science). Skinner (1974) stated,

> Radical behaviorism . . . does not insist upon truth by agreement [intersubjective verifiability] and can therefore consider events taking place in the private world within the skin. It does not call these events unobservable, and it does not dismiss them as subjective. It simply questions the objects observed and the reliability of the observations. (p. 15)

Thus, according to Skinner, cognitions have a legitimate role in science. However, they are seen as behavior to be explained rather than as behavior that explains other behavior. We will discuss this issue more thoroughly in Chapter 4.

Although Watson and Skinner were both behaviorists, they disagreed on many important matters. It is crucial to make distinctions between the various forms of behaviorism. Actually, there are quite a few such forms. The learning theorist Clark Hull advanced one form, Tolman another, and Kantor still another. Moreover, there are many current forms of behaviorism, such as Howard Rachlin's teleological behaviorism, John Staddon's theoretical behaviorism, and Steven Hayes's contextual behaviorism. Finally, philosophers such as Quine and Wittgenstein have advanced their own forms of behaviorism. Our point is that *behaviorism* is not an unequivocal term but rather describes a family of different philosophies. The reader needs to be careful in making any sweeping claims about these diverse positions. The reader is referred to *The Handbook of Behaviorism* (O'Donohue & Kitchener, 1999) for further information regarding the different kinds of behaviorism.

Thus, the influence of Watson on Skinner was actually less than may appear at first blush. Skinner adopted the word *behaviorism* to characterize his approach to psychology, but he distinguished it from Watson's behaviorism by terming Watson's form *methodological behaviorism* and his own form *radical behaviorism*. Watson worked to show the relevance of behavioral concepts and conditioning procedures to improving practical human problems, and Skinner strongly agreed that this was one of the most important features of behaviorism.

Skinner was influenced by these learning researchers in the following ways: (a) Most basically, these researchers showed that there was a phenomenon to be studied, that animals were predictably and relatively permanently influenced by their experiences. (b) The goal of the science of psychology become the prediction and control of behavior. (c) They—particularly Pavlov—showed that scientific controls were important to isolate the critical variables that participated in these orderly relations. (d) They showed that learning was not a monolithic process, because there appeared to be different kinds of learning, as well as different learning phenomena (e.g., extinction, generalization). (e) They showed that the same principles of learning applied to all mammals. That is, subhuman species could be studied as convenient experimental preparations for understanding human learning.

THE INFLUENCE OF CHARLES DARWIN: THE SELECTION BY CONSEQUENCES

Skinner saw psychology as a branch of biology. The most basic component of Skinner's account is Darwinian evolution. *Evolution* is the process by which the environment selects certain features in organisms (e.g., opposable thumbs, depth perception, being active during the day) because they overcome survival problems. Organisms with these features then reproduce and are competitive with other organisms. As a result, these attributes change the population distribution of future generations.

There are three basic mechanisms in any evolutionary process. There needs to be: (a) some variability in the phenomenon that will be selected (selection implies that some things are picked out and some are not—thus there needs to be a range of these things), (b) a mechanism for retaining what is selected, and (c) something that does the selecting. In modern biological evolutionary theory, the variability is genetic, phenotypic, or environmental variability. The mechanisms for retaining what is selected are genes. Finally, it is the environment that selects.

It is very important to note that the environment does the selecting. Let us give a few examples of how the environment selects out certain characteristics and how this results in a different frequency of characteristics in future generations.

Example 1: The Evolution of a Phenotypic Characteristic of a Species Based on Differential Survival

Imagine a species of moth that is generally white (Howlett & Majerus, 1987). Very importantly, however, there is some variation. (If you look at most features in living organisms, they are not identical from individual to individual. Rather, there is some variability. People are of different heights, weights, and hairiness. Variation is necessary for evolution to occur.) If one were to measure the exact color of all members of this species, one would find that their coloration forms a distribution. Some are very white, others a bit less white, and some a bit gray. Now let us suppose that these moths have predators that use visual information to detect and eat these moths. Let us also assume that because of pollutants resulting from industrialization, the environment has become sootier and blacker. Predators now find the whiter moths easier to spot and consume, because they contrast more with the darker environment. We would then expect to see a shift in this population in subsequent generations. This species would evolve into a darker species, because darker moths are more successfully surviving and reproducing. In fact, this is what actually happened. Note, again, that it is the environment (in the form of predators) that selects some for survival and some for termination.

Example 2: Evolution Based on Differential Reproduction and Sensitivity to a Particular Reinforcer

Imagine two groups of organisms that reproduce sexually. One group finds the sexual act very pleasurable, whereas the other group finds the sexual act unpleasant. Also assume that the sexual act has a natural connection to reproduction. Which group will increase in number in future generations? This change in frequency is an example of the group's evolution. The environment is selecting the group in which members find sex reinforcing, because this allows them to more readily experience pleasure. An important point to note is that you should not think of the environment as consisting merely of rocks, food, air, germs, and so forth (e.g., how it is defined in environmental studies). The environment includes all this as well as other organisms. Note that survival is not the entire story: Differential reproduction is the process responsible for evolution in this example. If you survive but produce no offspring, then your genes do not survive into the next generation.

Example 3: Extinction

Several species of plants and animals become extinct each day. This may occur because the environment has changed in a way that interferes with their survival or reproduction, and no favorable mutations occur that allow them to adapt to the new environment. Environmental activists are quick to point out that pollution, deforestation, ozone depletion, and other problems caused by modern humans' profligate ways cause species to become extinct. This is certainly true. But although nothing should justify the unnecessary pollution of our natural environment, some environmental activists sometimes miss the point that extinction is a natural process. Even before the advent of humankind, species came into existence, and some, because of their inability to solve problems posed by environmental circumstance, became extinct.

Example 4: The Evolution of Reflexes

Imagine two groups of organisms in a species. One group does little reflexively. The other responds automatically (without slower, apparently "voluntary" responses) to certain environmental stimuli. For example, when puffs of air hit the eyes of members of this group, they reflexively blink. Blinking can have enormous survival advantages, because it is important to protect the integrity of one's eyes, and objects moving toward one's eyes push air in front of them. Thus, blinking quickly (reflexively) can increase the probability that one can protect one's eyes. Organisms that do not have these reflexes would have a harder time surviving.[1]

Example 5: The Evolution of Learning From Consequences

Imagine two groups of the same species of organisms. One group cannot learn from experience. Suppose that the animal spends a lot of time looking under all sorts of things for food: rocks, logs, leaves, and so forth. Suppose further that each time the organism looks under a rock for food, it is successful and finds food, and each time it looks under logs, it does not find food. Imagine that the first group of organisms, learning nothing from this, keeps looking under rocks and logs. This group is wasting a lot of time and energy, because it has not learned from experience—looking under logs never produces food. Imagine that the second group can learn from the consequences of its behavior: It spends increasingly less and less time looking under logs. This is evolutionarily advantageous, because it allows food to be found more efficiently (more calories gained per calorie used in foraging). This learning, in which behavior is sensitive to its consequences, Skinner called *operant conditioning*, and it is itself an evolutionary adaptation. That is, the ability to learn from the consequences of behavior was an evolutionary development that proved advantageous. It is important to note two things here: (a) operant conditioning mirrors natural selection—it is the environment selecting in on the basis of consequences, and (b) operant conditioning is not the only learning mechanism that evolution has produced. Others include:

1. *Habituation*—learning that certain repetitive stimuli are not important and thus to decrease one's response to these. At first one attends to the loud repetitive ticking of a clock, but soon attention habituates, i.e., one no longer attends to this constant stimulus.

2. *Classical conditioning*—sometimes the environment pairs two stimuli, and it is important to learn this pairing. Pavlov paired the stimulus of ringing a bell with presenting food. At first, dogs did not respond to the bell by salivating. However, after repeated pairings the dogs began salivating to the bell.

The important thing is to see how these learning processes have evolutionary advantages: Organisms that lack these compete poorly with organisms that do have them. Thus, the environment selects organisms with the ability to be changed by experience—that is, the ability to learn. The other important thing is to see that evolution does not merely select for changes in anatomy—it also selects for behavioral tendencies (enabled by anatomical features). Malott, Tillema, and Glenn (1978) stated,

Some rewards and aversives control our actions because of the way our species evolved; we call these unlearned rewards or aversives. We inherit a biological structure that causes some stimuli to be rewarding or aversive. This structure evolved because rewards helped our ancestors survive, while aversives hurt their survival. Some of these unlearned rewards, such as food and fluid, help us survive by strengthening our body cells. Others help our species survive by causing us to produce and care for our offspring—these stimuli include the rewarding stimulation resulting from copulation and nursing. And many unlearned aversives harm our survival by damaging our body cells, such aversives include burns, cuts and bruises. (p. 9)

Example 6: The Evolution of Societies

Societal characteristics can also be selected. Social groups that are warlike, but not very good at combat, will tend to disappear. However, our favorite example involves two religious groups: Shakers and Roman Catholics. Shakers believe that all sex is immoral—even sex within marriage. They have a strict prohibition against all forms of sex. Roman Catholics, on the other hand, believe that many kinds of sex are immoral, but that sex within marriage for the purpose of procreation is perfectly moral, perhaps even a marital duty. They also believe that the use of most forms of birth control is immoral, both because the proper function of sex is reproduction and because some of these forms of birth control kill a human being (the fetus). Now, guess which of these religions over the years has the most members? The Shakers have about six members living on a farm in Maine, and the Catholics have hundreds of millions. The social practices of a group can have drastic implications for its survival and success. In his later writings, Skinner discussed the problematic tendencies in Western society that might have grave implications (no pun intended) for the future of the species. We will talk more about this later.

Example 7: Evolutionary Selection: Advantageous at One Time but Disadvantageous at Another

A very important point is that evolution is a slow process, and what was selected at one point in time may now be less advantageous and may even be disadvantageous at another time. Finding the taste of fat as reinforcing is advantageous in environments in which there are consistent or periodic food shortages. These food-scarce environments were quite common in the history of our species. It is only in the past 80 years or so that food has not been a primary survival problem.

Organisms that did not find it reinforcing to eat the most high-calorie foods possible would be at a selective disadvantage because preferring and eating low-calorie foods (e.g., lettuce) places them at greater risk of starvation during food shortages. Organisms that prefer to eat more high-calorie foods (and store more fat) can better survive during these periods.

Currently in Western society there are no longer food shortages for most people. Rather, there is a surplus of food. Now preferring high-calorie foods such as fats is a selective disadvantage. People eat these foods (potato chips, bacon, mayonnaise, etc.), become overweight, and die of coronary problems. Eiseley (1958) stated,

> [The] evolutionary past of every species of organism—the ghostly world of time in which animals are forever slipping from one environment to another and changing their forms and features as they go. But the marks of the passage linger, and so we come down to the present bearing the traces of all the curious tables at which our forerunners have sat and played the game of life. Our world, in short, is a marred world, an imperfect world, a never totally adjusted world, for the simple reason that it is not static. The games are still in progress and all of us, in the words of Sir Arthus Keith, bear the wounds of evolution. Our backs hurt, we have muscles which no longer move, we have hair that is not functional. All of this bespeaks another world, another game played far behind us in the past. We are indeed products of "descent with modification." (p. 197)

Now, remember our earlier points about a faithful reading of what Skinner actually said. Did Skinner actually say these things? Skinner (1984) stated,

> Human behavior is the joint product of (i) contingencies of survival responsible for natural section and (ii) contingencies of reinforcement responsible for the repertoires of individuals, including (iii) the special contingencies maintained by an evolved social environment. Selection by consequences is a causal mode found only in living things, or in machines made by living things. It was first recognized in natural selection. Reproduction, a first consequence, led to the evolution of cells, organs, and organisms reproducing themselves under increasingly di-

verse conditions. The behavior functioned well, however, only under conditions similar to those under which it was selected. Reproduction under a wider range of consequences became possible with the evolution of processes through which organisms acquired behavior appropriate to novel environments. One of these, operant conditioning, is a second kind of selection by consequences. New responses could be strengthened by events which followed them. When the selecting consequences are the same operant conditioning and natural selection work together redundantly. But because a species which quickly acquires behavior appropriate to an environment has less need for innate repertoires, operant conditioning could replace as well as supplement the natural selection of behavior. Social behavior is within easy range of natural selection, because other members are one of the most stable features of the environment of a species. The human species presumably became more social when its vocal musculature came under operant control. Verbal behavior greatly increased the importance of a third kind of selection by consequences, the evolution of social environments or cultures. The effect on the group, and not the reinforcing consequences for individual members, is responsible for the evolution of culture. (p. 477)

Skinner (1984) also stated,

Each of the three levels of variation and selection has its own discipline—the first, biology; the second, psychology; and the third, anthropology. Only the second, operant conditioning, occurs at a speed at which it can be observed from moment to moment. Biologists and anthropologists study the processes through which variations arise and are selected, but they merely reconstruct the evolution of a species or culture. Operant conditioning is selection in progress. It resembles a hundred million years of natural selection or a thousand years of the evolution of a culture compressed into a very short period of time. (p. 478)

It is no small matter that Skinner explicitly links psychology with evolutionary biology. Neither truth nor reality divides along the lines of university divisions. What is biologically true about organisms should have relevance for those studying the behavior of these organisms. Thus,

Skinner's reliance upon evolution allows a synthesis between evolutionary psychology and behavioral psychology in which each helps sustain and enlarge the other. However, although Skinner linked his psychology to evolutionary biology, the relationship between physiology and his psychology is more complex. We turn to this next.

Skinner's Views on Physiology

Some critics have misconstrued Skinner by stating that he thought an attempt to understand the physiological mechanisms associated with behavior was wrongheaded. This was not his argument. Skinner believed that when an intact organism interacts with its environment there is both a molar behavior act and a physiological act occurring at the same time. The physiological act needs to be studied scientifically and will be explained in terms of nerves, muscles, biochemicals, and so forth. Skinner, however, did argue against those who thought that the physiological level of analysis was an inherently superior level of analysis. There are those who believe that one doesn't really understand behavior until one understands the physiological processes involved in the behavior. Skinner argued that this is a problematic form of reductionism. Skinner argued that if one can completely predict and control behavior at a molar level (that is, by examining environmental-behavior relationships), then that is a perfectly fine kind of understanding. It is in no way fundamentally incomplete. Moreover, it gives the physiologist an important research question—What physiological mechanisms are behind this environment-behavior relationship?—that the physiologist would not have known if this behavioral analysis had not occurred. That is, physiology can be incomplete without a behavioral analysis. Thus, Skinner argued that a physiological analysis and a behavior analysis are equally important.

CONCLUSION

Skinner was influenced by Darwinian evolution in four ways: (a) Most fundamentally, Skinner agreed that all species are the products of evolution. That is, historically they have been biologically and behaviorally shaped by their environments. (b) The answers to many questions about organisms can be found in evolution. Organisms have certain phenotypic characteristics, certain reflexes, certain learning capabilities, and certain societal practices because of the selective action of the environment. (c) Operant conditioning arose because of the survival advantages it bestows. It allows organisms to be sensitive to environmental selection that can be more transitory and variable. (d) Operant conditioning mirrors natural selection. That is, environmental contingencies select behaviors from some initial behavioral distribution.

Note

1. "Learning" is also involved in this survival advantage.

References

Bacon, F. (1960). *The new organon* (F. H. Anderson, Trans.). New York: Liberal Arts Press. (Original work published 1620)

Catania, A. C. (1992). *Learning* (3rd ed.). Englewood Cliffs, NJ: Prentice Hall.

Eiseley, L. (1958). *Darwin's century*. New York: Doubleday.

Hergenhahn, B. R. (1992). *An introduction to the history of psychology*. Pacific Grove, CA: Brooks/Cole.

Howlett, R. J., & Majerus, M. D. (1987). The understanding of industrial melanism in the peppered moth. *Biological Journal of the Linnean Society, 30,* 31-44.

James, W. (1890). *The principles of psychology*. New York: Holt.

Kuhn, T. (1970). *The structure of scientific revolutions* (2nd ed.). Chicago: University of Chicago Press.

Leahey, T. H. (1987). *A history of psychology: Main currents in psychological thought*. Englewood Cliffs, NJ: Prentice Hall.

Mach, E. (1942). *The science of mechanics* (5th ed.; T. J. McCormack, Trans.). La Salle, IL: Open Court. (Original work published 1883)

Mach, E. (1959). *The analysis of sensations*. New York: Dover. (Original work published 1886)

Malott, R. W., Tillema, M., & Glenn, S. (1978). *Behavior analysis and behavior modification: An introduction*. Kalamazoo, MI: Behavior Delia.

O'Donohue, W., & Kitchener, R. F. (Eds.). (1999). *Handbook of behaviorism*. San Diego, CA: Academic Press.

Skinner, B. F. (1950). Are theories of learning necessary? *Psychological Review, 57,* 193-216.

Skinner, B. F. (1970). An autobiography. In P. B. Dews (Ed.), *Festschrift for B. F. Skinner* (pp. 1-21). New York: Irvington.

Skinner, B. F. (1974). *About behaviorism.* New York: Knopf.

Skinner, B. F. (1984). Selection by consequences. *Behavioral and Brain Sciences, 7,* 477-510.

Smith, L. D. (1995). Inquiry nearer the source: Bacon, Mach, and "The Behavior of Organisms." In J. T. Todd & E. K. Morris (Eds.), *Modern perspectives on B. F. Skinner and contemporary behaviorism* (pp. 39-50). Westport, CT: Greenwood.

Thorndike, E. L. (1911). *Animal intelligence.* New York: Macmillan.

Urbach, P. (1987). *Francis Bacon's philosophy of science.* La Salle, IL: Open Court.

Watson, J. B. (1913). Psychology as the behaviorist views it. *Psychological Review, 20,* 158-177.

Watson, J. B. (1919). *Psychology from the standpoint of a behaviorist.* Philadelphia: Lippincott.

Wundt, W. (1862). *Contributions toward a theory of sense perception.* Leipzig, Germany: Winter.

CHAPTER 4

Skinner's Philosophy of a Science of Human Behavior— Radical Behaviorism

❖

In the previous chapter we reviewed the major intellectual influences on Skinner. We will see in this chapter that although the work of Bacon, Mach, Pavlov, Thorndike, Watson, and Darwin all had major impacts on Skinner's thinking about a number of philosophical and scientific problems, Skinner's ultimate responses to these problems diverged somewhat from the thinking of each of these scholars.

WHAT IS MEANT BY RADICAL BEHAVIORISM?

Skinner called his philosophy of science *radical behaviorism*. He used the term *behaviorism* because he argued that psychology should be the study of behavior. For Skinner, behavior is anything the organism does. This approach diverges most sharply from that of psychologists who think the proper subject matter of psychology is consciousness or the stream of consciousness (such as Wundt and James) and from psychologists who think the unconscious should be the focus of study (such as Freud and his disciples).

Skinner said that a distinction can be made between overt behavior (i.e., behavior capable of being observed by two people) and covert behavior (i.e., behavior that occurs "within the skin"). Skinner thought that psychologists should study both kinds of behavior. This is surprising to

55

some people who think that Skinner was "against cognitions." However, Skinner thought that cognitions (covert behavior) were legitimate to study scientifically. What he denied was their potential to serve as explanations of other behavior—particularly of overt behavior. That is, cognitions do not explain overt behavior but rather are more behavior to be explained. We will discuss this more in Chapter 5.

Skinner called his kind of behaviorism *radical* because *radical* can mean "root," and Skinner thought that his behaviorism was a thorough-going, "deep" behaviorism. As Skinner stated,

> Behaviorism is not the science of human behavior; it is the philosophy of that science. Some of the questions it asks are these: Is such a science really possible? Can it account for every aspect of human behavior? What methods can it use? Are its laws as valid as those of physics and biology? Will it lead to a technology, and if so, what role will it play in human affairs? (Skinner, 1974, p. 3)

Skinner further stated that "behaviorism is a formulation which makes possible an effective experimental approach to human behavior. It is a working hypothesis about the nature of a subject matter" (Skinner, 1970, p. 18).

It is important to keep clear about what kind of thing radical behaviorism is and is not. It is not a scientific law or set of empirical findings. It is, rather, a *meta*scientific position that attempts to define what the science of behavior should look like. A metascientific position is "beyond" or "above" science and is the level upon which general questions about science are examined. It answers questions such as: What should the psychologist study—behavior, consciousness, unconsciousness? What methods should the psychologist use to study this domain—introspection, paper-and-pencil questionnaires, large social surveys, experiments? What are the most general organizing principles for this science—evolutionary biology, physiology, physics, or sociology?

These rather abstract matters are philosophical questions, and answers to these can be called a *philosophy of science*. Thus, radical behaviorism is a philosophy of science, or more exactly, a philosophy of psychology. Skinner calls the science based on this philosophy *the experimental analysis of behavior* or *behavior analysis*. We will discuss the major content of this science in the next chapter.

A fundamental claim of radical behaviorism is that the proper subject matter of psychology is behavior, both overt and covert.

DARWINIAN EVOLUTION PROVIDES
THE CONTEXT FOR RADICAL BEHAVIORISM

As discussed in Chapter 2, radical behaviorism depends heavily on evolutionary biology, and in fact, Skinner viewed his psychology as a branch of evolutionary biology. Evolutionary biology explains a significant amount regarding the organism's behavior (e.g., what limitations and abilities its body has, what it finds as primary reinforcers, what learning mechanisms it possesses, etc.). Skinner called the mechanisms by which the organism learns through its interaction with the environment *contingencies of reinforcement.* (A *contingency* is a dependency or an "if-then" relationship. That is, if x happens, then y will happen; another way of saying this is that y happening depends on x happening.) Skinner called evolutionary influences *the contingencies of survival.*

Radical behaviorism, like evolutionary theory, emphasizes the important role of the environment and the organism's interactions with the environment in understanding the current status of the organism. In the history of the species, the environment has selected certain biological features (the contingencies of survival). In the individual organism's lifetime, the organism is continuously interacting with its environment. (Review what you did so far today and try to see how this can be viewed as a series of interactions with your environment.) The environment sometimes provides stimuli that are sufficient to elicit a reflex. More frequently, the environment provides stimuli that alter the probability of a response. And quite importantly, in operant behavior, the environment provides consequences to behavior. All this is to point out that radical behaviorism is a kind of *environmentalism.*

Radical behaviorism's environmentalism does not imply that the organism passively reacts to the environment. The relationship between the organism and the environment is interdependent and reciprocal (Bijou, 1993). That is, although the organism interacts with its environment, its reaction also changes the environment. The organism is then influenced by an environment changed by its own behavior, behaves again, changes its environment again, and so on. Thus, the organism's relationship to its environment is one of mutual influence.

Evolution produces a unique type of causality. Causation in natural selection is not a "pushing or pulling," like one billiard ball hitting another and causing it to move. Rather, causation in radical behaviorism is selecting or surviving. For example, it is a demonstrated fact that newborn human babies spontaneously produce all the sounds that occur in all the world's languages (biological endowment). In addition, Skinner would claim that evolution has provided babies with a vocal musculature that is influenced by its consequences. Different language communities (environments) then select different sounds. In English, the sounds /m/ and /a/ are selected (i.e., they increase in frequency) because they are part of the English word *mama*. When a baby makes these sounds, the behavior is reinforced by the mother's getting excited, coming closer to the baby, and picking the baby up. On the other hand, in English language communities the guttural German phoneme goes unreinforced and soon disappears. The important thing to note here is that there is no pushing or pulling in this causal relation. What causes the baby to say one thing and not another is a selection by an environmental contingency.

Radical behaviorism is closely linked to evolutionary biology. Radical behaviorism looks for explanations in the contingencies of survival and the contingencies of reinforcement. The causal mechanism in radical behaviorism is selection.

WHAT IS GOOD SCIENCE ACCORDING TO SKINNER?

One of the most basic claims in radical behaviorism is that behavior should be studied scientifically. There are many different practices (methodologies), all of which have been considered scientific by some reputable psychologist. For example, one can conduct case studies and attempt to generalize regularities from one's observations of an individual case. Freud used this as his method of inquiry and thought it constituted good science (O'Donohue & Halsey, 1997). On the other hand, one can conduct correlational studies, that is, measuring the extent to which two or more variables change together. Knowing correlations can be useful, because one can predict the value of one of the variables from the value of the other.

However, Skinner suggested that neither of these approaches is the best way to make progress in psychology. Rather, he argued that experiments are necessary to discover nature's regularities. That is why he called his science the *experimental* analysis of behavior. An experiment involves manipulating one variable (the independent variable) while holding all other variables constant. This allows the experimenter to see if the independent variable is a cause for the observed changes in the dependent variable. The dependent variable (so called because its value can depend on the value of the independent variable) is the variable that we are interested in predicting and controlling. For example, the number of cookies eaten can be the dependent variable, and the amount of sugar in them can be the independent variable. That is, we can manipulate the amount of sugar in the cookies and see if this variable causes more or fewer cookies to be eaten.

An experiment in which a variable is manipulated (sometimes called the *true experiment*) is thought to be the best way to uncover what causes what. (Again, causes for Skinner are represented in functional relationships.) The independent variable is usually graphed on the *x*-axis, and the dependent variable is graphed on the *y*-axis. For example, here is a graph in which one manipulates the amount of reinforcement (i.e., the independent variable) and finds that this changes the rate of behavior (i.e., the dependent variable). This is a functional relationship and, for Skinner, a causal relationship (see Figure 4.1).

Discovering causes is important, because it allows us to predict and control phenomena. Skinner considered the practical aims of science to

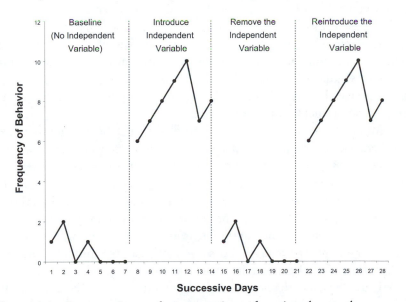

Figure 4.1. An experiment demonstrating a functional-causal relationship.

be prediction and control. Prediction allows us to have advance knowledge and accurate expectations of what will happen in certain situations. Control allows us to shape situations according to our preferences.

Thus, the aims of science are prediction and control. The scientific experiment is the method of choice to achieve these aims.

ALL BEHAVIOR IS DETERMINED

Skinner stated that one reason we believe in free will is that we know much about our behavior but little about its causes. Because we are often ignorant of how our behavior is caused, we jump to the conclusion that our behavior is not caused. That is, we presume that our behavior is a product of our "free will" and "choices." However, our lack of knowledge of causes does not imply, much less prove, that our behavior is not caused.

Science uncovers systematic regularities. That is, science uncovers statements like the following: If situation x occurs (say an object is in free fall near the earth's surface, or a person with strep throat is given an antibiotic), then either y must occur (the object will accelerate at 9.8 m/s^2) or the probabilities will systematically change (the strep will likely die soon). Science cannot occur if the entities it studies have free choice. Science is based on the view that given certain initial conditions, a predictable, regular situation will follow. If the entities can choose to do as they darn well please, that is, to behave in a willy-nilly fashion, then no systematic predictable relationships exist.

Although for Skinner all behavior is determined, he thought that operant behavior encompasses what most people term *voluntary behavior*. Skinner (1986) stated that "operant behavior is the field of intention, purpose and expectation" (p. 716). That is, operant behavior is "voluntary" in that it is not reflexive behavior. It is not an automatic response to a stimulus. Second, operant behavior is purposive in the sense that its function is to change the environment and bring about a consequence. However, purposive behavior does not entail that the individual has free will or that his or her behavior is not caused.

Thus, the view that behavior is determined is a necessary view for making it reasonable to study behavior scientifically. Therefore, another fundamental belief of radical behaviorism is that all behavior is determined.

THE EXISTENCE AND IMPORTANCE OF THE MIND

Some scholars have asserted that there is a special realm of being called the *mental*. The philosophers René Descartes and Bishop Berkeley and the psychologists Freud and Wundt are a few examples of such individuals. These men argued that the mind is an important part of the life of human beings, and because mental phenomena are some of the most important causes of human behavior, they argued that psychology should be the study of the mind.

These scholars also argued that mental phenomena differ from physical phenomena in that physical phenomena (like chairs, hairs, and bears) have both a physical location and a temporal location, whereas mental phenomena have only a temporal location. That is, it makes sense to say that my bathtub is located in such and such a place at such and such a time. However, it only makes sense for you to say that your thought of your bathtub occurred at such and such a time. You cannot locate the place that the thought occupies.

There is an important distinction to be made here. Many contemporary cognitive scientists do not believe in the existence of the mental. They believe that there is a distinction between the mental and the cognitive. Mentalists believe that there is a unique kind of stuff—the mental—that, as we noted above, has only temporal properties. Most cognitive psychologists, on the other hand, believe that there is no special kind of stuff that composes the mental, but rather, that there is only one kind of stuff—the physical. They believe that the phenomena that they study have a physiological substrate that does not require them to posit the existence of a special class of entity.

Skinner, like many cognitive psychologists, argued that there is not a special mental world with special properties. He also articulated further problems with the notion of the mind:

> But where are these feelings and states of mind? Of what stuff are they made? The traditional answer is that they are located in a world of nonphysical dimensions called the mind and that they are mental. But then another question then arises: How can a mental event cause or be caused by a physical one? If we want to predict what a person will do, how can we discover the mental causes of his behavior, and how can we produce the feelings and states of mind which will induce him to behave in a given way? (Skinner, 1974, p. 8)

Skinner further argued that cognitions are not made of special mental stuff. Covert behavior is the experience of one's own bodily states and is allowed by a nervous system that is only roughly suited for this task:

> To agree that what one feels or introspectively observes are conditions of one's own body is a step in the right direction. . . . A severe limitation is to be seen in the organs a person uses in observing himself. After all, what are the anatomy and physiology of the inner eye? So far as we know, self-observation must be confined to the three nervous systems . . . an interoceptive nervous system going to the viscera, a proprioceptive nervous system going to the skeletal frame, and an exteroceptive system bringing a person mainly into contact with the world around him. These three systems arose through natural selection as the human species evolved, and they were selected because of the role they played in the internal and external economy of the organism. But self knowledge arose much later in the history of the species, as the product of the social contingencies arranged by the verbal community, and those contingencies have not been active long enough to permit the evolution of an appropriate nervous system. (Skinner, 1974, p. 22)

There is no special kind of thing called the mind. Internal experiences are physiological processes that have no special status. Because of evolutionary developments we have, as part of our nervous systems, ways that allow us to respond covertly.

WHAT IS KNOWING?—SKINNER'S INDIGENOUS, PSYCHOLOGICAL EPISTEMOLOGY

If radical behaviorism is a philosophy of science, it should provide an answer to the question "What is knowledge?" All scientists must answer this question, because their aim is to discover knowledge as well as to discover methods that best yield knowledge. Traditionally, *epistemology* has been the branch of philosophy that studies knowledge. Its primary concerns have been problems such as: What is knowledge? Is knowledge even possible? If so, what are the legitimate sources of knowledge? There has been an interest in discovering what special properties (e.g., truth, justification, survival of attempted falsifications) and procedures (e.g., unbiased empirical observation, Cartesian methodical doubt, revelation, conjecture and refutation) distinguish knowledge from that which is not knowledge (e.g., false claims, unjustified assertions, misperceptions, accurate lucky guesses).

Epistemology dates at least as far back as Plato in the fourth century B.C. Plato argued that knowledge is justified, true, belief. However, in the 20th century there have been two dramatic changes in the study of knowledge. First, science has become a major subject of study for epistemologists, because it is commonly viewed as having produced an unprecedented acceleration in the growth of knowledge. Philosophy of science is concerned chiefly with epistemology and often takes as its starting point the question of what is special about science that allows such an unparalleled growth of knowledge.

The second major development in the 20th century is that not only has science been the focus of study, but it has also increasingly become the method for the study of epistemological questions. The study of knowledge is no longer the exclusive province of philosophers. Linguists, neurologists, biochemists, computer scientists, evolutionary biologists, and—as we shall see—psychologists have provided their own answers to the major questions of epistemology. Part of the underlying rationale for this move has been that if science is the best method for producing knowledge, then it should be used to gain knowledge about knowledge. Skinner attempted to naturalize epistemology. That is, he viewed knowing as a natural phenomenon (literally, a part of nature) that can be studied and accounted for in the same ways as other natural phenomena. Science (see previous section) has proven to be the best method for studying natural phenomenon, and thus one should attempt a scientific, rather than philosophical, account of knowledge. Skinner attempted to derive a natural, causal, and empirical account of knowledge, rather than a normative account. Normative accounts contain valuative concepts that cannot be reduced to empirical properties (such as truth, soundness, or validity).

Skinner thought that his account of learning could translate into an account of knowledge. That is, he realized that his learning research was essentially research into the growth of knowledge. To say that an organism has learned is to say that the organism has gained knowledge. Knowledge becomes effective behavior that is shaped through the contingencies of survival and reinforcement. Knowledge claims are behavior—verbal behavior—that is conditioned by the verbal community. Skinner made several statements on the subject: "A proposition is true to the extent that with its help the listener responds effectively to the situation it describes" (1974, p. 235). "We confirm any verbal response when we generate additional variables to increase its probability" (1957, p. 425). "If it turns out that our final view of verbal behavior invalidates our scientific structure from the point of view of logic and truth value then so much the worse for logic, which will also have been embraced by our analysis" (1945, p. 274). Skinner is remarkably consistent in that he also claims that the behavior of the scientist—including Skinner's own verbal behavior about verbal behavior—is just additional effective behavior. "Science is a corpus of rules for effective action" (Skinner, 1974, p. 235). For Skinner, there is never any metalevel or "first philosophy" from which his system could be evaluated by normative, philosophical concerns:

> It would be absurd for the behaviorist to contend that he is in any way exempt from his analysis. He cannot step out of the causal stream and observe behavior from some special point of vantage. . . . In the very act of analyzing human behavior he is behaving. (Skinner, 1974, p. 234)

It is also important to note that Skinner is not alone in his attempt to naturalize epistemology. The prominent social psychologist Donald Campbell (1987) and the leading analytical philosopher Wilford Van Orman Quine (1981) have also proposed to study knowledge scientifically. For example, Quine stated,

> Naturalism does not repudiate epistemology, but assimilates it to empirical psychology. Science itself tells us that our information about the world is limited to irritations of our surfaces, and then the epistemological question is in turn a question within science: the question is how we human animals can have managed to arrive at science from such limited information. Our scientific epistemologist pursues this inquiry and comes out with an account that has a good deal to do with the learning of language and with the neurology of perception. He talks of how men posit bodies and hypothetical particles, but does not mean to suggest that the things thus posited do not exist. Evolution and natu-

ral selection will doubtless figure in this account, and he will feel free to apply physics if he sees a way. (p. 72)

Quine clearly agrees with Skinner that epistemology should be studied in the psychological laboratory and that evolution should provide the overall context for this study.

Donald Campbell (1987) also agreed that we should only be interested in epistemologies that are

> compatible with the description of man and of the world provided by contemporary science. Modern biology teaches us that man has evolved from some simple unicellular or virus-like ancestor and its still simpler progenitors. In the course of that evolution, there have been tremendous gains in adaptive adequacy, in stored templates modeling the useful stabilities of the environment, in memory and innate wisdom. Still more dramatic have been the great gains in mechanisms for knowing, in visual perception, learning, imitation, language, and science. (p. 47)

Campbell (1987) also gives a quite interesting explanation of the evolutionary forces that have contrived to make humans particularly influenced by vision. Vision is important to understand from the point of view of epistemology because we learn so much through our eyes. We use expressions like "Let me see" and "Do you see what I mean?" that essentially refer to knowing rather than to literal "seeing":

> We once saw through the fumblings of a blind protozoan, and no revelation has been given to us since. Vision represents an opportunistic exploitation of a coincidence which no deductive operations on a protozoan's knowledge of the world could have anticipated. This is the coincidence of locomotor impenetrability with opaqueness, for a narrow band of electromagnetic waves. For this band substances like water and air are transparent, in coincidental parallel with their locomotor penetrability. For other wavelengths, the coincidence, and hence the cue value disappears. The accidental encountering and systematic cumulations around this coincidence have provided in vision a wonderful substitute for blind exploration. In this perspective, clear glass and fog are paradoxical—glass being impenetrable but transparent, fog being

the reverse. Glass was certainly lacking in the ecology of evolution. Fog was rare or nonexistent in the aqueous environment of the fish where most of this evolution took place. (Campbell, 1987, p. 48)

Thus, we are visual creatures that are sensitive to a small band in the spectrum of electromagnetic radiation because of the survival value of exploiting the coincidence involved in this band: The opaque is also the impenetrable.

Skinner was in agreement with these scholars and argued that many of the answers to questions of epistemology must be answered from the perspective of evolution. Distinctions can be made between ultimate questions and answers, that is, questions and answers in which a longer-term, evolutionary perspective is taken, and proximate questions and answers, that is, questions and responses that look at the more immediate processes. Skinner would argue that his research interest was largely in proximate questions and answers, that is, in selection processes that occurred in the organism's lifetime (the contingencies of reinforcement). However, he would also argue that these would need to be set in an ultimate context, provided by the contingencies of survival.

Thus, for Skinner, epistemology should be studied from a scientific, psychological point of view. Darwinian evolution (the contingencies of survival) provide answers to some epistemological questions. Learning (the contingencies of reinforcement) provides supplementary information about how organisms gain knowledge in their lifetime.

In order to provide a brief overview of Skinner's philosophy of psychology, we will provide a list of the central claims of this philosophy. Some of these points will be discussed further in other parts of this book:

1. Psychology is a branch of biological science. Skinner (1963) asserted that psychology is "part of biology, a natural science for which tested and highly successful methods are available" (p. 956).

2. The goals of science are prediction and control.

3. According to Skinner (1972), the proper subject matter of psychology is behavior, that is, what the organism does. Skinner stated that "behavior is not simply the result of more fundamental activities, to which our research must therefore be addressed, but an end in itself" (p. 326).

4. All behavior is determined; that is, all behavior is caused. There is no such thing as free will.

5. The behavior of all animals, including humans, is the result of evolution (natural selection, or what Skinner terms the *contingencies of survival*) and of learning that occurs in the animal's lifetime (or what Skinner calls the *contingencies of reinforcement*).

6. Behavior should be studied by manipulating environmental variables that precede and follow behavior to attempt to identify functional relationships between these environmental variables and behavior.

7. Cognitions are behavior; more specifically, they are covert behavior (i.e., behavior that cannot be seen by others). Cognitions have a legitimate status in a science of behavior. However, they are more behavior to be explained, rather than behavior that explains other behavior.

8. The rate at which an organism behaves is often the most useful dependent variable.

9. Scientists should identify general laws of conditioning by studying simple responses under controlled circumstances.

10. Scientists will be most effective if they proceed inductively and avoid hypothesis testing.

11. Scientists should analyze the behavior of individual subjects and avoid the averaging of data and the use of statistics.

12. Scientists will be most effective if they focus on accessible, manipulable variables.

13. Scientists ought to pay close attention to observables and avoid loosely defined theoretical constructs and metaphors. This is part of Skinner's insistence on Mach's dictum of using the most economical description of the facts.

14. Scientists should reject inner causes and explanations, particularly mentalistic ones, and should instead look to the environment for the causes of behavior.

15. Scientists should translate and, when necessary, revise mentalistic statements and everyday explanations into behavior statements. Speaking of nonbehavioral statements, Skinner stated that some

can be "translated into behavior," whereas others can be discarded as unnecessary or meaningless.

16. Scientists ought to regard private events as physical and lawful and ought to treat subjective states and events as collateral byproducts of other behavior.

Finally, it is also important to note what Skinner's philosophy was not. Some have taken his philosophy of science to be a species of logical positivism or derived from logical positivism. It was not. Skinner was influenced by Mach, and the logical positivists were also influenced by Mach. However, the logical positivists had other influences (e.g., the early Wittgenstein) who clearly did not influence Skinner.

B. F. SKINNER WAS NOT A LOGICAL POSITIVIST

Logical positivism was an influential philosophy of science in the first half of the 20th century. The temporal coincidence of the rise of behaviorism and the rise of logical positivism might have contributed to the false belief that they are closely related. Logical positivism, however, is a branch of linguistic philosophy that claims that many philosophical problems are due to problems in language, or, to use Wittgenstein's colorful phrase, to "language gone on holiday." Logical positivists argued that only scientific statements are meaningful. Other seemingly syntactically well-formed sentences (e.g., "God is three" or "It is immoral to kill") are actually meaningless (equivalent to "The green greens while sleeping furiously"): They appear to be grammatically well formed, but because they cannot be confirmed by empirical evidence (and thus cannot be determined to be true or false), they are actually meaningless. The logical positivists stated that only sentences that are *analytic* (i.e., true by logic; e.g., "A square is a square" or "Bachelors are unmarried") or *empirical* (i.e., that can be verified by sense experience; e.g., "Some copper conducts electricity" or "I am 6 feet tall") are meaningful. This criterion of meaningfulness was called the *verifiability principle*.

However, logical positivism was generally regarded to have died by 1950 for a number of reasons: (a) The verifiability criterion, when applied to itself, judged itself to be meaningless (i.e., the criterion itself is not the product of sense experience and therefore should, according to its own terms, be regarded as meaningless); (b) The verifiability criterion had other logical problems (see, e.g., Ayer [1946] and the paradox of the ravens or Hempel's [1965] lottery paradox);[1] (c) Quine (1951) argued that analytic statements could not be clearly defined and that single sentences do not derive their meaning from sense experience; (d) Popper (1959) argued that there is no logic of induction; (e) The verifiability principle rendered some perfectly legitimate scientific sentences meaningless. For example, the scientific law "All copper conducts electricity" is, according to the verifiability criterion, meaningless, because it is impossible to observe all copper. Thus, the verifiability criterion failed to work, because it judged certain perfectly legitimate scientific sentences as meaningless.

Unfortunately, some quite reputable scholars have argued that B. F. Skinner was a logical positivist, or at least that he was so influenced by logical positivism that when logical positivism died, Skinnerian psychology died, too. The historian of behaviorism Laurence Smith (O'Donohue & Smith, 1992; Smith, 1986) has suggested that historians such as Koch (1964) and Leahey (1980) have advanced three theses about the affiliation between logical positivism and radical behaviorism: (a) the importation thesis, which states that Skinner imported his philosophy and methodology from logical positivism; (b) the subordination thesis, which states that Skinner regarded his psychological views as subordinate to these prior philosophical views; and (c) the thesis of linked fates, in which the fate of Skinner's behaviorism was therefore linked to the fate of logical positivism.

Smith argues that these theses are all false. Although for the complete case we would recommend reading Smith's excellent book, *Behaviorism and Logical Positivism* (1986), we will give one piece of refuting evidence for each thesis. Regarding the importation thesis, Skinner never spoke positively about the verifiability criterion, never cared to develop a demarcation between meaningful and meaningless statements, never carried out logical analysis of constructs, and, in short, never extrapolated the central tenets of logical positivism into his psychology. Instead, as described previously, he developed an indigenous, psychological analysis of epistemology and psychology. Skinner did talk about the operational definitions of psychological terms, but he cashed this out in terms different than those of the logical positivists; that is, he did not want to define psychological terms intersubjectively. Rather, he wanted an analysis of the scientists' verbal behavior to discover environmental variables that govern its emission and effectiveness.

Regarding the subordination thesis, Skinner never viewed his work as subordinate to philosophical concerns. An anecdote is very revealing of his priorities here: When the young Skinner was told by Alfred North Whitehead that a psychologist should closely follow developments in philosophy, Skinner replied, "It is quite the other way around—we need a psychological epistemology" (Skinner, 1984, p. 29). Finally, because the alleged links between logical positivism and Skinner's work do not exist, they do not share linked fates.

Furthermore, the logical positivists took physics as the most important science. They thought that all other scientists should mimic the way physicists were doing science and that all other sciences should be reduced to physics. Skinner, in contrast, thought that biology was the most important science for psychology. Thus, although Skinner was influenced by Mach's biological positivism, he was not influenced and his theory was not derived from logical positivism.

Note

1. Kyburg (1964) raised a further problem with the probabilistic interpretation of induction known as the "lottery paradox." Suppose that there are 100 lottery tickets numbered consecutively from 1 to 100 and that in a fair drawing one is chosen. Now let us consider the ticket numbered 1. The probability that it is the winner is 1/100. Moreover, this entails that the probability that another ticket was drawn is 99/100. Assuming that .99 is a sufficiently high probability to confirm the conclusion that some other ticket is drawn, let us infer from this that some other ticket was drawn. (Notice that the probability of .99 is not essential to our argument. If one insists upon a higher probability for confirmation, all we need to do is to construct an example with more lottery tickets.) Now let us consider the ticket numbered 2: By the same reasoning, we conclude that some other ticket was drawn. We can use this same reasoning for tickets numbered 3, 4, 5, and so on, up to 100. In each case, the conclusion that some other ticket was drawn seems to be confirmed by its high probability. However, this set of conclusions is inconsistent with our knowledge that one ticket was drawn. Therefore, we cannot argue that something is the case simply because it has a high probability of being so.

   Carl Hempel's (1965) paradox of the ravens points out a further problem with induction. "All ravens are black" is logically equivalent to the proposition "All nonblack things are nonravens." The second proposition can be deduced from the first using the logical law known as the law of contraposition. The law of contraposition asserts that the statement "All As are Bs" is logically equivalent to "All non-Bs are non-As." Because these two propositions are logically equivalent, evidence that confirms one must confirm the other. Therefore, the observation of a yellow pencil—a nonblack thing that is a nonraven—would appear to confirm the hypothesis that all ravens are black.

Similarly, "All ravens are black" is logically equivalent to "Every object is either black or not a raven." Thus, "All ravens are black" seems to be confirmed by any black object (whether a raven or not) as well as by any nonraven (whether black or not). Critics of induction have taken these examples to show that certain logically proper "confirmations" seem to be substantively irrelevant.

References

Ayer, A. J. (1946). *Language, truth and logic* (2nd ed.). London: Victor Gollancz.

Bijou, S. W. (1993). *Behavior analysis of child development* (2nd rev. ed.). Reno, NV: Context Press.

Campbell, D. T. (1987). Evolutionary epistemology. In G. Radnitzky & W. Bartley (Eds.), *Evolutionary epistemology, rationality, and the sociology of knowledge* (pp. 36-53). La Salle, IL: Open Court.

Hempel, C. (1965). *Aspects of scientific explanation and other essays in the philosophy of science.* New York: Free Press.

Koch, S. (1964). Psychology and emerging conceptions of psychology as unitary. In W. T. Wann (Ed.), *Behaviorism and phenomenology* (pp. 1-41). Chicago: University of Chicago Press.

Kyburg, H. E., Jr. (1964). Recent work in inductive logic. *American Philosophical Quarterly, 1,* 1-39.

Leahey, T. H. (1980). *A history of psychology: Main currents in psychological thought.* Englewood Cliffs, NJ: Prentice Hall.

O'Donohue, W., & Halsey, L. (1997). The substance of the scientist-practitioner relation: Freud, Rogers, Skinner and Ellis. *New Ideas in Psychology, 15*(1), 35-53.

O'Donohue, W., & Smith, L. D. (1992). Philosophical and psychological epistemologies in behaviorism and behavior therapy. *Behavior Therapy, 23*(2), 173-194.

Popper, K. (1959). *The logic of scientific discovery.* New York: Harper & Row.

Quine, W. V. O. (1951). Two dogmas of empiricism. *Philosophical Review, 60,* 20-43.

Quine, W. V. (1981). *Theories and things.* Cambridge, MA: Harvard University Press.

Skinner, B. F. (1945). The operational analysis of psychological terms. *Psychological Review, 52,* 270-276.

Skinner, B. F. (1957). *Verbal behavior.* New York: Appleton-Century-Crofts.

Skinner, B. F. (1963). Behaviorism at fifty. *Science, 140,* 951-958.

Skinner, B. F. (1970). B. F. Skinner, an autobiography. In P. B. Dews (Ed.), *Festschrift for B. F. Skinner* (pp. 1-21). New York: Appleton-Century-Crofts.

Skinner, B. F. (1972). *Cumulative record: A selection of papers* (3rd ed.). New York: Appleton-Century-Crofts.

Skinner, B. F. (1974). *About behaviorism.* New York: Knopf.

Skinner, B. F. (1984). *A matter of consequences*. New York: New York University Press.
Skinner, B. F. (1986). Is it behaviorism? *Behavioral and Brain Sciences, 9,* 716.
Smith, L. D. (1986). *Behaviorism and logical positivism: A reassessment of the alliance.* Palo Alto, CA: Stanford University Press.

CHAPTER 5

Operant Conditioning and the Experimental Analysis of Behavior

❖

This chapter will introduce many of the empirical regularities that were discovered in the experimental analysis of behavior as well as the experimental methods and procedures used to uncover these. These empirical regularities have names, such as *reinforcement, discrimination,* and *extinction*. These are not just names for concepts that need to be researched to see if they actually describe reality. All of these have been well researched for the past 40 years or so, and it is no longer controversial to assert that behavior is lawful in the ways described by these terms.

We are including an overview of these empirical regularities and of this behavioral research methodology because we want you to see the entire web of Skinner's work. The many regularities that exist between an organism's environment and an organism's behavior that Skinner and his students discovered is an important part of this web. We also want you to understand the research methodologies used to uncover these regularities, because they are still being used and are still yielding new information.

The success of the experimental analysis of behavior provides evidence for the value of Skinner's philosophy of science. If his philosophy of science failed to produce a science that could achieve its goals of prediction and control, then this failure has to have some (negative) relevance for how good the philosophy of science actually is. Conversely, if his philosophy of science is unappealing, yet the science based on this philosophy is successful, then this information needs to be used to reappraise judgments regarding the worth of the philosophy. When something works, (especially when it works better than its competitors), then its conceptual basis deserves a closer look. Moreover, we want you to see the consistency between Skinner's philosophy of science and the methodology he used. We turn first to a brief overview of the major elements of Skinner's research methodology.

RESEARCH METHODS IN THE
EXPERIMENTAL ANALYSIS OF BEHAVIOR

The Use of Infrahuman Organisms

Most of Skinner's research was conducted with rats and pigeons. Skinner studied nonhumans, not because he was primarily interested in rats and pigeons, but for the same reasons that other scientists (e.g., physiologists) study nonhumans. First, it is more convenient to use nonhumans. They are always around to be run in experiments. Second, these animals are cheap to use (they don't require payment for their participation). Third, it is ethically permissible to use nonhuman animals in ways not permissible with humans. For example, most regard it as ethical to deprive animals of food and water, and it is ethical to have them participate in the experiment for many hours. One can use deception and (obviously) not inform the nonhuman animal of the purpose of the experiment. Fourth, evolutionary theory suggests that there is some behavioral continuity across species, because species are not distinct but rather have a common ancestry. Physiologists and physicians have successfully exploited this concurrence regarding origins for a century or so. Thus, there is reason to believe that the study of infrahuman species can reveal reasonably accurate information about humans. This is not to say that there is nothing unique about humans. There is. Some of this uniqueness will be discussed in Chapter 7, on verbal behavior.

Therefore, Skinner, like many basic researchers, used nonhuman animals in his experiments. However, Skinner was also keenly interested in human behavior. He regarded his animals as a convenient experimental preparation to study human behavior. Skinner recognized that there is an important extrapolation or generalization question: Does the regularity found with this nonhuman species also hold for humans? Skinner and his students sometimes answered this question by conducting experiments with humans, and their results generally indicated that the results also apply to humans.

Figure 5.1. The interior of an operant chamber.
NOTE: Reprinted by permission of the B. F. Skinner Foundation.

The Apparatuses

Skinner studied the behavior of his animals in what is called an *operant chamber* or *Skinner box* (see Figure 5.1). The operant chamber is a small, boxlike structure with one or two features that the animal can manipulate. For example, the operant chamber used with rats has a bar that the rat can press. The operant chamber for pigeons has a disk that the pigeon can peck. The bar and the disk provide something the animal can manipulate. This is important, because in order to study operant behavior, the experimental apparatus must have something that the animal can potentially manipulate (because, as you remember, operant behavior *operates* on the environment). The operant chamber also contains a mechanism to provide reinforcers such as food, water, visual stimulation, or sound.

Often the operant chamber has a light that signals the availability or absence of reinforcement. The light is called a *discriminative stimulus* and will be discussed more later. Sometimes, in order to study punishment, the floor of the operant chamber is fitted with an electrical grid so that shocks can be delivered to the animal.

The bar or disk in the chamber is connected to a *cumulative recorder,* a device that records and displays the total number of responses the organism makes as a function of time. As discussed previously, Skinner was interested in measuring the rate of response, and the cumulative recorder provides an easy-to-read display of the ongoing rate of responding and changes in the rate of responding (see Figure 5.2).

This experimental setup creates an idealized situation for studying operant behavior. The operant chamber allows (a) control of key parameters to determine if these are functionally related to changes in the rate of behavior, and (b) isolation from extraneous variables. Scientists often seek to isolate their experimental preparations from the complexities that occur in the natural environment, because such complexities can obscure orderly relations. For example, physicists study gravitational forces in vacuums so that the confounding factors of air friction and the aerodynamic properties of the object can be avoided. The purpose of the operant experimental preparation is to allow the experimenter to manipulate independent variables to see their effects on the dependent variable. The purpose is not to create an artificial situation.

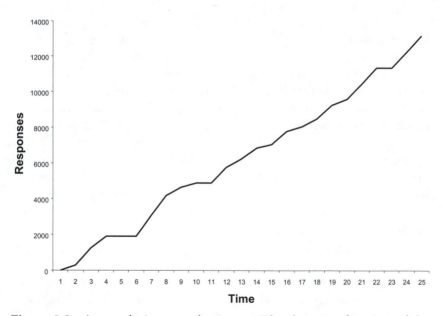

Figure 5.2. A cumulative record printout: The slope is a function of the number of responses over time (rate of response).

Functional Classes

What is selected in operant conditioning is a *functional response class,* not a response defined topographically. Defining a response *topographically* involves describing the specifics of what the particular response looks like. For example, we can topographically define a "greeting response" that you make by stating, "You make eye contact for two seconds, you move your right hand in such and such direction at such and such speed, while you say 'Hi' at a certain volume."

Topographically, each greeting is unique and occurs only once. It is highly unlikely that you will ever again behave with identical topographical details. Similarly, the rat in the Skinner box will sometimes press the bar with its right paw and sometimes with its left, sometimes with a certain force and sometimes with a slightly different force. Thus, defining a response topographically leads to the problem that no two responses are exactly alike, which seems to obscure the reality that conditioning involves learning to respond more frequently or less frequently.

Skinner solved this problem by demonstrating that what is learned is a class of responses defined functionally. For example, when a food-deprived rat presses a bar and receives a food pellet, what occurs is that the class of responses that function to depress the bar (e.g., certain right paw movements, certain left paw movements, etc.) will occur more frequently.

The same is true about stimulus classes that precede or follow the response. Seeing someone smiling may be an antecedent condition for us to greet them. However, no two smiles are exactly the same. This general class of antecedent responses can function to increase the probability of certain responses. Thus, in the experimental analysis of behavior, particular stimuli and responses are elements of classes that are defined functionally.

Rate of Responding as Key Dependent Variable

Skinner argued that rate of responding should be the key dependent variable, because he regarded learning as involving changes in the probabilities of responding. A rate (or frequency) is the number of responses per unit of time. Four bar-presses per hour is an example of such a rate.

The probability of a response is indexed by examining the rate (or fre-quency) of the response. *Frequency* is the number of responses that occur in a certain time interval. Skinner did not think that, in the contingencies of reinforcement, stimuli invariably elicited responses. Rather, the con-tingencies of reinforcement express probabilistic relationships between antecedent stimuli, responses, and consequences. Learning involves changes in these probabilities. Skinner (1953) stated,

> The rate at which a response is emitted in such a situation comes close to our preconception of the learning process. As the organism learns, the rate increases. As it unlearns (for example, in extinction) the rate falls. Various sorts of discriminative stimuli may be brought into con-trol of the response with corresponding modifications of the rate. Motivational changes alter the rate in a sensitive way. So do those events which we speak of as generating emotion. The range through which the rate varies significantly may be as great as an order of 1000:1. Changes in rate are satisfactorily smooth in the individual case, so that it is not necessary to average cases. . . . Rate of responding appears to be the only datum that varies significantly and in the expected direction under conditions which are relevant to the "learning process." . . . It is no accident that rate of responding is successful as a datum, because it is particularly appropriate to the fundamental task of a science of behav-ior. If we are to predict behavior (and possibly to control it), we must deal with "probability of response." The business of a science of be-havior is to evaluate this probability and explore the conditions that determine it. (pp. 45-46)

Skinner regarded rate of responding as a dependent variable that is sensi-tive to learning phenomena and a natural dimension of behavior.

Single-Subject Designs

The final piece of Skinner's experimental procedure is the research designs he utilized. These are often called *single-subject experimental designs*. They are *single-subject* because the behavior of only one subject is usually being studied. (However, single-subject designs can also be used with more than one subject—see Johnston & Pennypacker, 1980, for details.) They are *experimental* because only one variable is manipulated at a time. Skinner's designs allowed him to uncover causal (functional) relationships.

Behavioral researchers wish to uncover principles that have generality, that is, principles that cover a large number of cases or situations. The goal of research is not to discover idiosyncratic information about the particular situation under study. Rather, researchers wish to uncover general principles to make accurate predictions and to exert beneficial control in a wide variety of situations.

To do this, the researcher must use a valid research design. A valid research design allows alternative explanations to be ruled out. An experimental analysis, as discussed in the previous chapter, allows the experimenter to make valid conclusions about causation.

Research designs allow the experimenter to arrange experience so that it is less ambiguous. To discover causal relations, the researcher first simplifies the situation so that a manageable number of causes are operating. The researcher then manipulates one and only one (independent) variable and accurately measures the target (dependent) variable to see if the manipulated variable is functionally related to the dependent variable.

Skinner studied the behavior of the individual organism. Part of the rationale for doing this is that groups do not behave—individuals do. Thus, it makes more sense to study one organism. Although general principles may be true about a group of organisms, the specifics and particulars of these principles may vary from organism to organism.

Note that the physical sciences do not face the problem of the individuality of the entities under study. For example, the only way a hydrogen atom is unique is that it has a unique physical location. In all other ways hydrogen atoms are indistinguishable. There is virtually no "individuality" about many physical entities, and therefore their individuality, such as it is, can safely be ignored.

This is not true about most biological organisms. No two humans, for example, are the same. In a very important sense we are all individuals—unique entities who are distinct in many ways. An appropriate research design in behavioral science must account for these individual differences in a way that still yields any general principles that may be present. Skinner argued that the single-subject research strategy achieves this goal.

For example, many organisms engage in emotional behavior when punishment is delivered, but the specifics and intensity of this emotional behavior may differ from organism to organism. A single-subject experimental design can reveal the general principle and account for individual differences. Derived measures such as a group average are viewed as artificial contrivances that obscure important information about actual behavior.

The extent to which principles generally hold is discovered through replications with other subjects. If an orderly relationship is found with one subject, then a series of subjects can be run in similar experiments to see if this relationship consistently holds. Subjects in the replication studies can be chosen to be maximally different from one another in ways thought to be relevant; this is the best test of the generality of the principles. A combination of single-subject experimental designs and replications can account for both general principles and important individual differences.

Baseline Data

Single-subject experimental designs evaluate the effects of an independent variable by imposing it on ongoing behavior. For example, if one were testing the effectiveness of paying a fourth-grader $1 for each book she read, one would start by measuring for a number of days or weeks the number of books she read before "treatment" started. The first part of this process—the initial period of time, during which the treatment is absent—is called the *baseline*. The baseline serves as a comparison for the period of time when treatment is implemented. Logically, it is not possible to say that treatment increased, decreased, or had no effect on behavior without knowing the status of behavior before treatment was implemented. Ideally, one hopes to observe a stable baseline, that is, one in which there is no upward or downward trend and in which all of the responses fall into a small range. This creates the least ambiguous standard for comparing the effects of treatment.

A stable baseline allows the experimenter to make an important prediction: The behavior will continue as it is, given that nothing affecting it changes. That is, the belief is that a stable baseline shows that behavior will not change unless something that plays a causal role is added or subtracted.

Graphically, this can be illustrated as follows:

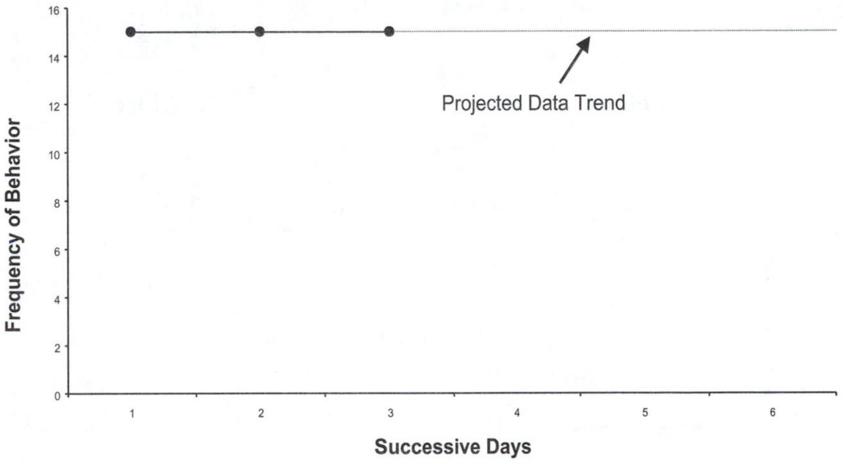

Figure 5.3. Baseline data. On the basis of the three initial data points (observations), one would expect performance to continue at this level for some time (indicated by the dotted line).

Let's examine the following case. A researcher has collected data and found a stable baseline. Next, the researcher applies an intervention and finds an immediate increase in the rate of behavior. Can the researcher now validly conclude that the treatment caused (is functionally related to) the rise in the target behavior? The answer is, No! A sound experimental design must rule out all plausible rival hypotheses. In this case, a rival hypothesis that has not been ruled out is *temporal coincidence*. It may be the case that some other event, which coincided with the treatment, actually caused the behavior change.

However, the researcher can rule out the plausible rival hypothesis of temporal coincidence. The researcher does this by *verification* (Cooper, Heron, & Heward, 1987). Verification is accomplished by showing that the baseline level of response would have remained unchanged if the independent variable had not been introduced. One way this can be accomplished is by withdrawing the treatment. In many cases, if the treatment was responsible for the change and it is withdrawn, then the baseline level of responding should reappear.

Graphically, this can be illustrated as follows:

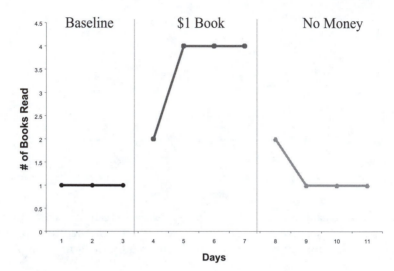

Figure 5.4. A withdrawal design. Ideally, performance will drop to baseline levels once the intervention is withdrawn. Of course, this isn't the case when a skill set is taught (e.g., reading, spelling, a second language)—you can't take skills away.

If the experimenter withdraws treatment and behavior returns to baseline, but the experimenter is still not convinced that he or she has ruled out temporal coincidences, then the experimenter can conduct replications within the experiment by repeating the procedure. That is, within practical limits, the experimenter can repeatedly add and remove treatment while observing the resulting behavior. This can be structured so that a variable amount of time occurs in each baseline and treatment period, making temporal coincidence even less plausible. Although there may be a regular process in temporal coincidence with the behavior change (e.g., every two weeks the subject works a night shift), it is less likely that there is an extraneous process that exactly mirrors an irregular temporal pattern of reversals. If the behavior changes in a systematic way (i.e., when there is no treatment, baseline levels are observed, and when there is treatment, different levels are observed), then eventually the experimenter could conclude that the plausible rival hypothesis of temporal coincidence has been properly ruled out.

What the experimenter has shown is a *constant conjunction*. That is, when treatment is implemented, behavior changes in a certain way, and when treatment is removed, behavior is restored to its previous state. This constant conjunction is what Hume regarded as a causal relationship. Thus, by showing a constant conjunction, the single-subject research design allows the experimenter to uncover causal relationships.

This basic design is called a *withdrawal* or *ABAB design*. The elements of this design involve the measurement of responding in a particular setting during three phases:

1. (A) a baseline period in which the independent variable is absent;
2. (B) a treatment phase in which the independent variable is introduced and remains present;
3. (A) a return to the initial baseline conditions, in which the independent variable is removed; and
4. (B) a reintroduction of the independent variable.

Graphically, this design can be depicted as shown in Figure 5.5 on the following page.

The major problem with this design is either the impossibility or the impracticality of the reversal, because it is sometimes impossible or unethical to reverse treatment effects. For example, if the intervention provides the subject with rules to follow, it is difficult to reverse. One cannot simply say, "Forget the rule."

Another design commonly used is the *multiple-baseline design*. This design can be used in cases in which the behavior cannot be reversed. Baer, Wolf, and Risley (1968) described this design in the following way:

> In the multiple baseline technique, a number of responses are identified and measured over time to provide baselines against which changes can be evaluated. With these baselines established, the experimenter then

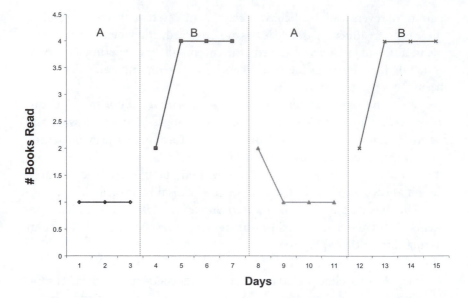

Figure 5.5. An ABAB design. Ideally, performance increases with the introduction of the intervention into the first B phase.
Performance drops when the intervention is withdrawn (second A phase). There is an increase in performance once the
intervention is reintroduced into the second B phase (the first
and second A and B phases are commonly indicated with the
subscripts 1 and 2, respectively—$A_1B_1A_2B_2$).

applies an experimental variable to one of the behaviors, produces a
change in it, and perhaps notes little or no change in the other baselines.
If so, rather than reversing the just-produced change he instead applies
the experimental variable to one of the other, as yet unchanged, responses.
If it changes at that point, evidence is accruing that the experimental
variable is indeed effective, and that the prior change was not simply a
matter of coincidence. The variable then may be applied to still another
response, and so on. The experimenter is attempting to show that he has
a reliable experimental variable, in that each behavior changes maximally only when the experimental variable is applied to it. (p. 94)

Graphically, the logic of this design can be illustrated as shown in
Figure 5.6):

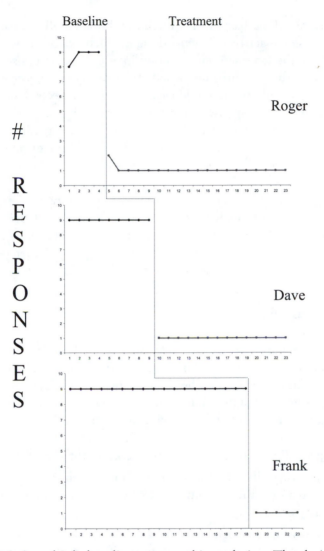

Figure 5.6. A multiple-baseline-across-subjects design. The design logic holds if it is across behaviors or settings. In this example, the intervention is staggered across subjects. Baseline is briefly taken for Subject 1 (Roger). The intervention is introduced into Subject 1's baseline while Subjects 2 (Dave) and 3 (Frank) are still in baseline. Next, the intervention is introduced into Subject 2's baseline while baseline is taken for Subject 3. Last, the intervention is introduced into Subject 3's baseline.

There are three basic forms of the multiple-baseline design: (a) a multiple-baseline-across-behaviors design, which examines two or more behaviors of the same subject; (b) a multiple-baseline-across-settings design, which examines the same response of the same subject in two or more settings; and (c) a multiple-baseline-across-subjects design, which examines the same response of several different subjects.

In the multiple-baseline design, verification of the predicted level of baseline responding is made by the observation of little or no change in the other behaviors (or subjects or settings) that are still under baseline conditions.

Cooper et al. (1987) argue that in order to properly use the multiple-baseline design, the experimenter must (a) select independent but functionally similar baselines, (b) not apply the independent variable to the next behavior too quickly, (c) significantly vary the length of the baselines, and (d) intervene at the most stable baseline first.

Visual Analysis

Skinner argued that it is not necessary to analyze data statistically. He thought that statistical analysis was an artificial manipulation of data that often was arbitrary and obscurantist. Instead, he suggested a visual inspection of graphs of the data. Cooper et al. (1987) claimed that immediately graphing data has the following advantages:

1. providing a complete, ongoing record of the subject's behavior;
2. allowing direct and immediate contact with the data, which in turn allows the experimenter to investigate important changes as they occur;
3. allowing a fast, readily learned method of data analysis that does not introduce arbitrary levels of significance and problematic statistical assumptions;
4. allowing a more conservative analysis of the data, in that only variables that repeatedly produce large effects are judged to be significant, and all weak and unstable effects are screened out;
5. encouraging independent judgments and interpretations by all consumers of the data;

6. allowing, in applied behavior analysis, graphical displays of data that can provide meaningful feedback to clients.

Skinner argued for an important departure from traditional psychology. Data are not analyzed statistically, but rather visually. In the history of science, most important scientific discoveries did not depend upon statistical analysis:

> It is not the obligation of the research worker to bow to the dictates of statistical theory until he or she has conclusively established its relevance to the techniques of inquiry. On the contrary, the onus lies on the exponent of statistical theory to furnish irresistible reasons for adopting procedures which still have to prove their worth against a background of three centuries of progress in scientific discovery accomplished without their aid. (Hogben, as quoted in Parsonson & Baer, 1978, p. 344)

Finally, there are many other single-subject research designs. We recommend that you look at the following texts for more information: Barlow, Nelson, and Hayes (1984); Cooper et al. (1987); Johnston and Pennypacker (1980); and Sidman (1960).

THE IMPORTANT REGULARITIES

Skinner studied operant conditioning. Skinner called the behavior *operant* because operant behavior operates on the environment. An operant response always changes the environment. When you talk, you change the environment, because now the environment has sound in it. When you put on a coat, you change the environment because now your environment includes a coat covering you. When you write, your environment changes, because now the computer screen contains words it did not previously. All these are examples of operant behavior, because in all these the response changes the environment.

So far we might conclude that Skinner studied a two-term relation:

Response → Environmental Consequence

However, Skinner realized that responses do not arise willy-nilly. We do not say "Yes" unless we have first heard a question. We do not open our umbrellas unless it is raining. We do not engage in typing motions with our fingers unless our computer is turned on and a keyboard is under our fingers. That is, we engage in responses only when the environment has certain characteristics—there is a question posed, it is raining, or the computer is on.

Thus, Skinner studied what is known as a *three-term contingency*:

Environmental Setting Event $\rightarrow$ Response $\rightarrow$
Environmental Consequence

Schematically, Skinner expressed this as:

$$SD \rightarrow R \rightarrow Rf+$$

SD is the symbol for a discriminative stimulus, *R* for response, and *Rf+* for reinforcer. Notice that, consistent with his philosophy, Skinner studied environmental-behavior relationships. He studied how the environment sets the occasion for a response, and he studied how the environment gives consequences to responses. He also studied the probability relationships between these and how these probabilities change.

Another important feature of the experimental analysis of behavior is that it searches for changes. Skinner (1969) stated,

> Any stimulus present when an operant is reinforced acquires control in the sense that the rate will be higher when it is present. Such a stimulus does not act as a goad; it does not elicit the response in the sense of forcing it to occur. It is simply an essential aspect of the occasion upon which a response is made and reinforced. The difference is made clear by calling it a discriminative stimulus (or SD). An adequate formulation of the interaction between an organism and its environment must always specify three things: (1) the occasion upon which a response occurs; (2) the response itself; and (3) the reinforcing consequences. The interrelationships among them are the "contingencies of reinforcement." (p. 7)

Another important feature of the experimental analysis of behavior is that it searches for changes in probability. In science, there are two types of laws. The first kind is a universal law. This kind of law states a necessity. That is, if certain conditions are met, inevitably a certain effect will follow. The law of gravitation is a universal law. If certain conditions are met (no countervailing force is acting on an object that is close to the earth's surface), the object will, without exception, fall toward the earth accelerating at a constant rate. The second type of law is probabilistic. That is, science can identify conditions that will (often dramatically) affect the probability of events. Physicians often use probabilistic laws. For example, if you have strep throat, a physician will prescribe an antibiotic, because the probability is very high (although it is not certain—the physician is not relying on a universal law) that if you take a regimen of antibiotics the strep will go away. But we need to emphasize that this is not certain: Some people (although a small minority) take the antibiotic and strep remains. However, we have useful information if, prior to gaining scientific knowledge, there is little probability of bringing about an event, but with the addition of scientific information, we can greatly increase the probability of controlling the event. Probabilistic laws are informative and useful.

Environmental antecedents do not universally bring about a response; rather, they affect the probability of the event. When it rains, you don't inevitably open an umbrella. (You might, for example, think it is too much of a hassle, as you have only a short distance to go to your car.) However, the frequency with which you open an umbrella when it doesn't rain compared to the frequency with which you open an umbrella when it does rain shows that raining does increase the probability of your opening an umbrella.

Events that follow the behavior also affect the future occurrence of the behavior probabilistically. If a professor responds to your question by saying "Shut up—that's a stupid question!" this will (in the typical case) affect the probability of your asking another question in the future. However, there is no universal, exceptionless law. One cannot say in all cases that if a professor says very negative things about a student's question, the student will never ask that professor another question. However, one can say, "If a professor says very negative things about a student's question, it will tend to decrease the probability of that student's asking another question."

A terminological distinction: If the environment can universally, without exception, cause some behavior to occur, that behavior is said to be *elicited* by the environment. Reflexes are generally elicited by the environment. If a strong puff of air is directed at your eyes, this elicits an eye blink. Behavior that is related to the environment probabilistically, like operant behavior, is said to be *emitted*. We (usually) emit umbrella opening behavior when it rains. Operant responses are emitted rather than elicited.

Reinforcement—The Most Important Principle

When behavior acts on the environment, the consequences it produces can be classified into three types according to the functions the consequences have on future behavior: (a) neutral—the consequences do not decrease or increase the future frequency of the behavior; (b) reinforcement—the consequences increase the future frequency of the behavior; and (c) punishment—the consequences decrease the future frequency of the behavior.

Skinner thought that reinforcement was the most important function. Reinforcement is important because it is the only one that has a constructive function. That is, neutral consequences, by definition, have no effect on how the organism behaves in the future, so they are not interesting. Punishment causes behavior to decrease or disappear, and thus, although it is interesting, it isn't directly responsible for building a behavioral repertoire. Reinforcement, on the other hand, selects behavior to increase in frequency and to be maintained in the behavioral repertoire.

Skinner also thought reinforcement was the most important function because organisms do not like to have their behavior punished. Skinner found that organisms would engage in negative emotions, escape, or avoidance behavior (see the discussion of escape and avoidance later in the chapter) when they learned that their behavior might be punished. For example, if a child learns that hitting his sister will be punished by his parents, he might escape the situation by running away from his parents when they are about to spank him. He might avoid his parents by remaining away from home. Or, if he is punished or thinks punishment is imminent, he may cry, be anxious, and generally be distressed.

For these and other reasons, Skinner thought that reinforcement, rather than punishment, was a better way to control behavior. Organisms display either neutral or positive emotions when their behavior is reinforced, and they do not try to avoid or escape from reinforcement. Moreover, reinforcement functions positively to construct a behavior repertoire, rather than negatively to temporarily inhibit some response from occurring. Skinner (1953) stated,

> Civilized man has made some progress in turning from punishment to alternative forms of control. Avenging gods and hell-fire have given way to an emphasis upon heaven and the positive consequences of the good life. In agriculture and industry, fair wages are recognized as an improvement over slavery. The birch rod has made way for the reinforcements naturally accorded the educated man. Even in politics and government the power to punish has been supplemented by a more positive support of the behavior which conforms to the interests of the governing agency. But we are still a long way from exploiting the alternatives. . . . Direct positive reinforcement is preferred because it appears to have fewer objectionable by-products. (p. 192)

There are two common mistakes made in trying to understand reinforcement. The first is to think that reinforcement is the same thing as reward. It is not, for two reasons: (a) Rewards do not necessarily increase the future frequency of behavior, and by definition, a reinforcer must increase the frequency of future behavior. For example, we can reward your asking questions by giving you some nice consequences, for example, giving you a good daily grade. However, these consequences might not actually increase the rate of your asking questions. Thus, although we are rewarding your question asking, we are not reinforcing it. (b) Rewards are generally considered to be pleasurable consequences, but reinforcement does not have to be pleasurable. We think of rewards as pleasurable things such as candy, money, tasty drinks, pats on the back, and so forth. However, reinforcing events need not be pleasurable—they only need to increase the frequency of the behavior. Our favorite example here involves writing with a pen. The pen leaves an ink trail on the paper. The ink trail reinforces your writing behavior. That is, if there were no ink trail you would stop, and if there were an ink trail you would have a higher probability of continuing. However, the ink trail on the paper does not typically cause you to feel pleasure.

The second mistake that people make is that they talk about reinforcing people rather than behavior. One always reinforces behavior, not people. Remember the definition of reinforcement: It causes an increase in the frequency of the response—not an increase in the frequency of a person, whatever that may mean!

Now let us look at some subtleties regarding reinforcement and punishment. Reinforcement and punishment can be classified into positive and negative subcategories. This distinction is made on the basis of whether the reinforcer or punisher is added or subtracted from the organism's environment to achieve the reinforcing or punishing effect. *Positive* simply means that something new is presented to the organism. Thus, *positive reinforcement* means that a stimulus such as food is presented to the organism after the organism responds. *Positive punishment* means that a stimulus such as a electrical shock is presented to the organism after it responds.

Negative simply means that something is taken away. *Negative reinforcement* means that some stimulus is taken away from the organism's environment, and this serves to increase the rate of response that follows. For example, a mother's giving a toy is negatively reinforced by a child having a tantrum, because the child's yelling and screaming goes away. Your speeding in your car is negatively punished when the police take away some of your money.

This distinction is important, because some people make the mistake of thinking that negative reinforcement means the same thing as punishment. It does not. Negative reinforcement will increase the frequency of the behavior it is contingent upon by removing something (crying). Positive or negative punishment, on the other hand, will decrease the frequency of the behavior it is contingent upon.

This distinction is useful, because it gives us increased options for influencing behavior. We can either take away or add something to influence behavior.

Two other important distinctions should be discussed. The first concerns the temporal delay between the consequences and the behavior. Some consequences occur quite close in time to the behavior. These are called *proximate consequences*. Others occur only after some delay and are called *distal consequences*. Some behaviors have both proximate and distal consequences. An interesting case is when the valence of these consequences changes; for example, the proximate consequences are reinforcers and the distal consequences are punishers. For example, the proximate consequences of eating cake can be reinforcing (it tastes good), whereas the distal consequences can be punishing (gaining weight). Or the proximate consequences can be punishing (pain during exercise), but the distal consequences can be positive (losing weight).

In general, proximate consequences are more powerful in controlling behavior. This is why many of us eat too much and exercise too little. The proximate consequences of these behaviors control their frequency more than the distal consequences do. Attempting to make distal consequences have more control is part of self-control, which will be discussed in Chapter 9. When behavior has mainly distal consequences, it is generally not correct to call these effects either punishers or reinforcers, because these distal effects generally do not influence the frequency of behavior. We have heard many parents say that they tried reinforcement to improve the behavior of their child, but it did not work. When we ask them exactly what they did, they often say something like, "I told him if he started studying harder now and if at the end of the semester he received As and Bs, I would buy him a minibike." However, no matter how much the child desires a minibike, the interval between the targeted behavior (studying now) and the putative reinforcer (the bike) is so long that it generally will have little or no effect. In the laboratory, effective reinforcers typically come within one second of the response.

Another distinction is between *natural* and *artificial* reinforcers and punishers. A natural reinforcer is a consequence that follows the behavior without some special arrangement. For example, the natural consequence of touching a burning ember is pain. A natural consequence of being rude is that people will avoid you. On the other hand, an artificial consequence for asking a question is getting a piece of candy. Another artificial consequence is getting 10 points for doing your homework. This distinction is important, because research has found that special therapy environments that use artificial consequences are problematic. When the client functions in real-life environments that do not contain these artificial consequences, his or her behavior changes will not be maintained. Reinforcers are not bribes.

A final distinction is between secondary (or conditioned) and pri-mary reinforcement. *Primary reinforcement* is said to occur when no learning is necessary for the reinforcement to have its effects. Mother's milk is a primary reinforcer for a baby's suckling. A *secondary reinforcer* needs to be learned. Five-dollar bills are secondary reinforcers, as are verbal responses such as "Good job." We need to learn the reinforcing value of secondary reinforcers. Saying "Good job" will not reinforce the behavior of a one-year-old, and a five-dollar bill will not reinforce the behavior of someone who has not learned the value of money.

So far we have discussed two terms of the three-term contingency. We have seen that the organism's response can be operant in that it operates on the environment. And we have seen that the environmental changes function as consequences that can affect the future probability of the re-sponse. We will now discuss the first term—the discriminative stimulus.

DISCRIMINATION AND GENERALIZATION

Skinner found that organisms do not emit behavior in a willy-nilly fash-ion. Rather, their behavior is influenced by stimuli that are present in the environment. These stimuli are said to set the occasion for the response. They are called *discriminative stimuli*. For example, a green light is a discriminative stimulus for behavior involved in proceeding through the intersection. The ringing sound ending and someone saying "hello" are discriminative stimuli for talking to begin. Note, again, that these do not elicit behavior (there is no reflex involved here, but rather, these increase the probability that an operant response will be emitted).

Organisms can learn to have a greater or lesser range of antecedent stimuli to influence their behavior. When organisms learn to have a smaller range of stimuli serve as discriminative stimuli, this is called *discrimina-tion learning*. When organisms learn to have a larger range of stimuli influence their behavior, it is called *generalization*. Discrimination learn-ing is taught through *differential reinforcement*. For example, let's say a one-year-old who is learning her first words is calling all men "Daddy." This causes some embarrassment to all concerned. Note that the child is still under the influence of antecedent stimuli. She does not call dogs, coats, and so forth "Daddy," just men. Differential reinforcement occurs when the family does not reinforce certain behavior (calling anybody else but her father "Daddy") and instead reinforces only proper target behavior, that is, calling her father "Daddy." This is how we learn to "make distinctions" and to respond differentially to a wide variety of antecedent stimulus conditions. Note here how the three-term contingency is involved in discrimination and generalization learning.

Sometimes, however, we want responses to generalize. This is often the case in behavior therapy. For example, let's say that we are treating a person who is afraid of dogs and we use exposure therapy to help her reduce her fears. Exposure therapy involves presenting the feared stimulus to the person until the person no longer feels fearful. Let's say we use a collie named Pooch to do this, and the client is soon unafraid of Pooch. What we want is for this lack of fear to generalize to all (friendly) dogs. Generalization is taught by reinforcing approach behavior in a wide range of antecedent conditions. In this example, to help the response generalize, we would need to expose the client to a wide variety of dogs. Keller and Schoenfeld (1950) stated, "In the ever changing environment, the generalization of stimuli gives stability and consistency to our behavior . . . in contrast with generalization, the process of discrimination gives our behavior its specificity, variety, and flexibility" (pp. 116-117). Now that you know the fundamentals of operant conditioning, we will present some other interesting findings.

Shaping

Before the environment can select a response class, it must first occur. Some behavior is so complex that there is little chance it will occur spontaneously. For example, it is unlikely that a person will spontaneously emit a proper tennis serve. Shaping is a procedure through which behavior can be generated from early approximations. *Shaping* can be defined as the differential reinforcement of successive approximations. For example, rats don't naturally press bars in the operant chamber. Usually, the experimenter must shape this response. This is how shaping is done: First, the experimenter reinforces responses that are close to the final, desired response. Thus, the experimenter may first reinforce standing close to the bar. After the rat is doing this reliably, the experimenter changes the criterion for reinforcement. Now standing close to the bar is no longer sufficient for gaining reinforcement. The experimenter now only reinforces standing close to the bar and making a paw movement in the direction of the bar. The experimenter can repeatedly raise the criteria for reinforcement in these successive approximations until the final, target behavior is performed. Note how differential reinforcement occurs in shaping: Some responses are reinforced and others are not.

Extinction

What happens if we reinforce a behavior for some time and then stop reinforcing it? Skinner found that eventually the organism stops responding. This is called *extinction* (note the evolutionary metaphor). For example, if we give a pigeon food each time it pecks a key and if we do this several hundred times, the pigeon will peck the key when hungry. However, Skinner found that if he stopped giving the pigeon food after it pecked the key, the pigeon would soon stop pecking the key.

Often before the behavior ceased there would be an *extinction burst*. Extinction bursts occur when the organism responds to the cessation of reinforcement by temporarily increasing the rate and intensity of responding. Extinction bursts may have evolutionary advantages. Often in the natural environment contingencies shift slightly. Extinction bursts, with their increases in the variability, intensity, and frequency of responding, increase the probability that the organism's behavior will successfully come into contact with the new contingencies.

SCHEDULES OF REINFORCEMENT

What happens if the experimenter reinforces some of the responses only every other response? Skinner, in his book with the late Charles B. Ferster titled *Schedules of Reinforcement* (Ferster & Skinner, 1957), studied the effects of procedures that specify which instances of an operant response will be reinforced. There are several kinds of schedules of reinforcement:

1. Continuous-reinforcement schedule: In this schedule, every instance of the operant response will be reinforced. For example, every time the rat presses the bar it will receive food.

2. Intermittent-reinforcement schedules: This is the opposite of a continuous-reinforcement schedule in that some instances of the operant response do not receive any reinforcement. There are two types of intermittent-reinforcement schedules:

   a. Ratio schedules: In this schedule, every second, or third, or sixteenth, response is reinforced.

   b. Interval schedules: In this reinforcement schedule, the key is the passage of time, not the number of responses. So in an interval schedule of two minutes, after the passage of two minutes the next response will be reinforced. The rat can respond many times or not at all during the two minutes, but none of these will be reinforced. After the time limit elapses, the very next response will be reinforced.

For one more level of complexity, ratio and interval schedules can be either *fixed* or *variable*. Here's what these two terms mean.

In a fixed schedule, the reinforcer is always delivered after the same ratio or interval. For example, in a "fixed-ratio schedule 3," the reinforcer is always delivered after the third response. In a "fixed-interval five minutes," the reinforcer is always delivered after the first response that occurs after five minutes has elapsed.

In a variable schedule, the ratios or intervals can vary within the schedule and are described by their mean value. For example, a "variable ratio 4" means that, on average, the fourth response is reinforced. However, when one actually looks at the delivery of reinforcement, sometimes the reinforcer was delivered after the second response, sometimes after the sixth response, and so forth, but when all these are averaged, the schedule delivered a reinforcer on average after the fourth response. Similarly for variable-interval schedules, on average the response is reinforced after some mean amount of time has elapsed.

The importance of understanding schedules of reinforcement is threefold:

1. In the real or natural world, there are many different schedules of reinforcement, and thus to understand the natural world we must understand all of these schedules. A perfectly functioning soda machine works on a continuous-reinforcement schedule. A slot

machine works on a variable-ratio schedule. Fishing works on a variable-interval schedule. Waiting for your computer to boot is tantamount to a fixed-interval schedule. Jobs that pay by piece-work—for example, every three bags of fruit earns the worker $5—work on a fixed-ratio schedule.

2. Different schedules of reinforcement produce different patterns of responding:

   a. In fixed-ratio schedules, we typically see a high rate of response until reinforcement occurs. Then a relatively long post-reinforcement pause occurs. Thus, if reinforcement comes only after you paint three pictures, typically you will work hard to get the three done. After you receive your reinforcement, you will take a break or pause for a while before beginning your next batch of three (called *break and run*).

   b. In variable-ratio schedules, the organism tends to respond at a high rate, but there is typically no pausing after reinforcement occurs.

   c. In fixed-interval schedules there is also a post-reinforcement pause. However, responding occurs at a lower rate than on ratio schedules, except toward the end of the interval, when responding briefly increases to "meet the reinforcer."

   d. In variable-interval schedules, there are usually no pauses either pre- or post-reinforcement. However, the rate of responding tends to be low.

3. The final reason why schedules of reinforcement are important to study is that the way in which the organism responds to extinction depends upon the schedule by which the organism was being reinforced. The various reinforcement schedules produce various *resistances to extinction*. The most interesting finding is known as the *partial-reinforcement extinction effect*: Intermittent-reinforcement schedules will result in many more responses during extinction than continuous reinforcement schedules will. It is thought that this phenomenon occurs because in intermittent schedules it takes many more responses for the organism to come into contact with the change in the contingencies. For example,

in a ratio schedule of 100, the organism must respond 100 times before it comes into contact with the extinction schedule, whereas in a continuous schedule it immediately comes into contact with the change in contingencies.

It is also important to note that Skinner recognized the existence of other learning processes, although he did not study these to any great extent. Thus, he acknowledged the existence of Pavlovian conditioning (although he usually called this *respondent conditioning*) and habituation in his explanation of behavior, although he rarely researched these processes.

ESCAPE AND AVOIDANCE

Skinner also studied escape and avoidance. In *escape conditioning,* the animal learns to make an operant response that changes the situation from one in which an aversive stimulus is present to one in which it is absent. For example, if a loud, aversive noise is present, rats can learn to press a bar to terminate the noise.

In *avoidance conditioning,* the organism learns to emit an operant response that prevents the occurrence of an aversive stimulus. Usually there is some signal of the impending occurrence of an aversive stimulus. For example, a mother can learn to give a baby a pacifier when it begins to stir. This behavior produces an avoidance of the baby's crying.

DEPRIVATION

It was common for Skinner to deprive his organisms of food or water before using them as subjects in his experiments. Skinner thought deprivation was a necessary condition for making something an effective reinforcer. Skinner's rats were maintained at 80% of free-feeding weight and were thus food deprived. Skinner found that for these rats, food pellets were effective reinforcers.

CONCLUSION

This chapter dealt with the empirical regularities that were demonstrated by the methods and procedures used in the experimental analysis of behavior. *Reinforcement, discrimination, extinction,* and *punishment* were terms for these regularities. These regularities would have likely remained obscure if experimental strategies other than single-subject methodology (e.g., group designs with statistical analysis) had been employed. The success of the experimental analysis of behavior provides evidence for the worth of Skinner's philosophy of science, radical behaviorism.

References

Baer, D. M., Wolf, M. M., & Risley, T. (1968). Current dimensions of applied behavior analysis. *Journal of Applied Behavior Analysis, 1,* 91-97.

Barlow, D. H., Nelson, R. O., & Hayes, S. C. (1984). *The scientist-practitioner.* New York: Pergamon.

Cooper, J. O., Heron, T. E., & Heward, W. L. (1987). *Applied behavior analysis.* New York: Macmillan.

Ferster, C. B., & Skinner, B. F. (1957). *Schedules of reinforcement.* New York: Appleton-Century-Crofts.

Johnston, J. M., & Pennypacker, H. S. (1980). *Strategies and tactics of human behavioral research.* Hillsdale, NJ: Erlbaum.

Keller, F. S., & Schoenfeld, W. N. (1950). *Principles of psychology.* Englewood Cliffs, NJ: Prentice Hall.

Parsonson, B. S., & Baer, D. M. (1978). The analysis and presentation of graphic data. In T. R. Kratochwill (Ed.), *Single subject research: Strategies for evaluating change* (pp. 101-165). New York: Academic Press.

Sidman, M. (1960). *Tactics of scientific research.* New York: Basic Books.

Skinner, B. F. (1953). *Science and human behavior.* New York: Macmillan.

Skinner, B. F. (1969). *Contingencies of reinforcement: A theoretical analysis.* New York: Appleton-Century-Crofts.

CHAPTER 6

Skinner on Cognition

❖

Various behavioral approaches (e.g., Watson's, Hull's, Skinner's) dominated psychology from approximately the 1920s to the 1960s. Many psychologists believe that in the 1960s a "cognitive revolution" occurred in psychology (Baars, 1986). In this revolution, experimental psychologists who studied humans began to argue that the behaviorists' views of the legitimate subject matter of psychology were wrong. They proposed that cognitive constructs such as *information processing, memory storage,* and *executive functioning* would provide a fuller, more accurate understanding of human activity. An important part of their argument was that, although behavior must make up the actual data of psychology, it is legitimate and even necessary to make inferences from these data to unobserved constructs that serve to better explain the behavior. For example, although no one actually observes memory, cognitive psychologists argued that this construct is useful and even necessary to explain behavior.

O'Donohue, Naugle, and Ferguson (2000) maintained that there were two major components of the cognitive psychologists' arguments during the so-called revolution. First, there were arguments about the recent accomplishments and future promise of a scientific approach that focuses on cognition. We will not discuss this component here, as it would take us too far afield. Rather, we refer you to Baars (1986) for a sympathetic account of the cognitive revolution and to O'Donohue et al. (2000) for an account that is critical of the substance of this revolution.

Second, there were arguments aimed at showing the inadequacy of the behavioral approach. A major focus of these arguments was that the behavioral approach mishandles cognitions. These arguments, in order to be exegetically correct, would have to properly characterize the behavioral approach to cognitions and its putative limitations. O'Donohue et al. (2000) argued that cognitive psychologists' exegesis regarding Skinner's views on cognitions was poor. Although there has been a revolution in a sociological sense—that is, although the number of behaviorists has decreased and the number of cognitively inclined psychologists has increased—there was little substantive material behind this shift. Behaviorism was not drowning in a sea of anomalies, and there were no clear demonstrations of the superiority of the cognitive approach with regard to prediction and control.

This chapter is devoted to Skinner's treatment of cognitions, because the proper role of the cognitive is, and has been, one of the most controversial issues in psychology. For example, some critics of Skinner (e.g., Chomsky, 1959; Dennett, 1978; Ellis, 1977; Fodor, 1983; Rogers & Skinner, 1956) have indicated that the basis of their rejection of behaviorism is that Skinner has failed to recognize the importance of cognitions, especially their explanatory potential. Even today, there is still considerable tension and debate between radical behaviorists and cognitive psychologists. Because this issue is still current, it is important to understand Skinner's position on cognitions.

O'Donohue, Callaghan, and Ruckstuhl (1998) have suggested that in this debate, the "cognitive side" has the advantage for two reasons. First, the cognitive position is more consistent with folk psychology. Our society teaches us in many ways that our thoughts are important because they cause overt behavior. However, it is another matter whether this inchoate folk psychology is true. Second, cognitive psychology has a prima facie plausibility. Cognitions often precede behavior, and thus they are in the proper temporal position to act as causes. However, the logical fallacy known as post hoc ergo propter hoc (literally, "after this, therefore because of this") states that simply preceding another event is insufficient evidence to conclude that the earlier event caused the later event.

Because of these factors, Skinner's position on cognitions, admittedly, does not enjoy prima facie appeal. However, as was discussed in the first chapter, often science forces us to accept conclusions that initially are not plausible.

SKINNER AND COGNITIONS

Skinner advanced several arguments regarding the role of cognitions in human behavior and in the science of human behavior. We suggest that there are two distinct kinds of claims in this web: (a) claims regarding the proper relation between science and cognitions, and (b) claims regarding the status of cognitions as natural events. Because of the multiplicity and interdependence of many of these arguments, it is best to view Skinner's position on cognition as consisting of a web of interdependent claims. We will see that Skinner has not one, but rather several, arguments regarding the proper status of cognitions in a science of human behavior. We will also see that some of these arguments concern the proper relations between science and cognition, whereas others have to do with the status of cognitions and are independent of any concerns about their scientific study. Moreover, we will also see that many of these arguments are interrelated in key aspects.

SKINNER'S METASCIENTIFIC ARGUMENTS

First, we will describe Skinner's arguments concerning the relationship between science and cognition. Skinner explicitly acknowledged that part of his writings were philosophical. Thus, in this first section we will attempt to faithfully describe how Skinner's philosophy of science treats cognitions.

I. Cognitions Are Not Directly Manipulable and Therefore Cannot Have a Causal Role in a Scientific Analysis

Skinner stated that the goals of science are description, prediction, and control. However, control is the preeminent goal because (a) when a phenomenon can be controlled, the other goals of science (prediction and description) can also be achieved; and (b) the control of some phenomenon allows humans to change conditions so that they are more to their liking (e.g., to reduce the incidence of self-abusive behavior). However, to control some phenomenon, the causes of that phenomenon must be understood. Moreover, to identify causes, true experiments must be conducted. Behaviorists and nonbehaviorists agree that the sine qua non of a true experiment is that a hypothesized causal variable must be manipulated.

Thus, only variables that can be manipulated can be candidates for causes in scientific analyses. Now, the question becomes "Are cognitions directly manipulable?" Skinner argued that they are not. Skinner (1974) stated that a scientist cannot directly alter or manipulate cognitions:

> No one has ever directly modified any of the *mental* activities or traits.
> . . . There is no way in which one can make contact with them. The
> bodily conditions felt as such can be changed surgically, electrically, or
> with drugs, but for most practical purposes they are changed only
> through the environment. (pp. 229-230)

For example, the scientist cannot "inject" a belief or thought into a subject's awareness. The scientist can possibly *indirectly* affect cognitions through the *direct* manipulation of the environment. A scientist can, for example, have some subjects read about aversive events and others read about pleasant events, or subjects can be instructed to recall disappointing events in their lives. But in these cases the scientist has not directly manipulated feelings or any other kind of cognitions. The scientist has directly manipulated environmental stimuli (e.g., reading material and instructions). Therefore, it can rightly be said that environmental events can play causal roles with respect to subsequent behavior. When cognitive psychologists claim they are manipulating cognitions, they are misspeaking in an important way (see arguments in Section IV of this chapter regarding inferential misdescription).

Therefore, because cognitive variables cannot be directly manipulated, and because the manipulation of an independent variable is a necessary condition of valid causal inference, cognitions cannot be identified as causes in science. On the other hand, to the extent that manipulable environmental variables can allow a large degree of control of the dependent variable of interest, then cognitive variables become correspondingly uninteresting as causal entities.

II. Transitivity Argument

The transitivity argument refers to the idea that if A is lawfully related to B and B is lawfully related to C, then A is lawfully related to C. Skinner (1953, 1977) argued that there is a causal chain, involving behavior and the environment, consisting of four links: (a) an environmental change, (b) an inner condition, (c) a class of behavior, and (d) an environmental consequence. Skinner argued that if each of these linkages is lawful, then nothing will be lost if the second link is bypassed. That is, if an environmental condition causes an inner condition, which in turn causes a particular behavior, which in turn operates on the environment to cause a change, then nothing is lost if the second link is ignored. All the information needed to understand the behavior of an organism are facts that can be objectively observed (i.e., physical acts in the environment), which requires extended observation of the environment-behavior relationship.

Consider the following example. Say it is known that a particular organism has not eaten for a long time. If it is also known that this condition leads the organism to feel hungry, and that when this organism is hungry the probability that it will eat is high (i.e., the organism's learning history), then we know that when the organism has not eaten for a long time, it will probably eat. Because food deprivation is lawfully related to hunger, which is then lawfully related to eating behavior, then knowledge of the first and third link is sufficient for predicting and controlling the behavior of the organism. Knowing that the organism experiences hunger is not necessary in predicting and controlling, and consequently understanding, the behavior of the organism. Skinner (1953) did point out, however, that if we could obtain independent information about the second link (i.e., hunger), this would obviously permit us to predict the third link without looking to the first link. In addition, Skinner (1953) argued, this information would actually be preferred, because it would be nonhistorical information. That is, the first link may lie in the past history of the organism, but the second link is something that is current. However, direct information about the second link is seldom, if ever, available (see argument regarding verbal community inaccessibility in Section IX for more on the nature and importance of this inaccessibility).

Skinner (1953) also pointed out that one does not need to completely ignore inner conditions. Knowledge of inner conditions can be used as collateral information for predicting behavior. That is, if certain inner conditions are reliably correlated with certain behaviors, then this information (if it is sufficiently precise and accurate itself, since it can usually be obtained only through self-report) can be used to help predict certain behaviors. Going back to the previous example, if it is known that depriving an individual of food lawfully results in the individual's eating, knowing that the individual is hungry is useful to the extent that if the organism has reported hunger in the past he or she has then eaten. This information, however, is not necessary for explaining why the individual ate and in fact appears to be redundant information. That is, we can still predict and control behavior if we have direct knowledge about the history (i.e., the past relationship between the environmental contingencies and that behavior) to which those inner conditions (e.g., hunger) are to be traced.

Consequently, the objection to inner states is not that they do not exist, but that they are not relevant in a functional analysis. Skinner argued that unless there is a weak link in the causal chain (e.g., the first link does not lawfully determine the second, or the second cause the third), then the first and third links must be lawfully related. Valid information about the second link may provide additional clues regarding the relationship between the first and third link, but it does not alter the relationship. Note that Skinner stated that cognitions are legitimately involved as causal entities in the causal chain. Skinner's argument is a metascientific one, because it attempts to establish that the cognitive causal link can be ignored without the loss of explanatory power.

III. Cognitions as More Behavior to Be Explained

Critics of Skinner frequently state that he devalued the role of cognition in psychology. The problem with this criticism is that it is too vague. However, it is possible to respond to the more specific criticism that Skinner's radical behaviorism has no role for cognitions. This criticism is false. Although in Skinner's system cognitions cannot be independent variables (see Section I), they can serve as dependent variables (Skinner, 1974). That is, cognitions do not explain other behavior but rather are more behavior to be explained.

Thus, Skinner admits covert behavior as legitimate data for scientific analysis. This distinguishes his radical behaviorism from the methodological behaviorism of John Watson. Watson, for methodological reasons, argued that cognitions should have no role in a science of behavior. The reason, in brief, is that cognitions are not intersubjectively verifiable, and thus the reliability and validity of these private events cannot be checked.

Skinner rejects the criterion of intersubjective verifiability—the psychology of the other one—and is satisfied simply with the report of the person who experiences the private event. Again, the private behavior needs to be explained (it can legitimately serve as a dependent variable), but because it cannot be manipulated, it cannot serve as an explanatory, causal, or independent variable:

> Mentalism kept attention away from the external antecedent events which might have explained behavior, by seeming to supply an alternative explanation. Methodological behaviorism did just the reverse: by dealing exclusively with external antecedent events it turned attention away from self-observation and self-knowledge. Radical behaviorism restores some kind of balance. It does not insist upon truth by agreement and can therefore consider events taking place in the private world within the skin. It does not call these events unobservable, and it does not dismiss them as subjective. It simply questions the nature of the object observed and the reliability of the observations. The position can be stated as follows: what is felt or introspectively observed is not some nonphysical world of consciousness, mind, or mental life but the observer's own body. (Skinner, 1974, pp. 18-19)

In sum, Skinner's claims are metascientific, in that his view about cognitions' proper role in science is that although they are unacceptable as independent variables, they can function in science as proper dependent variables.

IV. Cognitions as Inferential Misdescriptions

Individuals can speak in an imprecise and misleading manner when they use the cognitive idiom. For example:

A passage from a recent discussion of the development of sexual iden-
tity in a child might be translated as follows: "The child forms a concept
based upon what it has observed and been told of what it means to be
a boy or girl." (A child's behavior is affected by what it has observed
and been told about being a boy or girl.) "This concept is oversimpli-
fied, exaggerated, and stereotyped." (The contingencies affecting the
behavior are simplified and exaggerated and involve stereotyped behavior on the part of parents and others.) "As the child develops
cognitively, its concepts, and consequently its activities, become more
sophisticated and realistic" (As the child grows older, the contingencies
become more subtle and more closely related to the actual sex of the
child.) (Skinner, 1977, p. 2)

In his parenthetical remarks, Skinner attempted to translate claims expressed in the cognitive idiom to more accurate claims regarding behavior
and its interaction with the environment. However, people count these
inferential misdescriptions as successes of the cognitive approach. The
account in the previous quote, to the extent that it does accurately describe or predict behavior, is taken as evidence in favor of the cognitive
account.

However, Skinner argued that the cognitive inferences involved in
this description are problematic for several reasons: (a) they fail to point
to manipulable conditions that allow valid causal inference; (b) they are
misdescriptions, in that what should be described are the observed behavior-environment relations, which can be described in a less inferential
manner; and (c) the leap to the inferred cognitive construct is not supported by any independent evidence and hence is unwarranted. Thus, the
scientist speaks more precisely when the description involves a lower level
of inference.

V. Pseudoexplanations

As discussed later in this chapter, one of the reasons Skinner (1974,
1977) argued against inner explanations was that they are difficult (but
not impossible) to observe (see argument in Section IX regarding verbal
community inaccessibility). Second, according to Skinner, to explain some-

thing is to show its causes. However, covert behavior cannot be manipulated directly (see Section I) and therefore cannot have a role in causal explanation. In addition to the difficulty in observing putative inner causes, Skinner argued that inner causes have obscured the variables that *are* immediately available for scientific analysis. That is, in contrast to variables located within the organism, these variables are directly observable and can be found in the immediate environment of the organism and in its environmental history. Importantly, these variables are manipulable and therefore can potentially be shown to be causes. Skinner (1974) stated, "The objection to the inner workings of the mind is not that they are not open to inspection but that they have stood in the way of the inspection of more important things" (p. 182). Consider the following example provided by Skinner (1977):

> A British statesman recently asserted that the key to crime in the streets was "frustration." Young people mug and rob because they feel frustrated. But why do they feel frustrated? One reason may be that many of them are unemployed, either because they do not have the education needed to get jobs or because jobs are not available. To solve the problem of street crime, therefore, we must change the schools and the economy. But what role is played in all this by frustration? Is it the case that when one cannot get a job one feels frustrated and that when one feels frustrated one mugs and robs, or is it simply the case that when one cannot earn money, one is more likely to steal it—and possibly to experience a bodily condition called frustration? (p. 4)

In contrast to inner explanations (e.g., frustration), these external variables (e.g., unemployment, level of education, amount of money or resources) have the physical status that is needed in order to apply the usual techniques of science. Consequently, the use of these externally located variables, unlike internally located variables, makes it possible to explain behavior as other subjects are explained in science (Skinner, 1953).

Why then have feelings, cognitions, and so forth typically been invoked as the causes of behavior; that is, why have they served as pseudoexplanations for behavior? Skinner (1974) observed that most people appear to believe that if one thing follows another it was probably caused by the first thing (the fallacy of post hoc ergo propter hoc), and because feelings or thoughts typically immediately precede behavior, these inner conditions are taken to be the causes of behavior. Skinner (1974) argued, however, that these feelings, thoughts, and other cognitive phenomena are not causative but instead merely accompany behavior. That is, these inner conditions provide us with collateral information, not information regarding why the behavior itself occurred. For example,

> Salivation is elicited by certain chemical stimuli on the tongue . . . because the effect has contributed to the survival of the species. A person may report that a substance tastes good, but it does not elicit salivation because it tastes good. Similarly, we pull our hand away from a hot object, but not because the object *feels* painful. The behavior occurs because appropriate mechanisms have been selected in the course of evolution. The feelings are merely collateral products of the conditions responsible for behavior. (Skinner, 1974, p. 52)

Feelings, thoughts, and so forth, however, are part of the immediate situation, whereas the consequences that shape and maintain the behavior are not usually present in the setting in which a response occurs. Instead, they have changed the organism and become part of the history of the organism; they are much less salient and consequently are easily overlooked. For example, when a particular behavior is consistently reinforced (e.g., skillful athletic behavior), a person is said to have a feeling of confidence. When reinforcement stops, the behavior undergoes extinction, appearing much more seldom (e.g., the individual stops playing sports), and the person is said to have lost his or her confidence. The loss of confidence is then used to explain the absence of the behavior rather than the diminished level of reinforcement.

Finally, another reason cognitive explanations can be pseudoexplanations is that they can be redescriptions of the behavior to be explained. That is, a common form that these mentalistic pseudoexplanations take is a vicious circle that explains nothing. For example, one may seek an explanation for why Fred often behaves in a very outgoing, gregarious, friendly manner. The "explanation" might be that Fred has an extroverted personality. For some, this is a satisfying explanation. However, Skinner would ask, "And how do you know that this person has an extroverted personality?" If the answer is along the lines of "because he often behaves in a very outgoing, gregarious, friendly manner," then the explanation is circular. Skinner claimed that cognitive explanations are often pseudoexplanations in that the inner constructs are used to explain the behavior from which they were inferred.

VI. Cognitive Explanations Prematurely Allay Curiosity

Another reason Skinner (1974) argued against mentalistic explanations is that they tend to allay curiosity and bring inquiry to a stop. As discussed in the previous section regarding inner conditions as pseudoexplanations, it is easy to observe thoughts and feelings at a time and in a place that make them seem like causes (usually because they immediately precede or co-occur with the behavior), so that we are not inclined to inquire further about what actually was the cause of the behavior.

For example, when we say that a person eats because he or she is hungry or that a person drinks a great deal of alcohol because that individual has a drinking habit, we seem to be referring to causes. These putative "causes," however, are nothing but redundant descriptions (see Sections III and V). That is, nothing more is explained by referring to the inner condition (i.e., hunger, habit) than to the behavior (i.e., eating, drinking) itself. We have learned nothing new about how to predict, control, or understand why the behavior occurred; we have learned only that the person felt or thought something before he or she acted. Consider the following example regarding Pavlov's approach to explaining behavior:

> What Pavlov added can be understood most clearly by considering his history. Originally he was interested in the process of digestion, and he studied the conditions under which digestive juices were secreted. . . . He was handicapped by a certain unexplained secretion. Although food in the mouth might elicit a flow of saliva, saliva often flowed abundantly when the mouth was empty . . . this was called "psychic secretion." Perhaps the dog was "thinking about food." Perhaps the sight of the experimenter preparing for the next experiment "reminded" the dog of the food it had received in earlier experiments. But these explanations did nothing to bring the unpredictable salivation within the compass of a rigorous account of digestion. Pavlov's first step was to control conditions so that "psychic secretion" largely disappeared.

He designed a room in which contact between dog and experimenter was reduced to a minimum. The room was made as free as possible from incidental stimuli. The dog could not hear the sound of footsteps in neighboring rooms or smell accidental odors in the ventilating system. Pavlov then built up the "psychic secretion" step by step. In place of the complicated stimulus of an experimenter preparing a syringe or filling a dish with food, he introduced controllable stimuli which could be easily described in physical terms. In place of the accidental occasions upon which stimulation might precede or accompany food, Pavlov arranged precise schedules in which controllable stimuli and food were presented in certain orders. Without influencing the dog in any other way, he could sound a tone and insert food into the dog's mouth. In this way he was able to show that the tone *acquired* its ability to elicit secretion, and he was also able to follow the process through which this came about. Once in possession of these facts, he could then give a satisfactory account of all secretion. He had replaced the "psyche" of psychic secretion with certain objective facts in the recent history of the organism. (Skinner, 1953, pp. 52-53)

As pointed out by Skinner (1974), it has been objected that one could trace the cause of a person's behavior back not only to the physical conditions that shape and maintain the behavior but also to the causes of those conditions and the causes of those causes, ad infinitum. However, Skinner (1974) also pointed out that there is no point in going back beyond the point at which *effective action* can be taken, and that point is not to be found in the psyche (p. 231). Because we cannot manipulate the inner conditions of an individual directly, it appears that effective action must take place at a different level. For example, a therapist cannot directly manipulate the subjective reports of depression in another individual. The therapist can, however, help the individual to manipulate those conditions that may be affecting the level of depression (e.g., level of social support, amount of response-contingent positive reinforcement, etc.).

VII. Problems With the Mental

Skinner argued that there are difficult questions concerning what kind of thing cognitive or mental phenomena are. He suggested that the concept of mental phenomena is inconsistent with a physicalistic, scientific account of behavior and therefore should not be invoked by the psychologist:

> The practice of looking inside the organism for an explanation of behavior has tended to obscure the variables which are immediately available for a scientific analysis. These variables lie outside the organism, in its immediate environment and in its environmental history. They have a physical status to which the usual techniques of science are adapted, and they make it possible to explain behavior as other subjects are explained in science. These independent variables are of many sorts and their relations to behavior are often subtle and complex, but we cannot hope to give an adequate account of behavior without analyzing them. (Skinner, 1953, p. 31)

Thus, examining environment-behavior relationships avoids serious questions about the ontic status (i.e., do they exist at all?) of the mental and its relationship to physical events. An important advantage of this is that it allows the study of behavior to be consistent with the other sciences.

VIII. Cognitive Physiological Science Is Expensive and Impractical

Skinner argued that cognitions properly construed are bodily states—responses that do not explain other behavior but are more behavior to be explained (see Section III). Cognitive behavior can be studied by the physiologist and is a legitimate field of scientific inquiry. However, two qualifications need to be made. First, the physiological level of analysis deserves no hegemony: It is in no way better or "deeper" than the experimental analysis of molar behavior-environment relations. This point needs to be made, because some biological materialists claim that behavior is not really explained until its physiological mechanisms are understood.

Second, inquiry at the molar level has significant advantages over the physiological level. First, it is not physiologically intrusive. The intact organism can be studied, and the numerous side effects of invasive physical procedures can be avoided. This is an important practical matter because, for example, parents will be much more willing to change the environment of their children than to change their brain structure. Second, physiological mechanisms are not self-contained. Rather, when a mechanism's causal chain is tracked back, eventually one still needs to understand what environmental events it stands in relation to. Thus, eventually one must still understand the role of the environment.

SKINNER'S ARGUMENTS REGARDING THE STATUS OF COGNITIONS

Skinner argued that not only do cognitions present difficulties in their relationship to science but that they also present problems to the language community for teaching discriminations, as well as to the individual for accurately understanding the nature of the covert behavior. A possible implication of these arguments is to suggest that covert behavior may be a relatively impoverished domain in which to search for variables that aid in prediction and control (compared to the richness of the environment). We turn now to these two arguments.

IX. Verbal Community Inaccessibility

According to Skinner (1974, 1977), because the verbal community (i.e., the verbal practices of an area) does not have direct access to the inner conditions of an individual (e.g., the individual's thoughts, feelings, etc.), the verbal community must rely on the individual to communicate what those inner conditions are. That is, how does a person find out what is going on inside another if he or she does not have direct access to that information? One way to resolve this problem is to teach the individual to make distinctions between different experiences and then to relay that information to the outsider. For example, when teaching a child to correctly identify colors, one can show the child colored objects, ask him or her to respond with color words, and then give the child verbal feedback stating whether or not the responses correspond or fail to correspond with the colors of the objects. In this example, however, both the child and the teacher have direct access to the colored object (i.e., the colored object can be found in both of their environments). This is more difficult to accomplish when trying to get an individual to make distinctions and report states that the individual alone has access to—his or her own cognitions or feelings. Because the verbal community lacks direct information regarding these inner states, the community is in less of a position to help the individual make distinctions by providing differential consequences in order to teach a discrimination between these different experiences.

To some extent, however, the verbal community can solve this problem. For example, the verbal community may use collateral responses to stimuli. These collateral responses, then, can be used to help identify or describe an inner state. For example, one may observe that when a child receives a painful blow, he or she cries. The verbal community teaches the child to say "That hurts"; in so doing, the verbal community teaches the child, however imperfectly, to label his or her experience as pain. Similarly, if a child has not eaten for a long time or eats quickly and ravenously when given food, the verbal community can teach the child to say "I'm hungry" when he or she is in a similar situation. Later, when the child receives a painful blow or has not eaten in a while, he or she has learned to tell others that he or she is in pain or is hungry. The verbal community now has some access to information that previously was only available to the individual experiencing these states.

Although the verbal community has coped with the problem of privacy to some extent, the descriptions of these bodily states are still not very accurate (see also Section X on the problems of introspection). For example, when seeing a physician, one is given a great deal of latitude in explaining what "kind" of pain one is experiencing (e.g., sharp, dull). The crudeness of one's descriptions of the pain is not due to the vagueness of the pain; rather, it is attributable to the inaccessibility of that information to the verbal community, and consequently to the community's limited ability to teach the individual how to accurately discriminate and hence report on these inner states. Contrast this to the large number of discriminations possible regarding color. Two related problems include the verbal community's reliance on the individual to report his or her inner conditions truthfully and the ability of the individual to report on his or her inner states (Nisbett & Wilson, 1977). The latter of these two points will be discussed further in the next section.

X. Inability to Report—
The Problems of Introspection

According to Skinner (1953, 1974), not only does the verbal community have limited access to the internal processes (e.g., cognitions, feelings) of an individual, but the individual him- or herself has limited access as well. That is, when using introspection to gather information about one's internal processes, an individual does not come in contact with the actual processes of his or her nervous system; instead, all that one is aware of is just more stimuli and responses. Consider Skinner's (1977) comments regarding this issue:

> Those who see themselves thinking see little more than their perceptual and motor behavior, overt and covert. They could be said to observe the results of "cognitive processes" but not the processes themselves— a "stream of consciousness" but not what causes the streaming, the "image of a lemon" but not the act of associating appearance with flavor, their use of an abstract term but not the process of abstraction, a name recalled but not its retrieval from memory, and so on. We do not, through introspection, observe the physiological processes through which behavior is shaped and maintained by contingencies of reinforcement. (p. 10)

In other words, an individual can report on some of the products of his or her physiological processes, but not on the physiological processes themselves. For example, people have access to the pleasure they find in playing video games, but they do not have access to how the association between that feeling and that activity came about. When asked why they play video games, their likely response is that they find it enjoyable, not that this behavior has been maintained by contingencies of reinforcement, because they don't have access to information about the latter. A possible reason why we have limited access to our internal conditions may have to do with evolution (in Skinner's phrase, *contingencies of survival*). That is, systems that have persisted through the process of evolution are those that have played a role in the survival of the species. Systems that process information from the environment have been more important to the survival of the species than systems that process information regarding the internal conditions of the organism.

CONCLUSIONS

We have attempted to provide a faithful exegesis of Skinner's positions on cognition. We have argued that he presents two broad kinds of positions—one regarding the proper status of cognitions in a science of human behavior and the other dealing with problems in the relationships between cognitions and the language community and between cognitions and the individual's perceptual abilities.

One of our major interests in providing an accurate summary of Skinner's positions on cognitions is to provide a standard by which past and future criticisms of Skinner can be assessed. Valid criticism needs to accurately characterize the position in question. Skinner's positions on cognition are complex, and any useful criticism needs to adequately capture this intricacy.

Finally, we would like to suggest that this complexity derives from Skinner's appreciation of the complexity of the subject matter at hand:

> No one can give an adequate account of much of human thinking. It is, after all, probably the most complex subject ever submitted to analysis. . . . No matter how defective a behavioral account may be, we must remember that mentalistic explanations explain nothing. (Skinner, 1974, p. 246)

References

Baars, B. J. (1986). *The cognitive revolution in psychology.* New York: Guilford.

Chomsky, N. (1959). Review of Skinner's *Verbal behavior. Language, 35,* 26-58.

Dennett, D. (1978). Skinner skinned. In D. Dennett (Ed.), *Brainstorms* (pp. 53-70). Cambridge: Massachusetts Institute of Technology Press.

Ellis, A. (1977). The basic clinical theory of rational-emotive therapy. In A. Ellis & R. Grieger (Eds.), *Handbook of rational-emotive therapy* (pp. 3-34). New York: Springer.

Fodor, J. A. (1983). *The modularity of mind.* Cambridge: Massachusetts Institute of
     Technology Press.
Nisbett, R. E., & Wilson, T. D. (1977). Telling more than we can know: Verbal reports on
     mental processes. *Psychological Review, 84,* 231-259.
O'Donohue, W. T., Callaghan, G. M., & Ruckstuhl, L. E. (1998). Epistemological barriers
     to radical behaviorism. *Behavior Analyst, 21,* 307-320.
O'Donohue, W. T., Naugle, A. E., & Ferguson, K. E. (2000). *You say there was a cognitive
     revolution: A critique of the cognitive revolution.* Manuscript in preparation.
Rogers, C. R., & Skinner, B. F. (1956). Some issues concerning the control of human
     behavior: A symposium. *Science, 124,* 1057-1066.
Skinner, B. F. (1953). *Science and human behavior.* New York: Macmillan.
Skinner, B. F. (1974). *About behaviorism.* New York: Vintage.
Skinner, B. F. (1977). Why I am not a cognitive psychologist. *Behaviorism, 5,* 1-10.

CHAPTER 7

Skinner on Language

❖

The eminent 20th-century philosopher Ludwig Wittgenstein, who had a large influence on the development of logical positivism, is reported to have said that human beings have extreme difficulty in gaining a proper perspective on things that are commonplace—things that they almost can't help but take for granted (Moravcsik, 1990, p. 92). Language is an example of such a common phenomenon. Human beings, capable of language, talk constantly. We talk when others are around. We talk when no one is around. We talk on the phone. And now many of us talk on the Internet. We "think out loud" when solving problems ("thinking out loud" is the same as talking out loud). Some people even drink alcohol to encourage[1] themselves to talk more ("speak easy"). Human beings have such a proclivity to talk that we even talk to objects that are incapable of talking back. Children talk to their toys. Adults yell at their vehicles when on road trips. Some people even talk to their pets as if they were old school chums.

Indeed, because language is so common, we often forget how awe-inspiring it really is. Without this capacity, we would be little more than clever primates (as opposed to *really* clever primates). Cumulative knowledge, gained from countless life experiences built atop other life experiences, would not exist.

This all changed, however, once our ancestors developed the necessary apparatuses for speech (e.g., larynx, oral cavity, cerebral cortex) and began speaking with one another. In the words of W. V. Quine (1997), "with the development of language, thought proceeded to soar" (p. 172). As thoughts proceeded to soar, so too did cumulative knowledge for much of the species. Early on, we developed advanced agricultural practices (e.g., rotating crops) and animal husbandry (e.g., cross-breeding). We began fashioning sophisticated tools and weapons out of bronze and other metals. And, about 2,500 years ago, we began talking about talk—and spoken sounds were seen as "symbols of affectation in the soul" (Aristotle, as quoted in Moravcsik, 1990, p. 92). Most remarkably, language brought us into intimate contact with our distant past, through "historical" recollections (e.g., Herodotus, trans. 1924).

WHAT IS LANGUAGE?

Before proceeding to a behavioral definition of language, let us consider a more traditional definition. Indeed, the term *language* means different things to scientists of different orientations. To the linguist, "a language consists of a system of rules which relate sound sequences to meanings" (Hayes, Ornstein, & Gage, 1988, p. 2). Language is supposed to be a manner in which we communicate "thoughts" and "emotions" with each other (Chomsky, 1993, p. 9).

In the following passage, Skinner (1957) pointed out some critical flaws with this definition:

> But can we identify the meaning of an utterance in an objective way? A fair argument may be made in the case of proper nouns, and some common nouns, verbs, adjectives, and adverbs—roughly the words with respect to which the doctrine of ideas could be supported by the appeal to images. But what about words like *atom* or *gene* or *minus one* or *the spirit of the times* where corresponding nonverbal entities are not easily discovered? . . . Even the words which seem to fix an externalized semantic framework are not without their problems. It may be true that proper nouns stand in a one-to-one correspondence with things, provided everything has its own proper name, but what about common nouns? What is the meaning of *cat*? Is it some one cat, or the physical totality of all cats, or the class of all cats? Or must we fall back upon the idea of cat? Even in the case of the proper noun, a difficulty remains. Assuming that there is only one man named Doe, is Doe the meaning of *Doe*? Certainly *he* is not conveyed or communicated when the word is used. (p. 8)

In light of these problems, for Skinner (1957), language is a different matter entirely:

> The "LANGUAGES" studied by the linguist are the reinforcing prac-
> tices of verbal communities. When we say that *also* means *in addition*
> or *besides* "in English," we are not referring to the verbal behavior of
> any one speaker of English or the average performance of many speak-
> ers, but to the conditions under which a response is characteristically
> reinforced by a verbal community. (p. 461)

A verbal community includes members within a given geographic location (though not necessarily in this day and age—with modern communication technology like the Internet) who reinforce or withhold reinforcement (extinguish) for certain forms of verbal behavior while punishing others. For example, Ebonics (a dialect spoken by some people in the Bronx) would probably go unreinforced in London, United Kingdom (i.e., it would be ignored). Conversely, the dialect of English typically reinforced in London would likely not produce reinforcement if it were spoken in the Bronx.

According to Catania (1992), "Language is behavior" (p. 227). We might add that Skinner's formulation of language is wholly consistent with his science of behavior described elsewhere (Skinner, 1938, 1945, 1953, 1969, 1974).

HISTORICAL ANTECEDENTS

Skinner's formal work on language began in 1934, when he was 30 years old.[2] His commitment to understanding language can be dated to a conversation he had with the eminent philosopher Alfred North Whitehead while dining at the Harvard Society of Fellows (Skinner, 1957, pp. 456-460). While Skinner was expounding the principal arguments in favor of behaviorism, the conversation eventually came to a head when Professor Whitehead took a stand against Skinner on one critical point, namely, the viability of investigating language by means of science.

> Here, he [Whitehead] insisted, something else must be at work. He
> [Whitehead] brought the discussion to a close with a friendly challenge:

"Let me see you," he said, "account for my behaviour as I sit here saying, 'No black scorpion is falling upon this table.'" The next morning I drew up the outline of the present study. (Skinner, 1957, p. 457)

Even though it took 23 years for Skinner to publish his official "reply" to Professor Whitehead, by 1945 much of the content of his book on the subject, *Verbal Behavior* (1957), had been finished, and he later put his ideas to use in a summer course at Columbia University in 1947 (Michael, 1984). Skinner modified the crux of this material into his William James Lectures (Bjork, 1993). These lectures were mimeographed, and several hundred copies were distributed among his associates in the behavioral community. Even prior to its publication, Skinner's work on language was rapidly gaining currency among his followers (see Keller & Schoenfeld, 1950, pp. 376-400, as a case in point).

We now turn to Skinner's interpretation of verbal phenomena as outlined in *Verbal Behavior* and in his later work. The reader should note that, in Skinner's opinion, his book on language behavior was his greatest contribution to the science of behavior. And as we shall see, *Verbal Behavior* also invited much criticism from those unfamiliar with his brand of behaviorism.

PRINCIPLES OF THE ANALYSIS OF VERBAL BEHAVIOR

According to Skinner, the human species's crowning achievement came when its members began emitting verbal behavior.

The human species took a crucial step forward when its vocal musculature came under operant control in the production of speech sounds. Indeed, it is possible that all the distinctive achievements of the species can be traced to that genetic change. (Skinner, 1986, p. 117)

Although verbal behavior shares similar characteristics with other behavioral modalities (i.e., it can be reinforced and punished), it differs in how it influences the environment. Namely, verbal behavior requires the mediation of other persons to have any impact on the world at large. A *mediator* is someone or something that is required to achieve a particular end. If a glass is out of reach, way up high on a bookcase, we require a mediator (a person with long arms) to get it down for us.

In the following passage, Skinner (1957) made a distinction between nonverbal and verbal behavior:

> Behavior (nonverbal) alters the environment through mechanical action and its properties or dimensions are often related in a simple way to the effects produced. . . . All this follows from simple geometrical and mechanical principles. . . . Much of the time, however, a man acts only indirectly upon the environment from which the ultimate consequences of his behavior emerge. His first effect is upon other men. Instead of going to a drinking fountain, a thirsty man may simply "ask for a glass of water." . . . The ultimate consequence, the receipt of water, bears no geometrical or mechanical relation to the form of "asking for water." . . . Indeed, it is characteristic of such behavior that it is impotent against the physical world. (pp. 1-2)

Accordingly, verbal behavior is defined as behavior that is "reinforced through the mediation of other persons" (Skinner, 1957, p. 2)—persons who have been explicitly trained to do so (p. 225). This mediation takes place in what Skinner (1957) calls "a total verbal episode" (p. 2).

A Total Verbal Episode

Every study needs a unit of analysis. A *unit of analysis* is something you measure. Ideally, it should have a clear beginning and end. The unit of analysis in a football game is the yard. When studying speech, Skinner's unit of analysis was the total verbal episode. A total verbal episode can be understood using the three-term contingency. Importantly, this contingency applies to both speaker and listener. Recall that this contingency arrangement requires a discriminative stimulus (S^D), the response, and some consequence that is causally linked to any subsequent change in the probability of that behavior. In Figure 7.1, we illustrate a total verbal episode using a diagram comparable to those used in *Verbal Behavior* (Skinner, 1957; see pp. 38-39, 57, 84-85). Using Skinner's (1957, pp. 37-40) nomenclature,[3] the audience (the first S^D) sets the occasion for verbal behavior. The first ($\uparrow$) depicts the stimulation supplied by the listener (i.e., seeing or hearing him or her). The first ($\downarrow\downarrow$) indicates that the listener has been stimulated by the speaker's request (R^V). The speaker's request "Hand over the remote" (R^V) serves as a discriminative stimulus

(SPEAKER)

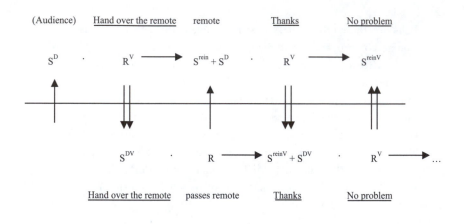

Figure 7.1. A total verbal episode
SOURCE: Adapted from Figure 1, Skinner, 1957, p. 38.

(S^{DV}) that sets the occasion for the listener to pass the remote to the speaker
(R). The second ($\uparrow$) indicates the point at which the remote changes hands.
The placing of the remote into the speaker's hand ($S^{rein} + S^D$) serves as a
reinforcer as well as a discriminative stimulus that evokes the verbal response (the second R^V) "Thanks." The second ($\downarrow\downarrow$) suggests that the
listener has been stimulated by the auditory stimuli produced by the
speaker (i.e., "Thanks"). Those stimuli (the second $S^{rein} + S^D$) serve as a
reinforcer and discriminative stimulus that evokes the response (the third
R^V) "No problem." The listener's response, in turn, reinforces (S^{reinV}) the
speaker's earlier verbal response (i.e., "Thanks").

The verbal episode just discussed depicts a simple request. Technically speaking, Skinner called this contingent relationship between the
speaker's behavior and the listener's responding a *mand* context. The
speaker is said to mand the remote control. Within this arrangement,
the speaker emits a verbal operant mainly because he or she is experiencing a condition of deprivation (i.e., being deprived of the remote)—but
more on mands in a moment. In addition to the mand, Skinner identified

six other classes of verbal operants: echoic, textual, transcription, intra-verbal, tact, and autoclitic. Skinner required these additional classes to account for other contingency relationships between speakers and listeners. These contingency relationships will be discussed in the following sections.

AN ANALYSIS OF THE SPEAKER'S BEHAVIOR

Verbal Behavior as Response Classes

Before outlining Skinner's seven classes of verbal operants, let us briefly review what he meant by classes of responding. Skinner (1938) commented early on in the development of his science of behavior that responding tends to vary from one moment to the next, and that therefore, the "identifiable unit is something more" (p. 33) than a precise description of the topographical characteristics of a particular individual response. *Topographical characteristics* are what a response looks or sounds like. Speaking quickly or slowly, or loudly or quietly, are topographical characteristics. They don't change the actual words spoken—they simply accent *how* they are spoken. For this reason, Skinner argued that the appropriate unit of analysis ought to occur above the level of individual responses to encompass larger classes of responses that serve similar functions. Functions of verbal behavior are simply what they *do*. "Milk, please," for example, gets you milk. This notion of class (different response forms that achieve similar ends), of course, is familiar ground and wholly consistent with the conventions of science (Quine, 1995). Flicking on a light switch and asking someone to do it for you belong to the same functional class. Both result in increasing the illumination in the room. Without class concepts, science could not adequately deal with most natural phenomena; instead, science would necessarily entail the study of isolated, wholly unique events, rendering anyone's ability to predict events impossible. As a case in point, the periodic table of elements enables chemists to predict the behavior of atoms of known classes—the "behavior" of elements when they combine into compounds.

In dealing with responses in class terms, Skinner (1953) set down the foundations for his concept of the *operant*:

> A response which has already occurred cannot, of course, be predicted or controlled. We can only predict that similar responses will occur in the future. The unit of a predictive science is, therefore, not a response but a class of responses. The word "operant" will be used to describe this class. (pp. 64-65)

In other words, "The term operant . . . is concerned with prediction and control of a *kind* of behavior. Although we observe only instances, we are concerned with laws which specify kinds" (Skinner, 1957, p. 20). As with other branches of science, without the concept of class, the analysis of verbal behavior dissolves, for formulating lawful relations becomes increasingly untenable as more and more "exceptions to the rule" enter into the picture. With that as background, let us turn to Skinner's (1957) seven classes of verbal operant behavior.

Functional Relationships Between Controlling Variables and Verbal Responding

Mands. The first type of verbal operant is called a *mand*. As a derivative of the words *command* and *demand,* among others, a *mand* is defined as a verbal operant in which the response is reinforced by a characteristic outcome and as such is under the momentary influence (Michael, 1993) of conditions of deprivation (e.g., hunger, thirst, lack of attention) or aversive stimulation (e.g., pain, skin irritation, distress; Skinner, 1957). Although not exclusively so, mands are easily identified because they usually specify the reinforcer. Crying out for a painkiller, asking for second helpings, and begging one's big brother to stop tickling are mands when they are under the control of specified consequences.

In the mand circumstance, verbal behavior is characteristically reinforced by those stimuli responsible for counteracting the condition of deprivation or eliminating aversive stimulation. By contrast, the next four functional relationships concern verbal behavior under the control of other verbal stimuli, whereby "a contingency is arranged between a verbal response and a generalized reinforcer" (Skinner, 1957, p. 53). An example of a generalized reinforcer is praise from others. Praise is usually associated with a host of other reinforcing events (e.g., the delivery of food, hugs, money), and as such, it has general reinforcing characteristics under a great variety of conditions of deprivation or aversive stimulation.

Echoic Behavior. The second type of verbal operant is called an *echoic.* According to Skinner (1957), "In the simplest case in which verbal behavior is under the control of verbal stimuli, the response (echoic) generates a sound-pattern similar to that of the stimulus" (p. 55). In other words, if a parent says "grape," and immediately thereafter a child says "grape" because of (i.e., under the control of) hearing the parent, this would constitute an instance of echoic behavior. The reader should note that there is a one-to-one correspondence between the stimulus produced by the parent ("grape") and the response emitted by the child ("grape"). Likewise, if a pet owner says "cracker," and his or her parrot produces a sound pattern similar to that stimulus because of (i.e., under the control of) hearing its owner, then this is echoic behavior.

What is most important to note here is that a verbal stimulus of corresponding form must immediately precede the response. Repeating the verbal stimulus an hour later would not be considered echoic behavior, because "a special temporal relation is lacking" (Skinner, 1957, p. 59).

Textual Behavior. The third type of verbal operant is *textual behavior.* Behavior is textual when the stimulus that sets the occasion for a vocal response is written or otherwise nonauditory (Catania, 1992).

> A text may be in the form of pictures (in so far as the response consists simply of emitting an appropriate vocal form for each picture), formalized pictographs, hieroglyphs, characters, or the letters or symbols of a phonetic alphabet (regardless of the accuracy or consistency with which the alphabet records vocal speech). . . . In the textual operant, then, the vocal response is under the control of a nonauditory verbal stimulus. (Skinner, 1957, pp. 65-66)

Upon closer inspection of Skinner's definition, it becomes plain that what is at issue is not so-called understanding, at least not in the conventional sense. That is to say, the appropriate response is simply evoked from a nonauditory discriminative stimulus—there is no requirement that the individual must "comprehend" the text.

Consider someone learning a second language. During the early stages of instruction, correct pronunciation is the most important thing. Such being the case, students usually read aloud lengthy passages with little or no appreciation for what the foreign words mean.

Skinner on Understanding

Given that the terms *understanding* and *meaning* refer to radically different things in behavior analysis, let us take a brief detour before returning to the next class of verbal operants. First, let us explain what we think Skinner meant by the term *understanding*. While reading the following, take notice that Skinner described levels of understanding, all of which suggest varying degrees of comprehension.

"In a simple sense of the word, I have understood what a person says if I can repeat it correctly" (Skinner, 1974, p. 146). Describing a deeper level of understanding, Skinner (1974) wrote: "In a somewhat more complex sense, I understand it if I respond appropriately" (p. 146). Or, worded differently,

> The listener can be said to understand the speaker if he simply behaves in an appropriate fashion. The behavior may be a conditioned emotional response. When, for example, the listener blushes at the mention of social error, he can be said to have understood what was said to the extent that his reaction was appropriate to the original event . . . the listener understands to the extent that he tends to act appropriately. (Skinner, 1957, p. 277)

It follows, therefore, that when someone is said to misinterpret a bit of text, according to the above formulation, what is meant by *misinterpretation* is that the reader does not respond in the same manner as the writer. In other words, the reader behaves in a given way "because of the operation of different variables" (Skinner, 1957, p. 278).

The same analysis can extend to when a listener is asked to do something and fails to understand what is expected of him or her. If, for example, a listener is told to "Go get bread" and returns from the market with a basket of fish, it is obvious that his or her behavior was influenced by variables apart from those responsible for the speaker's behavior.

The deepest level of understanding has to do with being able to specify contingencies of which behavior is a function. Behavior under the control of so-called contingency-specifying stimuli is *rule-governed behavior* (Pierce & Epling, 1995). Rule-governed behavior will be discussed at length in the latter part of this chapter. But for now, let us examine the relationship between verbal stimuli of this sort and how those stimuli participate in what Skinner called understanding.

Skinner (1974) described this deepest level of understanding in the following passage:

> Understanding sometimes means knowing reasons. If I throw a switch to put a piece of apparatus into operation and nothing happens, I may try the switch again, but my behavior quickly undergoes extinction, and I may then look to see whether the apparatus is connected with the power source, or whether a fuse is blown, or whether the starting switch is broken. In doing so, I may come to understand why it has not worked in the sense of discovering reasons. I have acquired understanding by analyzing the prevailing contingencies. . . . We also find it reinforcing when a rule, as a description of contingencies, makes them less puzzling or more effective. If a given situation has not evoked any very useful verbal behavior, we may be reinforced by what a writer says about it if we can then respond in the same way. We understand what he says in the sense that we can now formulate the contingencies he describes more exactly or respond to them more successfully. (pp. 146-147)

The point to notice here is that one does not simply respond to environmental events as dogs or cats would, but one also speaks to oneself or listens to others talk about what is going on (i.e., "knowing reasons"). And, based on the specification of the contingencies, a person then coordinates his or her actions with the prevailing contingencies, along with what was said. The part said is of chief importance, should it bring about more effective action on the part of the speaker. Practically speaking, those who demonstrate a greater understanding of the circumstances they are in are those individuals who respond most effectively to their circumstances.

Skinner on Meaning

In everyday discourse, we speak of "using" words as if they were objects, or, rather, we speak of words as if they were tools (Catania, 1992). For example, orators are said to "use" certain words to rouse interest in their audiences—such as *eye-popping, heart-stopping,* and *astounding.* These tools (words) are said to convey "ideas" from one "mind" to the next.

However, Skinner (1957) warned against such formulations in a scientific account of verbal behavior:

> We have no more reason to say that a man "uses the word *water*" in asking for a drink than to say that he "uses a reach" in taking the offered glass. In the arts, crafts, and sports, especially where instruction is verbal, acts are sometimes named. We say that a tennis player uses a drop stroke, or a swimmer a crawl. No one is likely to be misled when drop strokes or crawls are referred to as things, but words are a different matter. (p. 7)

In consideration of a behavioral analysis, such notions distract scientists from uncovering the controlling variables of which verbal behavior is a function, namely, environmental factors (Lee, 1981). Embracing such notions in a scientific enterprise forces us into dealing with nonmaterial, unobservable stuff. And importing nonmaterial stuff into science (if such stuff even exists) poses major problems. How, for instance, does one manipulate "invisible," intangible variables? As mentioned in Chapter 1, early chemists (known as *alchemists*) tried to understand combustion through "cooking up" an explanation that referred to the release of an element called *phlogiston* (which turns out not to exist) from the combusting substance. As it turned out, this approach was not a successful solution to any problem. The notion of phlogiston was abandoned.

According to proponents of behavior analysis, for a science of verbal behavior to exist, one must dispense with such concepts.

For Skinner (1974), "meaning" does not reside in words; rather,

> the meaning of a response . . . is to be found in its antecedent history. . . . In other words, meaning is not properly regarded as a property either of a response or a situation but rather of the contingencies re-

sponsible for both the topography of behavior and the control exerted by stimuli. To take a primitive example, if one rat presses a lever to obtain food when hungry while another does so to obtain water when thirsty, the topographies of their behavior may be indistinguishable, but they may be said to differ in meaning: to one rat pressing the lever "means" food; to the other it "means" water. But these are aspects of the contingencies which have brought behavior under the control of the current occasion. (pp. 93-94)

It follows, therefore, that "when someone says that he can see the meaning of a response, he means that he can infer some of the variables of which the response is usually a function" (Skinner, 1957, p. 14). It is important to emphasize here the fact that words do not hold meaning— the meaning is to be found in the circumstances in which a given speaker emits verbal behavior of a given form and function. So when a speaker says "I'm hungry," the meaning is not found in this configuration of words; rather, the so-called meaning will be found once we answer questions relating to the conditioning history of that particular speaker (e.g., when [time of day], where [context], and in the presence of whom does this speaker emit *I'm hungry,* and how do listeners characteristically respond to utterances of this sort?).

Transcription. Let us now return to our discussion of classes of verbal operants. The fourth type of verbal operant is called *transcription.* Skinner (1957) used the term to describe those instances in which written or vocal stimuli occasion written responding. When discriminative stimuli are written, "all the characteristics of echoic behavior follow, except that they are now expressed in visual rather than auditory terms" (Skinner, 1957, p. 70). In other words, as in the case of echoic behavior, there is a one-to-one correspondence between the stimulus and response (i.e., the configuration of letters found in the discriminative stimulus, whether cursive or typeset, is in the same order as those written).

When written responding is evoked by vocal stimuli, the writer is said to be taking dictation (Skinner, 1957). As with simply copying text, there is a point-to-point correspondence between the stimulus and response, though with dictation the correspondence entails different dimensional systems (Skinner, 1957, p. 71). For example, should the speaker say the word *air* (auditory dimensional system), the writer would respond in another dimensional system (visual) by writing the letters A-I-R (or perhaps in another circumstance, he or she would write H-E-I-R or E-R-R).

Intraverbal Behavior. The fifth type of verbal operant, the *intraverbal,* bears no one-to-one correspondence with the verbal stimuli that evokes it (Skinner, 1957, p. 71). The relationship between stimulus and response is entirely arbitrary (Catania, 1992). For example, a listener might respond "nine" to any of the following: "A stitch in time saves _____." "What whole number follows 8 and comes before 10?" "Beethoven's famous 'Ode to Joy' is part of Beethoven's Symphony Number _____." "How many planets are in our solar system?" Notice that the response *nine,* be it spoken or written, is not evoked from any particular word. The response *nine* is emitted, not the responses *bus, horse,* or *twenty-seven,* because of an arbitrarily established reinforcement history involving stimulus chains—a conditioning history in which the response *nine* eventuated in reinforcement when it immediately trailed the presentation of any of the above verbal stimuli.

Taking "How many planets are in our solar system?" as a case in point, children's vocal or written responses are reinforced by the teacher (via generalized reinforcement in the form of praise, a gold star, or grades) whenever the child says or writes *nine* upon being presented with that particular configuration of verbal stimuli. Similarly, should the teacher ask "What is the third planet in order from the sun?" then upon hearing this particular configuration of verbal stimuli, the intraverbal *Earth* would result in the delivery of generalized reinforcement.

Tact. The sixth verbal operant is called a tact. A tact is a verbal response of a particular form that is evoked by certain nonverbal stimulus or event characteristics (Skinner, 1957, pp. 81-82).[4] In other words, objects, people, and events evoke verbal responding upon sensory contact (via sight, sound, smell, touch [pain], and taste). The strength of the functional relationship between stimulus and response depends on a previous reinforcement history with respect to one's community. For example, overtly tacting peoples' blemishes generally does not engender praise; rather, it is censured in most instances. Accordingly, this functional relationship would be weakened, should censure serve as a punisher. Openly tacting someone's nice new hairstyle, by contrast, is likely to spur positive reciprocation, and therefore, the functional relationship between the tact and the stimulus is strengthened.

Tacting Private Events. Tacts are particularly useful to those around us when they are emitted in response to events taking place inside our bodies. Without a verbal repertoire of private stimulation, for example, how would a person be able to tell the physician "where it hurts"? How would we share our "thoughts" and "feelings" with others? How would we "know" when it is time to leave a room when "our blood boils"? How would we know when it is time to rest, when we are "feeling under the weather"?

The above are examples of so-called private events (Skinner, 1953). Private events are said to occur "within one's skin," and as such, they are of limited accessibility to the verbal community (Skinner, 1945, 1974). Though limited in accessibility (only the behaving individual has access to this behavior—no one else), private events, Skinner (1953) maintained, are of no special structure or nature, and in fact, they will someday become better understood with advances in the instrumentation of science. Of course, as is the case of physiological measurement, any measurement, invasive or otherwise, is partly an inference of what goes on inside. To arrive at some measure of blood pressure with a sphygmomanometer, for example, does not reflect one's private reaction when pressure is much higher than normal (i.e., how does one measure dizziness, nausea, numbness, tingling, or blurred vision with any instrument?).

Skinner (1957) suggested five ways in which the verbal community teaches its members to tact private events: One is by way of a common accompaniment (e.g., upon seeing a sharp object pierce the flesh, individuals are taught to say "That hurts!"; p. 131); the second is to use some collateral response to private stimulation (e.g., upon seeing a person rubbing his or her head, the verbal community teaches him or her to tact "I have a headache"; p. 131); a third way is when a speaker's behavior recedes in magnitude to covert form (e.g., saying something to oneself that was once said aloud; p. 133);[5] a fourth and fifth way one learns to tact private stimulation is via metaphorical and metonymical extension (p. 133). Because the concepts of metaphorical and metonymical extension are rather complicated, let us consider them at some length.

Metaphors are commonplace in our language. Athletes are said to possess "iron willpower." A food server is said to have a "bubbly" personality. The child, afraid to dive, is called a "chicken." We say that our opponent in a debate is merely "scratching the surface" of the issues at hand. Perhaps, "behind closed doors," we might also say that he or she is "shallow" in character. All of these examples share one thing in common:

We take a term from one context and *extend* it into another, when the second context shares some (not all, or even most) of the characteristics of the first.

In the following passage, Skinner (1957) described the process of metaphorical extension:

> An example of metaphorical extension is provided by the child who, upon drinking soda water for the first time, reported that it tasted "like my foot's asleep." The response *My foot's asleep* had previously been conditioned under circumstances which involved two conspicuous conditions—partial immobility of the foot and a certain pinpoint stimulation. The property which the community used in reinforcing the response was immobility, but the pinpoint stimulation was also important to the child. Similar stimulation, produced by tasting soda water, evoked the response. (pp. 92-93)

He elaborated further:

> When for the first time a speaker calls someone a mouse, we account for the response by noting certain properties—smallness, timidity, silent movement, and so on—which are common to the kind of situation in which the response is characteristically reinforced and to that particular situation in which the response is now emitted. . . . When a metaphorical response is effective and duly reinforced, it ceases to be primarily a metaphor. (Skinner, 1957, p. 93)

What is argued here is that, once a metaphorical extension has been made and reinforced by one's verbal community, it has thus run its course as a metaphor. Should the response occur again under a similar set of circumstances, then we would call it a conventional response, not a metaphorical one.

Like the concept of metaphorical extension, that of metonymical extension is a "slippery" one also. Here Skinner (1957) defined the concept:

> an extension of a tact occurs when a stimulus acquires control over the response because it frequently *accompanies* the stimulus upon which reinforcement is normally contingent. Thus, we say *The White House denied the rumor,* although it was the President who spoke, or *you*

haven't touched your dinner, when the important fact was that the dinner was not *eaten.* We account for such behavior by noting that the President and White House, and touching and eating, frequently occur together. (pp. 99-100)

And, as with metaphorical extensions, once a metonymical extension has been emitted and thus reinforced, it ceases to be a metonymical extension. Should the response arise again under similar circumstances, it becomes a conventional response. Let us now examine how metonymical extensions enable one to speak of private events. In the following passage, Skinner (1957) discussed how one might come to tact the experience of pain:

If the response *sharp* is first acquired in connection with certain objects with identifiable physical properties not related to their effect upon the human organism—for example, if a needle is called sharp if it shows a certain geometrical pattern in profile or easily penetrates paper or cloth, or if a knife is called sharp if it readily cuts wood, then the extension of the response to a certain type of painful stimulus generated by pricking or cutting is metonymical. Certain stimuli are frequently associated with objects having certain geometrical properties, and the response is therefore transferred from one to the other. *That is sharp* becomes synonymous with *That hurts,* where it was originally synonymous only with *That has a fine point* or . . . *a thin edge.* (pp. 132-133)

By this logic, when a dull object (one that shows a certain geometrical pattern) strikes the kneecap with full force, the hapless individual experiencing the blow might make a metonymical extension by calling the associated private event a "dull" pain. Of course, metonymical extensions of this sort, as they arise in this or other comparable circumstances, occur only once.

Tacting and Self-Awareness. One's ability to tact private events is wedded to Skinner's (1974) notion of *self-awareness.* Self-awareness arises out of a long-standing history of interacting with members of one's verbal community (Skinner, 1974, p. 226). Given that the community has already arranged the appropriate contingencies, a person is said to be self-aware in the event that he or she no longer merely participates in an activity, but also "sees" him or herself participating. The chief point here is that the ability to observe oneself behaving—by way of seeing, smelling, hearing, problem solving, imagining, reminiscing, and so on—is enabled through verbal behavior. With respect to emotions, other animals and nonverbal humans experience the "core" emotions as you or I do, although without verbal functioning, in all likelihood they do not experience themselves experiencing them. To our knowledge, human beings are the only animals who talk about their feelings and about the feelings of those around them. And more important, human beings are the only animals that are truly *aware* of how their behavior affects others.

Autoclitic. The *autoclitic* is the seventh type of verbal operant (Skinner, 1957). Autoclitics are said to "lean on" or otherwise depend upon other verbal behavior. In other words, in the absence of additional verbal behavior, autoclitics serve no discernible function. In the presence of other verbal behavior, however, autoclitics not only depend on other verbal behavior but also modify the effects of the verbal behavior upon which they depend (Catania, 1992). Adding *ly* to the following verbal stimuli illustrates this point. An *arrogant* man is said to speak *arrogant-ly*. A *graceful* prima donna is said to move about the stage *graceful-ly* during her aria. While hiking up a steep *hill*, we might say that it is *hil-ly*. Extracting the *ly* from the above contexts, and observing it in isolation, shows that, in and of itself, it serves no purpose. When might a person say *ly* in his or her natural environment? Conversely, an *arrogant* man, a *graceful* prima donna, and a *steep hill* all depict, among other things, instances of tacts that are capable of standing on their own, all of which can be emitted independently in response to a person's natural environment.

Skinner's (1957) treatment of the autoclitic is extremely complicated and rather lengthy; therefore, we cannot do it justice in a chapter of the present scope. For those readers interested in this topic, see Chapters 12, 13, and 14 of *Verbal Behavior*. Notwithstanding, in the interest of being somewhat thorough, we highlight two primary forms: the descriptive and the relational autoclitic.

Descriptive autoclitics are secondary tacts to ongoing verbal behavior—the effects of which modify the responses of the listener (Catania, 1992).

> Important examples are *I agree, I confess, I expect, I concede, I infer, I predict, I dare say, I must say, I can say, I admit, I reply, I should say,* and *I mean to say. . . .* All of these permit the listener to relate the response

which follows to other aspects of the current situation, and hence to react to it more efficiently and successfully. (Skinner, 1957, p. 316)

Take the phrases *I think it will rain* and *I know it will rain* as a case in point. In the former case, there is some uncertainty as to whether it will indeed rain. That is to say, upon hearing this, the listener may or may not pack an umbrella. In the latter case, because the speaker *knows* it will rain, the listener should be inclined to take an umbrella with him or her. Accordingly, in both instances, the listener will respond more effectively to the verbal behavior of the speaker: In the first case, he or she will probably have to "see for him- or herself" or ask someone else whether it is raining; in the second case the listener will have to "look no further" to take effective action.

The relational autoclitic serves "grammatical" functions. Agreements of case and tense are common examples of such. In the following Skinner (1957) expounded on this point:

An additional autoclitic function of such a grammatical tag as the final *s* in *runs* [*The boy runs*] is to indicate "agreement" in number between the verb and noun which serves as its subject. In our example, the -*s* indicates that the object described as *the boy* possesses the property of running. The fact that the boy and the running go together and that they are not isolated responses occurring accidentally is made clear to the listener by the grammatical device. In the response *The boy runs,* the -*s* has other functions as a minimal tact, but it also serves as a relational autoclitic in its "agreement" with the form of the verb. (p. 333)

Other examples are words and phrases such as *above, below, beside, to the right of,* and so forth. They are not tacts of events or properties of environmental circumstances; rather, they combine with other verbal stimuli, and only by virtue of this combination do they acquire their functions (Catania, 1992).

The Audience Variable

Verbal behavior does not arise in the absence of an audience (note that a speaker can also serve as his or her own audience). Accordingly, in light of its importance, no discussion on verbal behavior would be complete without some mention of the audience variable. Therefore, we will conclude this section with a brief survey of this critical variable.

According to Skinner, an audience is a discriminative and reinforcing stimulus in whose presence verbal behavior is characteristically strong. Though audiences do not simply increase the likelihood of all verbal behavior, they do increase the probability of certain subdivisions of a speaker's repertoire (e.g., his or her native tongue) and also influence the subject matter of a given verbal episode. By contrast, in the presence of certain audiences the emission of verbal behavior in general, of particular subdivisions of a repertoire, or of specific topics becomes less likely. Technically speaking, this type of audience is called a *negative audience,* because verbal behavior is punished in its presence. Under those contingencies, one should expect the following pattern of speaker behavior to emerge. According to Skinner, punishment converts stimulus products of verbal behavior into aversive stimuli. Therefore, any behavior that reduces such stimulation is automatically reinforced. So if a particular topic eventuates in punishment, the speaker will eventually change the topic. Likewise, should a particular dialect (e.g., slang) lead to punishment, then the speaker is more likely to emit verbal behavior that is more closely aligned with the prevailing contingencies (e.g., speaking formally). Of course, highly punishing audiences may bring forth ubiquitous silence.

The Impact of Skinner's Book *Verbal Behavior*

As mentioned in Chapter 1, the value of a scientist's contributions to his or her respective field can be appraised by counting the number of citations of his or her work found in the literature. In this vein, McPherson, Bonem, Green, and Osborne (1984) of Utah State University conducted such an analysis of *Verbal Behavior,* spanning January 1957 to August 1983. Their analysis revealed something rather striking. During this period, the total number of citations of the book (i.e., the number of other scientists referring to it) was 836. Of those 836, only 31 were empirical investigations. And of those 31, only 19 entailed an experimental analysis. Thus, over the course of 26 years, *Verbal Behavior* stimulated very little subsequent research in the behavioral community.

The most obvious question one might ask is "Why did *Verbal Behavior* not stimulate the same sort of experimental fervor as Skinner's other work did?" Not only did Skinner's (1938) first book, *The Behavior of Organisms,* for example, spawn a plethora of research programs, but also numerous technical and methodological advances proliferated from this germ. In answering this question, here are several hypotheses, among others, as to why behavior analysis has made so little headway in the experimental analysis of verbal behavior.

The first possible reason pertains to the fact that *Verbal Behavior* did not offer anything conceptually new (McPherson et al., 1984). That is to say, even though Skinner introduced novel terms, they were introduced within a familiar framework (e.g., using the three-term contingency). Therefore, behavior analysts might have simply "accepted" Skinner's interpretation without question. Verbal behavior, for example, came under the same functional control as any other behavioral modality. The analysis of the latter, therefore, could be applied to the former. Verbal behavior is reinforced—the probability that it will occur again increases. Verbal behavior is punished—the probability that it will occur again decreases. The following quote from Skinner (1957) lends support to this hypothesis:

> The basic facts to be analyzed are well known to every educated person and do not need to be substantiated statistically or experimentally at the level of rigor here attempted. . . . The emphasis is upon an orderly arrangement of well-known facts, in accordance with a formulation of behavior derived from an experimental analysis of a more rigorous sort. The present extension to verbal behavior is thus an exercise in *interpretation* rather than a quantitative extrapolation of rigorous results. (p. 11)

What is of great interest here is that the "orderly arrangement of well-known facts" to which Skinner referred are almost solely derived from nonhuman research, involving relatively simple experimental preparations (e.g., lever presses and key pecks). Skinner is called to task on this practice by his critics, as we shall see in Chapter 11.

The second possible reason for this lack of experimental progress has to do with methodological barriers imposed upon scientists by the nature of verbal phenomena. Simply put, "verbal behavior is the convergence of many concurrent and interacting variables in the natural environment" (Skinner, 1957, p. 85); as such, it does not lend itself well to experimental preparations. In other words, laboratory settings fail to get a grip around most, let alone all, of the relevant controlling variables of which verbal respondings are a function. How, for example, does one control for subtle influences (e.g., private events) arising in the current setting, or, more remotely, how does one control for historical factors, which undoubtedly play a role in present performance (e.g., environmental and genetic determinants)?

A third reason why many behavior analysts have yet to step up to experimentally analyze verbal phenomena has to do with difficulty in arriving at an appropriate unit of analysis. What, for example, are the "units" of verbal behavior as they arise in time (Leigland, 1989, p. 27)? Should our level of analysis entail word roots, prefixes, and suffixes, or, rather, are sentences more useful (e.g., "How are you?" is usually taught as one integrated unit)?

More fundamentally, Skinner's notion of a verbal stimulus as simply the product of verbal behavior (Skinner, 1957, p. 34) has the potential to lead us afield. Here, Skinner confused stimulus object with stimulus function (Hayes & Hayes, 1989). An example will help explain this point. Inserting an electrode into someone's brain and getting him or her to utter something (e.g., "Hello"—producing a stimulus product/object) is very different from hearing the individual respond "Hello" upon entering a room (also producing a stimulus product/object). In the latter case, the stimulus serves apparent functions (e.g., getting the listener's attention). In the former case, by contrast, what are the functions of "Hello"? Beyond neuronal firing, what are the contingencies that govern responding?

AN ANALYSIS OF THE LISTENER'S BEHAVIOR

Rule-Governed Behavior

The first part of this chapter dealt with the behavior of the speaker. About 10 years after the publication of *Verbal Behavior*, Skinner (1969) extended his analysis of verbal phenomena to include the actions of the listener; he did this by providing "an operant analysis of problem solving" or, rather, an analysis of rule-governed behavior. Incidentally, exactly 20 years thereafter, he followed up this analysis with a chapter entitled "The Behavior of the Listener" (Skinner, 1989)—published a year prior to his death. Let us look at rule-governed behavior.

Verbal stimuli in the form of rules are vital in complex social environments. Rules facilitate social interaction, and, more broadly speaking, rules play an integral role in cultural transmission from one generation to the next.

A rule is a special type of discriminative stimulus (i.e., verbal discriminative stimulus; Baum, 1994). Rules are "defined functionally, in terms of their roles as antecedent verbal stimuli, rather than structurally, by topographic or syntactic criteria" (Catania, Shimoff, & Matthews, 1989, p. 120). Rules are called *contingency-specifying stimuli*. Accordingly, behavior under the control of contingency-specifying stimuli is called *rule-governed behavior* (Pierce & Epling, 1995).

Rules come in many forms. Warnings (e.g., "Stop smoking before it kills you"), admonitions (e.g., "Remember to get plenty of rest before an exam"), exhortations (e.g., "Stop drinking and driving—you have a family to consider!"), and advice (e.g., "Buy low and sell high") are rules—they specify the circumstances in which a punisher or reinforcer will *likely* result contingent upon the emission or absence of a given operant. That is to say, rules operate probabilistically: "The more remote the predicted consequences, the less likely we are to follow [rules]" (Skinner, 1987, p. 5). More on this point in a moment.

Within the same rubric, goals are rules as well, in that they specify the contingencies with which behavior or behavioral chains will lead to the receipt of a deferred reinforcer. Along with goals, instructions can also be classified as rules. However, instructions are usually more explicit than goals, and as such, they break down complex chains of behavior into various components. Instructions describe precisely what behavior is involved, when the response should or should not be emitted, and when to anticipate the outcome. For example, a recipe describes the behavior (e.g., "add two eggs and mix"), under what conditions it should be emitted (e.g., "add water before mixing flour"), and when to anticipate the reinforcer (e.g., "after 10 minutes in the oven, take cookies out of the oven, let cool for 5 minutes, then ready to serve").[6]

Rules—in the form of manners, customs, values, governmental legislation, and religious and secular law—are what hold cultures together (Skinner, 1953). In a broader sense, rules govern the behavior of millions of people simultaneously (drive on the right side; stop on red). To illustrate this point, the Ten Commandments are found in both the Old Testament and the Torah. Christians and Jewish people who follow rules of this sort do not steal, kill one another, or revolt against those who own possessions. Instead, by following rules, they are more likely to live harmoniously and not emit any of the above transgressions.

Rule-governed behavior has evolved along with the formation of complex societies (Skinner, 1957). Developing systems of rules and evolving practices of reinforcement for rule following and of punishment for noncompliance have been critical in managing the growth of the human species. Rule-governed behavior has provided an evolutionary advantage in response to changing complexities in the composition of the species. For example, we require rules for effective social control (e.g., group control, government and law, religion, economic control, education; Skinner, 1953).

Rule-Governed Versus Contingency-Shaped Behavior

Gilbert Ryle (1949) made the distinction between two types of "knowledge": "knowing that" and "knowing how." What he meant by this was that individuals may, for example, know "how" a particular piece of equipment works and yet not be able to operate it if instructed to do so. This distinction has also been described as knowledge gained from books as opposed to knowledge (i.e., verbal and nonverbal behavior) shaped by way of contingencies occurring in the natural world. Knowledge by description and knowledge by acquaintance (Russell, 1912/1961) are called *rule-governed* and *contingency-shaped behavior,* respectively.

Consider the tasks of a lawyer and of a craftsman. A lawyer *must* get his or her knowledge out of books. The lawyer wouldn't keep food on the table if he or she relied on trial-and-error learning (contingency-shaped behavior). By contrast, the skill of a craftsman such as a sculptor cannot be acquired from a book. The craftsman must work with his or her hands to develop a complex skill set.

Many complex skills are originally taught as a series of rules before the individual can perform any activity with a high degree of fluency or before the individual's performance becomes automatic. Consider the many stages in shaping the virtuosic behavior of the concert pianist David Helfgott. At an early age, he was instructed by his father that if he played a certain configuration of keys, a song would "emerge." Like most children learning how to play the piano, he initially engaged in rule-governed behavior by "talking himself through songs" (e.g., "First middle C, next E, F#, and finally, a G major chord"). His self-talk constituted contingency-specifying stimuli because it described S^D: R → S^r relationships (whereby the S^Ds were stimuli associated with the piano and proprioceptive and kinesthetic stimulation, the response was the configuration of keys played, and the S^r was "hearing the music" or social reinforcement). Later, however, once the song had been "learned" from sheet music, the natural contingencies took over in maintaining his musical behavior. Indeed, what sets him apart from mediocre talent is his ability to detach himself from rule-governed behavior, coming under the control of both the audiences' response to his performance and the natural contingencies supplied by the instrument.

Over time, after operating under natural contingencies, he probably would not be able to explicitly describe the complex contingencies involved in playing Rachmaninoff's Piano Concerto No. 3 in D minor. Indeed, it would not even be necessary for him to describe the contingencies once he had achieved this level of mastery: The rules only served to prime his behavior.

Skinner (1978) described this same process in the shaping of a skillful equipment operator. Skinner suggested that although the operator must first learn how to operate the equipment by following instructions, he or she will "operate it skillfully only when [his or her] behavior has been shaped by its effects on the equipment. The instructions are soon forgotten" (p. 12). Indeed, if we went through life having to rely on rules all the time we would not be very effective in our day-to-day activities. In any event, rule-governed behavior plays an integral part in the acquisition of complex human behavior.

Why Follow Rules?

According to Baum (1994), rule-governed behavior always involves two sets of contingencies: a long-term, ultimate contingency and a short-term, proximate contingency for rule following. An example of an ultimate contingency can be found in the contingencies maintaining academic performance. Consistent with any type of academic endeavor, from grade school all the way through graduate school, "most students study to avoid the (ultimate) consequences of not studying" (Skinner, 1982, p. 4). Specifically, students study to avoid failing, which in turn may lead to innumerable problems later on in life (e.g., financial destitution, depressed social status, unemployment). These contingencies compete with conflicting proximal contingencies at lower payoffs, the effects of which are more immediately reinforcing in nature. Indeed, television, a boyfriend or girlfriend, parties, sporting events, or daydreaming might lead any individual down the path to academic failure.

As implied earlier, ultimate contingencies are rather "weak" because the specified consequence extends far into the future (Reese, 1989). To bridge this temporal gap, more immediate consequences are necessary for individuals to avoid the negative effects of *contingency traps.*[7] Within our culture, these immediate consequences, or proximal contingencies, are socially mediated. That is, proximal contingencies are usually provided by other members of the verbal community, whereby the rule coupled with the proximate reinforcer[8] prompts the listener to engage in the desired behavior (Baum, 1994).

Rule-Governed Behavior and Self-Management

Self-control is observed when an individual chooses a deferred, larger reward over an immediate, smaller reward, when a choice must be made between one or the other (Skinner, 1953). Examples of self-control abound. Prudent financial decisions almost always involve some degree of self-control. For instance, when an individual puts money into a retirement savings plan rather than buying a bigger television, he or she is demonstrating self-control. Likewise, successful dieters are those who judiciously self-manage their eating and buying behavior. Avoiding the cookie aisle during shopping excursions is one example.

As mentioned earlier, self-control is a necessary requirement for academic success. Students who show self-management by studying, opting out of carousing with friends when an important exam is forthcoming, usually perform better on the test than those who choose the latter option. One final example of self-control can be seen in an alcoholic undergoing rehabilitation. There are many discriminative stimuli in the person's environment with which he or she must, at some point, come into contact: The television is powerful in evoking beer-drinking behavior; temporally, he or she always had a "good stiff drink" after work; on the way home, he or she must walk past a bar or liquor store that had been frequented; or perhaps similar aversive contingencies (e.g., "pressures" at home or in the workplace) are in effect whereby alcohol consumption as a means of escape had been well established in the person's repertoire.

Before members of society can emit the necessary rules that prevent hapless spendthrifts from becoming financially destitute, dieters from regaining their weight, and alcoholics from hitting rock bottom, such rules must be primed by one's verbal community (Poppen, 1989). In the previous example, the alcoholic likely sought treatment after the following were modeled by his verbal community: from his boss, "Clean up your act, or you're fired!"; from his wife, "Shape up or ship out!"; and from his friends, "You have to sober up, because you're no longer any fun to be around." These rules, if effective at all, might precipitate a change in behavior for the better.

The alcoholic, or anyone else for that matter, should not rely solely on other people's rules; instead, he or she must extract rules for him- or herself—this rule is "a kind of metarule" (Poppen, 1989, p. 339). As used here, *metarules* means rules about making up our own rules (e.g., "rules are only valuable if they lead to effective action—otherwise they are of no use to us"). Eventually, our alcoholic must formulate his or her own rules: "Now that I've been sober for six months, I get to keep my job, my wife, and my friends."

This ability in extracting rules from the contingencies observed is an essential component in self-management. As will be discussed in Chapter 9, *self-management* (also known as *self-control*) is the "personal and systematic application of behavior change strategies that result in the desired modification of one's own behavior" (Heward, 1987, p. 517). In the dieter example, in order to maintain weight loss, he or she must reformulate his or her rule of avoiding sweets. The dieter cannot avoid sweets indefinitely; more realistic goals would probably involve buying only one bag at a time or eating sweets in moderation. Thus, with changing environments, rules must evolve as well, because they need to better specify the contingencies that currently prevail.

Concluding Remarks on Rule-Governed Behavior

Rule-governed behavior is intimately tied to cultural evolution, whereby members of the verbal community exert control over current members as well as transmitting cultural practices to future generations.

Cast in secular and canonical laws, injunctions, and maxims, among many other manifestations, rules have a profound impact on how we conduct ourselves with other human and nonhuman organisms and with the environment in which we coexist. At a microlevel, rules help us manage our own behavior in order to avoid choosing immediate but meager rewards at the expense of reinforcers of greater merit, although they are more deferred. In any event, rule-governed behavior is behind many wonders that have been actualized by the human species and is also the reason why we have thus far evaded so many pitfalls.

Let us turn to applied instances of Skinner's principles of behavior. We will revisit verbal behavior in Chapter 11 when we consider Chomsky's (1959) famous review of Skinner's book by this name.

Notes

1. *Encourage* at one point meant "to inspire with courage."
2. Ironically, this was Chomsky's age when he wrote his scathing review of *Verbal Behavior* in 1959, which, according to some (e.g., cognitivists), marked its death.
3. Note: A superscript V (^{V}) indicates that the stimulus or response is verbal—if there is no ^{V} consider the stimulus or response nonverbal.
4. As a side note, tacting is not the same as naming (Zettle & Hayes, 1982, p. 79), because the evoking stimulus must be present at the time of the utterance. With naming, the verbal response can occur outside of the physical presence of the stimulating object.
5. Consider language acquisition in an infant. When he or she begins learning the language, all vocal behavior is overt and is seldom punished. Eventually, however, the child is told to "quiet down." The same goes for reading. Eventually the child will be told to "read silently." Both of these examples illustrate the process by which behavior recedes in magnitude to covert form.
6. This example has been modified from Hayes, Zettle, and Rosenfarb (1989, p. 199).
7. See Baum (1994, pp. 157-160) for a discussion of contingency traps.
8. Proximate reinforcers are exemplified by the following verbal stimuli: "great job," a pat on the back, and a smile or nod of approval, among many others.

References

Baum, W. M. (1994). *Understanding behaviorism*. New York: HarperCollins.

Bjork, D. W. (1993). *B. F. Skinner: A life*. New York: HarperCollins.

Catania, A. C. (1992). *Learning* (3rd ed.). Englewood Cliffs, NJ: Prentice Hall.

Catania, A. C., Shimoff, E., & Matthews, B. A. (1989). An experimental analysis of rule-governed behavior. In S. C. Hayes (Ed.), *Rule-governed behavior: Cognitions, contingencies, and instructional control* (pp. 119-150). New York: Plenum.

Chomsky, N. (1959). Review of B. F. Skinner's *Verbal behavior. Language, 35,* 26-58.

Chomsky, N. (1993). *Language and thought.* London: Moyer Bell.

Hayes, C. W., Ornstein, J., & Gage, W. W. (1988). *The ABC's of languages and linguistics: A basic introduction to language science.* Lincolnwood, IL: National Textbook Company.

Hayes, S. C., & Hayes, L. J. (1989). The verbal action of the listener as a basis for rule-governance. In S. C. Hayes (Ed.), *Rule-governed behavior: Cognition, contingencies, and instructional control* (pp. 153-190). New York: Plenum.

Hayes, S. C., & Hayes, L. J. (1992). Verbal relations and the evolution of behavior analysis. *American Psychologist, 47,* 1383-1395.

Hayes, S. C., Zettle, R. D., & Rosenfarb, I. (1989). Rule-following. In S. C. Hayes (Ed.), *Rule-governed behavior: Cognition, contingencies, and instructional control* (pp. 191-220). New York: Plenum.

Herodotus. (1924). *The famous history of Herodotus* (Trans. B. R.). New York: Knopf.

Heward, W. L. (1987). Self-management. In J. O. Cooper, T. E. Heron, & W. L. Heward (Eds.), *Applied behavior analysis* (pp. 515-549). Columbus, OH: Merrill.

Keller, F. S., & Schoenfeld, W. N. (1950). *Principles of psychology.* New York: Appleton-Century-Crofts.

Lee, V. L. (1981). Prepositional phrases spoken and heard. *Journal of the Experimental Analysis of Behavior, 35,* 227-242.

Leigland, S. (1989). On the relation between radical behaviorism and the science of verbal behavior. *Analysis of Verbal Behavior, 7,* 25-41.

McPherson, A., Bonem, M., Green, G., & Osborne, J. G. (1984). A citation analysis of the influence on research of Skinner's *Verbal behavior. Behavior Analyst, 7,* 157-167.

Michael, J. (1984). Verbal behavior. *Journal of the Experimental Analysis of Behavior, 42,* 363-376.

Michael, J. (1993). *Concepts and principles of behavior analysis.* Kalamazoo, MI: Association for Behavior Analysis.

Moravcsik, J. M. (1990). *Thought and language.* London: Routledge.

Pierce, W. D., & Epling, W. F. (1995). *Behavior analysis and learning.* Englewood Cliffs, NJ: Prentice Hall.

Poppen, R. (1989). Some clinical implications of rule-governed behavior. In S. C. Hayes (Ed.), *Rule-governed behavior: Cognitions, contingencies, and instructional control* (pp. 325-357). New York: Plenum.

Quine, W. V. (1995). *From stimulus to science.* Cambridge, MA: Harvard University Press.

Quine, W. V. (1997). The flowering of thought in language. In J. Preston (Ed.), *Thought and language* (pp. 171-176). Cambridge, UK: Cambridge University Press.

Reese, H. W. (1989). Rules and rule-governance: Cognitive and behavioristic views. In S. C. Hayes (Ed.), *Rule-governed behavior: Cognitions, contingencies, and instructional control* (pp. 3-84). New York: Plenum.

Russell, B. (1961). Knowledge by acquaintance and knowledge by description. In R. E. Egner & L. E. Denonn (Eds.), *The basic writings of Bertrand Russell* (pp. 217-224). New York: Simon & Schuster. (Original work published 1912)

Ryle, G. (1949). *The concept of mind.* New York: Barnes & Noble.

Skinner, B. F. (1938). *The behavior of organisms.* New York: Appleton-Century-Crofts.

Skinner, B. F. (1945). The operational analysis of psychological terms. *Psychological Review, 52,* 270-276.

Skinner, B. F. (1953). *Science and human behavior.* New York: Macmillan.

Skinner, B. F. (1957). *Verbal behavior.* New York: Appleton-Century-Crofts.

Skinner, B. F. (1969). *Contingencies of reinforcement.* New York: Appleton-Century-Crofts.

Skinner, B. F. (1974). *About behaviorism*. New York: Knopf.

Skinner, B. F. (1978). *Reflections on behaviorism and society*. Englewood Cliffs, NJ: Prentice Hall.

Skinner, B. F. (1982). Contrived reinforcement. *Behavior Analyst, 5,* 3-8.

Skinner, B. F. (1986). The evolution of verbal behavior. *Journal of the Experimental Analysis of Behavior, 45,* 115-122.

Skinner, B. F. (1987). *Upon further reflection*. Englewood Cliffs, NJ: Prentice Hall.

Skinner, B. F. (1989). The behavior of the listener. In S. C. Hayes (Ed.), *Rule-governed behavior: Cognitions, contingencies, and instructional control* (pp. 85-96). New York: Plenum.

Zettle, R. D., & Hayes, S. C. (1982). Rule-governed behavior: A potential theoretical framework for cognitive-behavior therapy. In P. C. Kendell (Ed.), *Advances in cognitive-behavioral research and therapy: Vol. 1* (pp. 73-118). New York: Academic Press.

CHAPTER 8

Applied Behavior Analysis

❖

A*pplied behavior analysis* is the application of the principles and methodologies of the experimental analysis of behavior to practical situations and problems. Applied behavior analysis is concerned with three broad subject areas: (a) providing an understanding of normal processes that occur in everyday life, for example, how a child develops; (b) providing an understanding of the development and maintenance of abnormal behavior, for example, how a child may become unruly and oppositional; and (c) providing information on how to effectively intervene in problem situations to improve these, for example, how to teach daily living skills to adults with mental retardation. We will discuss each of these subject areas in this chapter.

There are a few terms that have meanings similar to, but not identical to, applied behavior analysis. *Behavior modification* is the closest in meaning, in that it is the application of behavioral principles to clinical problems. However, behavior modification is mostly concerned with the third subject area listed above. *Behavior therapy* can encompass applied behavior analysis but also covers cognitive change techniques and learning techniques derived from Hullian learning theory, such as systematic desensitization (Masters, Burnish, Hollon, & Rimm, 1987).

A BRIEF OVERVIEW OF THE
HISTORY OF SKINNER'S APPLIED WORK

Skinner provided the early impetus for applied behavior analysis by frequently writing about applications of the experimental analysis of behavior to practical situations. Many learning researchers speculated about the practical implications of their basic research, but Skinner was one of the few who actually attempted to develop and test practical programs derived from his research. Skinner was also uniquely successful in motivating other scientists and clinicians to develop research and clinical programs regarding designing and evaluating operant-based interventions.

One of Skinner's books was titled *The Technology of Teaching* (Skinner, 1968). In his autobiography, Skinner described the development of an effective technology of teaching as his most important practical effort. In *The Technology of Teaching,* Skinner saw teaching not as an art but as an applied science that could benefit from his operant research. Skinner thought that traditional teaching methods violated all the laws of learning. Skinner argued that learning should be active, so that the student could make responses that could be evaluated and shaped toward the pedagogical objectives. According to Skinner, in traditional teaching methods, rewards (e.g., grades) are typically too remote in time to serve as effective reinforcers for newly acquired behavior. Skinner thought that reinforcement was too scarce in traditional schools, and he thought that schools relied on aversive control (i.e., punishment and the threat of punishment), which taught students to dislike and avoid learning, at least in subjects in which they were not successful. The goal of education is to build behavioral repertoires, not to suppress behaviors, and thus reinforcement should be stressed. Skinner did not want to rely on artificial reinforcers. Instead, he thought that most students would find learning new behaviors (knowledge acquisition) naturally reinforcing. Finally, in Skinner's view, traditional learning methods were insufficiently sensitive to individual differences. Students have different starting points, proceed at different rates, and have different stumbling blocks. Teachers confronted with 20 or more students in a class must teach to the average student, and thus the educational environments of many students are not optimized. Skinner called the traditional group approach the *phalanx system* after the well-known military tactic of moving soldiers in large groups:

> Failure to provide for differences among students is perhaps the greatest single source of inefficiency in education. In spite of heroic experiments in multi-track systems and ungraded schools, it is still standard practice for large groups of students to move forward at the same speed, cover much the same material, and reach the same standard for

promotion from one grade to the next. The speed is appropriate to the average or mediocre student. Those who could move faster lose interest and waste time; those who should move more slowly fall behind and lose interest for a different reason. . . . One student must move at the same rate in several fields, although he may be able to move rapidly in one but should move slowly in another. Little or no room is left for idiosyncratic talents or interest, in spite of the fact that many distinguished men have shown an insularity not far from that of the *idiot savant*. (Skinner, 1968, pp. 242-243)

Skinner developed a teaching machine, based on operant principles, to overcome these difficulties. He (1984) thought that teaching should be governed by four rules: (a) be clear about what is to be taught; (b) teach first things first; (c) program the subject matter; and (d) stop making all students advance at essentially the same rate.

Based on these four rules, Skinner built teaching machines to help facilitate learning in the classroom. Teaching machines divided subject matter into individual frames, for example, a single proposition requiring students to respond to the content presented. These individual propositions would be ordered according to a logic that was conducive to learning. Each step was to be quite gradual and yet was designed to progress toward the final educational objective. This requirement would force teachers to be clear on what they want to teach. Skinner stated that, in the ideal program, the material would be broken down such that the student would make few or no errors. Items would be presented on a disk, and the student would be asked to respond to a question that tested his or her knowledge of that item. Students could not move to the next frame until they had correctly answered the previous frame. Students would return to frames they had not mastered.

With the use of teaching machines, learning could become active: Immediate feedback is given after every frame. Students can work at their own pace and repeat material they find difficult. Students can work on the machines when convenient for them and for as long as they like. Teachers would thus be freed to interact with students in more enriching ways. Teachers would also be more productive.

Unfortunately, teaching is one of the few professions that has not fully utilized machines and technology to enhance its productivity, and thus teachers teach now much as they did hundreds of years ago. One might argue with this point by claiming that there are in fact computers in most classrooms. However, in spite of all their chirps and whistles, most software is based on poorly constructed learning technology. The term *interactive learning technology* is functionally interchangeable with the term *interactive entertainment technology*. So the mere presence of computers in the classroom is not enough.

As classrooms, particularly in inner-city neighborhoods, get bigger, teachers become increasingly ineffective. As a corollary, because students have not acquired the necessary prerequisite skills for many ongoing learning activities, they tend to get off task. By getting off task, they fall farther behind and disrupt the learning environment of everyone around them. This inefficiency has tremendous social costs, because it produces citizens who are poorly educated and who have learned to dislike learning.

Skinner won an award for his humanism, and part of the rationale for this award should be clear from Skinner's ideas about teaching. Skinner's individualism should be apparent. It is ironic that behavioral interventions are sometimes criticized on the grounds that they mistreat people by ignoring their uniqueness. It should be clear that Skinner in fact criticized traditional teaching on the grounds of its insufficient attention to the person and that he proposed a teaching approach based on a profound appreciation for the value of individualism.

As another example of his applied interests, Skinner, in *Science and Human Behavior* (1953), provided an operant analysis of self-control. Skinner saw self-control as a class of operant behavior that influenced the probability of other behavior (see Chapter 9). Skinner suggested that effective behaviors that could alter the probability of other behavior included (a) using physical constraints, (b) removing oneself from the situation, (c) removing discriminative stimuli, (d) avoiding situations, and (e) engaging in competing behavior. For example, learning to shop for groceries when full increases the probability that the person will not eat junk food at home, because being relatively sated decreases the likelihood of buying high-calorie food. The reader is referred to Rachlin (1974), Logue (1997), and Mischel (1974) for other classic statements of self-control.

In *Walden Two* (1948), Skinner extrapolated from the principles of operant conditioning to designing a better society. Skinner's conception of a behavioral utopia will be discussed in Chapter 10. However, it is important to make clear that behavior analysts have not concerned themselves only with the problems of the individual; they have also addressed societal problems such as pollution and energy consumption.

With the exception of teaching machines, which Skinner actually built and tested, Skinner rarely empirically tested the ideas that arose from extrapolating from the principles of operant conditioning. An important exception to this occurred in the early 1950s, when Skinner and his students attempted to treat an electively mute schizophrenic by shaping his verbal behavior (Lindsley, Skinner, & Solomon, 1953). Today, the vast majority of applied behavior analysis follows this exemplar. That is to say, contemporary behavior analysts concern themselves with remediating problem behavior in institutions, schools, and the home.

THE ETHICS OF CHOOSING TREATMENTS

Applied behavior analysis has enjoyed great success. Behavior analysts have developed and demonstrated the effectiveness of a number of interventions with a number of different kinds of problems. Prior to the development of behavior analysis, few effective therapies existed. Individuals who had problems with developmental delays, autism, or schizophrenia, for example, were left without effective options to improve their situations. The advent of behavior analysis represented the advent of new hope for many individuals and their families.

Behavior analysts use single-subject experimental designs to show that their interventions are causing the problem behavior to improve. Thus, it does not rely on testimonial or case studies of treatment, which are vastly inferior forms of evidence. Moreover, behavior analysts, with their insistence upon graphical depictions, insist on large changes in the target behaviors.

Behavior analysts usually evaluate (or ought to) the social validity of their treatment effects. A treatment is socially valid when the individuals significantly affected by the intervention indicate that the treatment effect was satisfactory to them. For example, if a child is engaging in out-of-the-seat behavior in school, a socially valid treatment would involve teachers, parents, and the child indicating that the posttreatment level of behavior is now satisfactory. Thus, behavior analysts have had remarkable success in demonstrating that their therapies are actually causing behavior to improve.

WHAT IS APPLIED BEHAVIOR ANALYSIS?

Baer, Wolf, and Risley (1968), in an article that helped define applied behavior analysis, stated, "Obviously, the study must be applied, behavioral, and analytic. In addition, it should be technological, conceptually systematic, and effective, and it should display some generality" (p. 92).

Applied. Applied behavior analysts try to change behavior that people find important or problematic in some way. The range of behavior addressed by behavior analysis has been wide and varied, including a newborn baby's life-threatening vomiting, language acquisition of autistic children and those with mental retardation, academic skills, child-management skills for parents and teachers, skills of daily living for adults with mental retardation (dressing, self-feeding, grooming, social skills, etc.), communication skills for marital partners, littering, electricity consumption, and seat-belt use, among countless others.

Behavioral. Applied behavior analysis is "behavioral" in three ways: (a) Applied behavior analysts are attempting to change a behavior, rather than, say, an abstract concept such as self-esteem. (b) The principles used to change the behavior are behavioral learning principles derived from the operant laboratory. (c) The conceptual framework (philosophy, methodology used, etc.) is also behavioral.

Analytic. Applied behavior analysts attempt to analyze behavior by uncovering the functional relationships that exist between the target behavior and environmental antecedents and consequences. Behavior is said to be analyzed when its controlling conditions are identified by experimentally manipulating environmental conditions that are shown to affect the probability of the behavior. This is in direct contrast to intervention attempts that simply attempt to change the behavior without experimentally demonstrating the functional relationships. The behavior analyst uses single-subject experimental designs, which were described in a previous chapter.

Ullmann and Krasner (1975) have argued that when therapy is analytic and applied, as described previously, therapy is research and research is therapy. That is, when conducting research the researcher is attempting to identify controlling variables by experimental procedures, and when the therapist is attempting to understand what changes to make to improve the client's behavior, he or she also has to identify controlling variables by experimental manipulations. The advantage of this as a therapeutic paradigm is twofold: (a) First, and most important, the therapist is using the sophisticated epistemology of science (i.e., the therapist uses a scientific worldview). (b) Second, the client, therapist, and significant others gain important information about the variables that affect target behavior (i.e., environmental causes).

Technological. The treatment must be specified in sufficient detail that another behavior analyst could implement the treatment without needing further coaching from the treatment's designer(s). Implementing treatments is not to be an informal art, but rather a systematic technology. The treatment must include information about how to handle common problems encountered when implementing treatment. For example, when teaching parents how to more effectively manage their children, the treatment must specify how to handle problems such as temper tantrums (on the part of children and parents) and aggression.

Conceptually Systematic. Behavior analysis is not a "collection of tricks." Rather, it is a conceptually coherent system of procedures derived from general principles of behavior. In order to effectively intervene, the behavior analyst needs to understand how the specific techniques he or she is using relate to general principles of behavior. This allows other techniques to be derived from the same general principle or for the specific technique to be adapted to a particular clinical situation while remaining faithful to the underlying principle.

Effective. The behavior analyst seeks interventions that produce meaningful changes. The analyst is not seeking to produce small changes but rather large, consistent changes that clients or their significant others regard as satisfactory. Thus, if parents are complaining about their son's aggression toward his sister, and the behavior analyst implements an intervention that decreases these incidents from 10 a day to 7 a day, this is not an effective intervention. No one would judge the final state of affairs as satisfactory: Seven acts of aggression is still too many for the girl to experience. An effective intervention would reduce the behavior to zero or very near zero.

Generality. The behavior analyst realizes that an important discriminative stimulus may be the analyst's artificial intervention. If behavior is under tight stimulus control, the behavior may change only when the intervention stimuli are present. If clients learn to discriminate these intervention cues and change desirably only when these are present, then bad news awaits when the therapist considers the task finished and withdraws. The client can discriminate that the intervention is no longer present, and behavior can return to its pretreatment levels.

To prevent behavior from returning to pretreatment levels, behavior analysts train for generality. Called "programming for generalization" in behavioral circles, such training aims at broadening the scope of situations in which the target behavior occurs. Among others, specific training strategies include introducing the client to naturally maintaining contingencies, for example, getting him or her to ask for milk in the home, school cafeteria, and restaurant (this will establish the kind of contingency relationship one would contact without a trainer present); training sufficient exemplars, for example, teaching cooperative play, not only in the training condition but also on the playground, in the classroom, and at Sunday school, involving children of all ages; teaching techniques that mediate generalization (otherwise known as training self-management), for example, training a client in how to use self-instruction as a means of working through anger in a variety of different settings (Stokes & Baer, 1977; Sulzer-Azaroff & Mayer, 1991).

BEHAVIOR ANALYSIS RARELY RELIES ON PUNISHMENT

One common misconception about behavior analysis and behavior modification is that these approaches use punishment a lot. The caricature of these approaches is a cattle-prod-wielding Nurse Ratchet who shocks and threatens to punish in order to coerce behavior change. Although punishment is sometimes used, behavior analysts follow Skinner's recommendations and rarely use punishment as a first choice. Punishment has the following problems: (a) it often breeds escape and avoidance, and thus the behavior analyst will lose his or her client or have difficulties because the client will not want to participate in therapy; (b) it elicits emotional behavior such as anger and fear, which are aversive for all parties to deal with; and (c) it is not a constructive learning mechanism. That is, punishment decreases the frequency of some behavior (by definition). It does not necessarily increase the frequency of a more desirable behavior.

Thus, applied behavior analysts prefer to use a reinforcement-based intervention. However, at times, reinforcement has not worked, and the undesirable behavior is so serious that the behavior analyst feels that punishment must be used.

There are two forms of punishment used in behavior analysis: Type I and Type II (Foxx, 1982). Procedurally defined (without considering its effect on behavior), *Type I punishment* is the presentation of an aversive stimulus following the behavior targeted for intervention. Physical and mechanical restraint are examples of Type I punishment—both are extremely aversive to most people (and to animals, for that matter). Holding a child's arms when he or she flails illustrates Type I punishment.

Another way of looking at Type I punishment is to define it functionally—that is, in terms of the effect it has on the frequency of behavior. From a functional standpoint, Type I punishment occurs only when two conditions are met: (a) an aversive stimulus follows behavior, and that stimulus produces a (b) reduction in responding. Returning to our previous example, should holding a child's arms when flailing decrease the overall presentation of that behavior, then punishment has occurred. If there is no discernible change in responding or if flailing increases, then we would not call holding the child's arms punishment.

Procedurally, *Type II punishment* involves removing something positively reinforcing contingent on the problem behavior. By *positively reinforcing,* we mean something that an individual will work to obtain. Colloquially, the item is highly "valued." For example, a child will go out of his or her way to look for a favorite toy. Once it is in his or her possession, taking it away following a temper tantrum is an example of Type II punishment (from a procedural standpoint). Of course, a functional definition would require a behavioral reduction for us to call it "punishment." That is, (a) a positively reinforcing stimulus is removed after the child engages in problematic behavior, thus producing (b) a reduction in this behavior. As a side note, behavior analysts tend to examine behavioral reduction and skill-building procedures in functional terms.

THE BEHAVIOR ANALYSIS OF "NORMAL" PHENOMENA

Behavior analysts strive to determine the extent to which behavioral principles are useful in explaining everyday phenomena, such as how someone learns to drive an automobile or how two people communicate. The presumption is that the contingencies of survival (see Chapter 10) provide broad biological components that are necessary for the behavior (e.g., vocal musculature that is sensitive to consequences) and the contingencies of reinforcement explain much of the rest. That is, a very large percentage of behavior is learned by the organism's interaction with its environment.

In this chapter, we will illustrate the behavioral analysis of normal behavior by examining Sidney Bijou's (1993) account of child development. Bijou defined *development* as "progressive changes in interactions between the behavior of an individual and the people, objects, and events in the environment" (p. 12). Newborn babies engage in mostly reflexive behavior. When a nipple or nipple-like object touches near their mouths, they "root," that is, they move their mouths to enclose the nipple. A nipple in their mouths elicits suckling. As the baby engages in many trials of this, the baby's movements become more coordinated and efficient.

Babies also engage in exploratory behaviors, and the environment begins to select certain responses. They learn not to touch burning embers. In other words, they learn to avoid harm. As discussed in Chapter 2, they also come to make certain sounds more frequently (/mama/). These sounds are often shaped into complex speech patterns (should the child show "normal" development). While this is occurring, they are also learning movements that are necessary to grasp and hold objects. In short, the child's interaction with the environment builds increasingly sophisticated repertoires of behavior.

This psychological development does not occur independently of biological development. The two appear to be interdependent. Sometimes the baby cannot emit a response because he or she is insufficiently strong or coordinated. The baby has to wait for biology to catch up and potentiate the response. On the other hand, it is clear from cases of child neglect that if the child is not appropriately stimulated and challenged by the environment, his or her biological development is hampered.

The preceding is a brief example of how the behavior analyst relies on the use of learning processes to explain normal development. The view is that the child is constantly interacting with his or her environment and that this interaction changes the child. These changes are what is commonly referred to as "development." The reader is referred to Bijou (1993) and Bijou and Baer (1965) for a further discussion of these issues.

THE BEHAVIOR ANALYSIS OF ABNORMAL BEHAVIOR

Behavior analysts argue that what are called "abnormal behaviors" are "no different, either quantitatively or qualitatively, in their development and maintenance from other behaviors" (Ullmann & Krasner, 1975, p. 2). Thus, there is not the view that there is a set of "normal" processes that results in normal behavior and a set of "abnormal" processes that accounts for abnormal behavior. Rather, the same set of processes (learning processes) is used to explain both abnormal and normal behavior.

An example will help illustrate this point. Consider two scenarios: The first scenario involves running from a rattlesnake while hiking in the woods, and the other involves running from a rattlesnake that somehow ended up on your kitchen floor. In either case, any behavior that gets you the heck out of the situation unscathed will likely be repeated under similar circumstances. Technically speaking, effective escape behavior is negatively reinforced by removing contact with the aversive stimulus. Fundamentally then, the behavioral processes are identical in both cases.

Now consider this: The rattlesnake in the second scenario is rubber, and you know it. For the sake of argument, you flee because of a snake phobia. Even though escape is now deemed "abnormal" by most people, it does not change our basic behavior analysis of the situation. Namely, when confronted with an aversive stimulus assuming snake-like characteristics (or any other aversive properties, for that matter), you run. Because running is successful, you do it again in a similar situation.

THE MEDICAL MODEL OF ABNORMALITY

The behavioral model is in direct contrast with what is often called the medical or disease model of abnormality. According to this model, (a) abnormal behavior can be clearly distinguished from normal behavior based on objective criteria; (b) abnormal behavior is explained by different processes than normal behavior (i.e., a disease process); (c) psychopathology lies within the person, that is, there is something inherently wrong with the person; and (d) treatment for these pathological states involves identifying the source of the problem (i.e., diagnosis) and removing it.

Of course, there is a real danger in espousing this position: Attributions that do not give due emphasis to environmental variables may be considered "person-blaming," because they attribute the problem to a defect in the person (Chapter 10 explores this blaming attitude in greater detail). And insofar as a person is blamed for deficiencies in "character," the person doing the blaming disavows him- or herself of responsibility. This, of course, has its advantages for the individual doing the blaming. However, person-blaming merely masks a problem, obscuring more probable causes of deficient performance.

> 1. They [person-blaming interpretations] offer a convenient apology for freeing the government and primary cultural institutions from blame for the problem. 2. Since those institutions are apparently not the cause of the problem, it may be legitimately contended that they cannot be held responsible for amelioration. If they do provide such help, they are credited with being exceedingly humane, while gaining control over those being helped, through the manipulation of problem definitions in exchange for treatment resources. 3. Such interpretations provide and legitimate the right to initiate person-change rather than system-change treatment programs. This in turn has the following functions: (a) it serves as a publicly acceptable device to control troublesome segments of the populations, (b) it distracts attention from possible systemic causes, and (c) it discredits system-oriented criticism. (Caplan & Nelson, 1973, p. 202)

Attention is also called to the following fact:

> One should not presume that there is always a pathological physiological state that underlies what we call abnormal behavior. Some individuals may regard vegetarians as engaging in abnormal behavior (and vice versa) but there is in all likelihood no physiological cause of vegetarianism. The medical model has been strikingly unsuccessful in finding

physiological differences between individuals labeled abnormal and those labeled normal. (Caplan & Nelson, 1973, p. 202)

Haughton and Ayllon (1965) provided a very interesting demonstration of how an operant analysis can result in behavior that is commonly regarded as abnormal. In addition, their report shows how learning processes can be ignored by professionals. These investigators studied the behavior of a 54-year-old woman who had been diagnosed as "schizophrenic" and hospitalized for over 20 years. They were interested in studying the development of unusual, repetitive behaviors that appear purposeless, because these are often important in traditional diagnosis and are often seen as puzzling. For the previous 13 years, this patient had refused to participate in recreational or occupational activities. She would only lie on a couch and smoke cigarettes. First, the researchers deprived her of cigarettes, allowing her only one at mealtimes (this increased her motivation to respond to the intervention). Second, the authors chose broom holding as an arbitrary response and shaped the behavior of "holding the broom while in an upright position," using cigarettes and tokens that could be exchanged for cigarettes as reinforcers. Baseline revealed a frequency of zero, but after two months she was engaging in this behavior over 20 times per day.

Two psychiatrists were then called to observe and evaluate the patient. They were not told anything about the shaping procedure. The responses from both illustrate the danger of ignoring the environment's influence on problem behavior. The first psychiatrist's evaluation stated,

> The broom represents to this patient some essential perceptual element in her field of consciousness. How it should have become so is uncertain; on Freudian grounds it could be interpreted symbolically, on behavioral grounds it could perhaps be interpreted as a habit which has become essential to her peace of mind. Whatever may be the case, it is certainly a stereotyped form of behavior such as is commonly seen in rather regressed schizophrenics and is rather analogous to the way small children or infants refuse to be parted from some favorite toy, piece of rag, etc. (quoted in Haughton & Ayllon, 1965, p. 98)

The second psychiatrist stated,

Her constant and compulsive pacing holding a broom in the manner she does could be seen as a ritualistic procedure, a magical action. When regression conquers the associative process, primitive and archaic forms of thinking control the behavior. Symbolism is a predominant mode of expression of deep seated unfulfilled desires and instinctual impulses. By magic she controls others, cosmic powers are at her disposal and inanimate objects become living creatures.

Her broom could be then:

1. a child that gives her love and she gives him in return her devotion;

2. a phallic symbol;

3. the scepter of an omnipotent queen. (quoted in Haughton & Ayllon, 1965, p. 98)

CONCLUSION

Skinner's science of behavior can be applied to most practical problems where behavior change is the goal. In fact, simply describing "abnormalities" in objective behavioral terms brings us one step closer to fixing the problem, even if we do not bring such terms as *contingencies, antecedents,* and so on to the table. With behavior analysis, targeting a child's use of one-syllable, four-letter words, for example, is much easier to deal with (regardless of your orientation) than other attempts at "resolving unresolved conflicts," changing the child's "attitude," or prescribing excessive medication because the child's problem is deemed "organic." Skinner's technology of behavior offers parents, managers, teachers, and others considerable hope indeed, both in conceptualizing problems scientifically and in offering techniques that work.

References

Baer, D. M., Wolf, M. M., & Risley, T. (1968). Current dimensions of applied behavior analysis. *Journal of Applied Behavior Analysis, 1,* 91-97.

Bijou, S. W. (1993). *Behavior analysis of child development.* Reno, NV: Context Press.

Bijou, S. W., & Baer, D. M. (1965). *Child development: Vol. 2. Universal stage of infancy.* New York: Appleton-Century-Crofts.

Caplan, N., & Nelson, S. D. (1973). On being useful: The nature and consequences of psychological research on social problems. *American Psychologist, 28,* 199-211.

Foxx, R. M. (1982). *Decreasing behaviors of persons with severe retardation and autism.* Champaign, IL: Research Press.

Haughton, E., & Ayllon, T. (1965). Production and elimination of symptomatic behavior. In L. Ullmann & L. Krasner (Eds.), *Case studies in behavior modification* (pp. 94-98). New York: Holt, Rinehart & Winston.

Lindsley, O. R., Skinner, B. F., & Solomon, H. C. (1953). *Studies in behavior therapy: Status report 1.* Waltham, MA: Metropolitan State Hospital.

Logue, A. W. (1997). Self-control. In W. O'Donohue (Ed.), *Learning and behavior therapy* (pp. 252-273). Boston: Allyn & Bacon.

Masters, J. C., Burnish, T. G., Hollon, S. D., & Rimm, D. C. (1987). *Behavior therapy.* San Diego, CA: Harcourt Brace.

Mischel, W. (1974). Processes in delay of gratification. In L. Berkowitz (Ed.), *Advances in experimental social psychology: Vol. 7* (Vol. 7, pp. 197-208). San Diego, CA: Academic Press.

Rachlin, H. (1974). Self-control. *Behaviorism, 2,* 94-107.

Skinner, B. F. (1948). *Walden two.* London: Macmillan.

Skinner, B. F. (1953). *Science and human behavior.* New York: Macmillan.

Skinner, B. F. (1968). *The technology of teaching.* New York: Appleton-Century-Crofts.

Skinner, B. F. (1984). The shame of American education. *American Psychologist, 39,* 947-954.

Stokes, T. F., & Baer, D. M. (1977). An implicit technology of generalization. *Journal of Applied Behavior Analysis, 10,* 349-367.

Sulzer-Azaroff, B., & Mayer, G. R. (1991). *Behavior analysis for lasting change.* New York: Harcourt Brace.

Ullmann, L. P., & Krasner, L. (1975). *A psychological approach to abnormal behavior.* Englewood Cliffs, NJ: Prentice Hall.

CHAPTER 9

B. F. Skinner: Expert Self-Manager

❖

Much of daily life is about avoiding "temptation" (e.g., overeating, drugs and alcohol, gambling, unprotected sex) and forcing ourselves to do tasks we usually don't enjoy (e.g., getting up for work, paying taxes, cleaning the house, seeing the dentist). These tasks often involve some sort of "sacrifice" on our part for the good of others as well as ourselves. And the payoffs are usually deferred—from months to several decades. However, in our pursuit of doing "what's right," we almost always face these challenges alone. The reason society isn't there to lend support has to do with its fundamental beliefs about the causes of behavior. In particular, most of society embraces the notion that human beings are responsible for the majority of their actions. Hence, it is ultimately left up to the individual to "find the right path."

LIBERTARIANISM

This belief in human responsibility is termed *libertarianism*. This view holds that people have free will and denies that all human action is caused (Cornman & Lehrer, 1968, pp. 131 ff.). Therefore, when a person successfully avoids giving in to temptation, he or she is given credit. Conversely, when an individual fails to "live up to standards," he or she is socially reprimanded and is labeled a "sloth," "lazy," and generally "a waste of space." From a libertarian stance, the person is to blame—the individual is held accountable. Skinner (1971) articulated this libertarian attitude well in the following passage:

Unable to understand how or why the person we see behaves as he does, we attribute his behavior to a person we cannot see, whose behavior we cannot explain either but about whom we are not inclined to ask questions. We probably adopt this strategy not so much because of any lack of interest or power but because of a longstanding conviction that for much of human behavior there *are* no relevant antecedents. The function of the inner man is to provide an explanation which will not be explained in turn. Explanation stops with him. He is not a mediator between past history and current behavior, he is a *center* from which behavior emanates. He initiates, originates, and creates, and in doing so remains, as he was for the Greeks, divine. We say that he is autonomous—and, so far as a science of behavior is concerned, miraculous. (p. 14)

The point to notice here is that the behaving individual is seen as the "locus of control." In other words, even though we might say that a person is "influenced" by others (e.g., artists are influenced by other artists), ultimately, the decision to engage or not engage in a particular activity rests with the individual.

DETERMINISM

The antithesis of this belief is called *determinism*. Determinism "is the thesis of *universal causation,* the thesis that *everything is caused*" (Cornman & Lehrer, 1968, p. 120 [italics added]). From a deterministic stance, as it concerns a science of behavior, there is no such thing as "autonomous man." The locus of control is not in the individual but is instead found in the individual's environment. That is to say, present behavior is determined by variables in the history of the species (contingencies of survival) and variables in the individual's history (contingencies of reinforcement; Heward & Cooper, 1992, p. 352). This belief is necessary to advance a science of behavior:

Science . . . is an attempt to discover *order,* to show that certain events stand in *lawful relations* to other events. . . . We must expect to discover that what a man does is the result of *specifiable conditions* and that once these conditions have been discovered, we can anticipate and to some extent *determine* his actions. (Skinner, 1953, p. 6 [italics added])

Along with adopting a deterministic belief about behavior, "the inner gatekeeper (autonomous man) is replaced by the contingencies to which the [individual] has been exposed" (Skinner, 1971, p. 187). If the locus of control is not inside the individual but is instead in the individual's environment, then the individual is in a better position to modify behavior (the environment is easily modifiable—the "stuff" inside people isn't). In so doing, we can develop a behavioral technology (practical tools) that people can use to "avoid temptation" and live productive lives. Specifically, we call this technology *self-management*.

WHAT IS SELF-MANAGEMENT FROM A BEHAVIOR ANALYTIC PERSPECTIVE?

Self-management (also known as *self-control*), from a behavior analytic perspective, is the "personal and systematic application of behavior change strategies that result in the desired modification of one's own behavior" (Heward, 1987, p. 517). Self-management is considered a skill set, and therefore individuals must practice to become proficient in this area (Watson & Tharp, 1997, p. 4).

What is considered an actual "self-managed" response varies greatly. Self-management can be as simple as a one-time-only response, such as refusing a drag of marijuana. Or it can be something as complex as totally revamping one's lifestyle, including changing one's diet and sticking with an exercise regime. The following are just a handful of published studies demonstrating the power of self-management training for improving problems such as the following:

- ◆ Headaches (Blanchard, 1992)
- ◆ Developmental disabilities (Dixon et al., 1998)
- ◆ Binge eating (Allen & Craighead, 1999)
- ◆ Study habits (Richards, 1976)
- ◆ Weight loss (Fremouw, Callahan, Zitter, & Katell, 1981)

◆ Insomnia (Lacks, Bertelson, Gans, & Kunkel, 1983)

◆ Panic attacks (Gould, Clum, & Shapiro, 1993)

◆ Hypertension (Jacob, Wing, & Shapiro, 1987)

◆ Smoking cessation (CinCiripini, CinCiripini, Wallfisch, Haque, & Vunakis, 1996)

◆ Reducing tremors (Guercio, Chittum, & McMorrow, 1997)

SKINNER AS SELF-MANAGER

The remainder of the chapter describes Skinner's approach to self-management. Just as Skinner exhaustively studied the behavior of his subjects, he also examined his own behavior with the same rigor and enthusiasm:

> I have been as much interested in myself as in rats and pigeons. I have applied the same formulations, I have looked for the same kinds of causal relations, and I have manipulated behavior in the same way and sometimes with comparable success. (Skinner, 1967, p. 407)

Indeed, few, if any, of the competing views in psychology can say the same. It is one thing to talk about events as they unfold—doing something about those events is another matter entirely. To paraphrase Karl Marx, the task of the scientist is not simply to describe phenomena but to change them. Skinner's analysis of behavior is all about "doing"—it is a practical science. As such, it is of relevance to the behavior of everyone, including the scientist. In the following passage, taken out of his *Notebooks* (1980), Skinner reflected on this point. In an almost disdainful manner, he compared his experimental analysis of behavior with that of his critics:

> I have, I think, made good of my analysis of behavior in managing my own life, particularly my own verbal behavior. Can psychoanalysts and the cognitive and humanistic psychologists say as much? Did Freud ever report the use of his theory to influence his own thinking? Are cognitive psychologists particularly knowledgeable about knowledge? Are humanistic psychologists more effective in helping other people because of their theories? (p. 75)

Of course, Skinner's answer to all of the above questions, though not explicitly stated, would be a resounding "No!"

Skinner analyzed and managed his own behavior during practically every waking hour (Epstein, 1997). And to a large extent he believed that this self-management lifestyle contributed to his success and happiness. Even toward the last few months of his life, he remained highly active, as Julie Vargas (1990), his eldest daughter, recounted:

> The last few months my father continued the pattern of his "retirement;" up early to write, breakfast, a walk, appointments with visitors and mail until lunch. Afternoons he usually spent relaxing with music and light reading, getting in shape for the next morning's work. (p. 409)

As a side note, Julie probably placed quotes around the word *retirement* because Skinner never really retired. Skinner did in fact officially retire from Harvard in 1974, but in title only. He kept his office long after that. He continued walking to William James Hall for years (2 miles from home), where he spent several hours each week answering correspondence and seeing visitors (Bjork, 1993, p. 216). While at home, he stuck to his routine of rising each morning at 5:00 A.M. and then writing for two hours. During afternoons he rested. He retired early, at 9:00 P.M., only to roll out of bed once more at midnight to continue working for yet another hour (Vaughan, 1990).

In old age Skinner remained a prolific writer, which comes as no surprise in light of his superb skills in self-management. During the final 16 years of his life, in spite of a host of health complications, Skinner published roughly 70 works. Of these 70, 9 were books (including his three-volume autobiography, which spanned over 1,100 pages). He wrote over a half dozen invited chapters. The rest of the works were scientific papers. Most remarkably, Skinner wrote until the bitter end, up to the evening of his death (Vargas, 1990).[1]

Skinner seldom wasted any time. The following quotation, taken from his autobiography (Skinner, 1967) in editors Edwin G. Boring and Gardner Lindzey's *A History of Psychology in Autobiography*, illustrates this point nicely. In it, Skinner described his work ethic:

> I try not to let any day "slip useless away." I have studied when I did not feel like studying, taught when I did not want to teach. . . . I have

met my deadlines for papers and reports . . . I write and rewrite a paper until, so far as possible, it says exactly what I have to say . . . I freely change my plans when richer reinforcements beckon. My thesis was written before I knew it was a thesis. *Walden Two* was not planned at all . . . I emphasize positive contingencies . . . In short, I arrange an environment in which what would otherwise be hard work is actually effortless. (pp. 407-408)

We turn now to Skinner's discussion of self-management. First, we will consider the origins of self-management repertoires. Namely, we will answer the following questions: "Does self-management come from within?" In other words, "Is self-management an act of willpower or self-determination?" "Does society take any part in self-management?" If so, "What role does society play in teaching and maintaining such repertoires?"

In the second part of the chapter, we outline Skinner's kinds of self-management techniques. These techniques are seen in all industrialized societies. Given their prevalence and significance, they deserve some mention here. Finally, we will discuss at length how Skinner applied these principles and techniques to his own life. All through his productive life, he developed an armamentarium of clever little gadgets and "tricks" to assist him in his professional routines. We will cover many of these in the present chapter. In sum, we will trace how Skinner's self-management repertoire developed from early childhood and throughout most his professional life. This chapter closes with a discussion of his "retirement plan" for enjoying old age (Skinner & Vaughan, 1983). Indeed, Skinner left many gems for us to find, most of which are pertinent to the young and the aged alike.

FROM WHENCE IT (SELF-MANAGEMENT) CAME

Before the dawning of modern civilization, human beings were hunter-gatherers who roamed the earth as small nomadic tribes (Jaynes, 1976). As more and more people populated the planet and as tribes converged into larger collectivities, they became increasingly complex. As the eminent anthropologist Coon (1955) observed,

As these institutions grew in size and numbers, they also grew increasingly formal. While it is easy for members of a small intimate band to get along together on a personal informal basis of natural give and take, when people belong to different families and different face-to-face groups, such as neighborhoods or sections of a village, trouble can arise if rules are not formulated and observed. (p. 7)

This struggle between the "desires" of individuals and those of the group is best articulated in a dialogue between Frazier[2] and Castle[3] in Skinner's (1948) utopian novel *Walden Two*:

"Each of us," Frazier began, "is engaged in a pitched battle with the rest of mankind." . . . Each of us has interests which conflict with the interests of everybody else. That's our original sin, and it can't be helped. Now, 'everybody else' we call 'society.' It's a powerful opponent, and it always wins." (p. 97)

These "interests" Frazier is talking about refer to "selfish behavior—the product of the biological reinforcers to which the species has been made sensitive through natural selection" (Skinner, 1974, p. 181). Sexual contact is a perfect example. Sexual contact is one of the most powerful reinforcers known to humankind. To keep people from indiscriminately mounting each other whenever they get the "urge," society has deemed certain practices (e.g., sex in marriage for the purpose of procreation) as "good," "legal," or "moral," whereas under other circumstances (e.g., sex with a prostitute), sexual behavior is seen as "bad," "illegal," "immoral," or "sinful" (Skinner, 1953, p. 352). In the former case, sex between a man and woman is actually encouraged (sometimes through incessant prompts from relatives and friends). Newlyweds hear "Are you expecting yet?" ad nauseam. It goes without saying, in the latter case, that those who visit "houses of ill repute" are castigated by mainstream society.

Fortunately, many of us are taught a skill set called *self-control* or *self-management*. In applying these skills to daily life, one prevents most interpersonal conflicts by stifling one's selfish "impulses." Skinner (1974, p. 181) called this impulsive self the *managed self*, and he called the controlled self the *managing self* (see Figure 9.1). Elsewhere, he called the

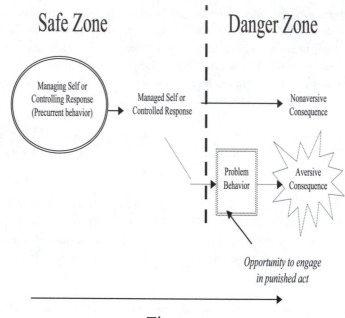

Figure 9.1. A temporal relationship between self-management and problem behavior (modeled after the procrastination-scallop
diagram in Michael, 1993, p. 114). As one moves along the
timeline from left to right, self-management efforts become
less effective. For example, an individual has little chance of
running out to the car to fetch condoms once both lovers are
naked in bed and in the throes of heavy petting.

former the *controlled response* and the latter the *controlling response*
(Holland & Skinner, 1961, p. 307). The managing self "is set up mainly
by the social environment, which has *its* selfish reasons for teaching a
person to alter his behavior in such a way that it becomes less aversive
and possibly more reinforcing to others" (Skinner, 1974, p. 181). Accordingly, self-control does not arise out of one's willpower or
self-determination, because "society is responsible for the larger part of
the behavior of self-control . . . little ultimate control remains with the
individual" (Skinner, 1953, p. 240).

A TAXONOMY OF SELF-CONTROL TECHNIQUES

In *Science and Human Behavior* (1953), Skinner examined nine behavioral techniques that are commonly used in self-management: physical restraint (physical aid), changing the stimulus, depriving and satiating, manipulating emotional conditions, aversive stimulation, drugs, operant conditioning, punishment, and doing something else. These techniques are used, for better or worse, in all industrialized societies, and, given their widespread adoption, they warrant some mention in the present chapter.

Physical Restraint (Physical Aid). Physical restraint is simply limiting the activity of one's body parts (Skinner, 1953, pp. 231-233). One can do this in order to avoid behaving in a manner that is normally punished by members of the community. Biting one's lower lip, for example, prevents a person from saying something he or she might later regret. Walking away prevents us from losing our cool. Another illustration of physical restraint is when people jam their fists into their pockets to prevent nail biting or picking at their faces. The point to notice here is that

> In each of these examples we identify a controlling response, which imposes some degree of physical restraint upon a response to be controlled. To explain the existence and strength of a controlling behavior we point to the reinforcing circumstances which arise when the response has been controlled. (Skinner, 1953, p. 231)

In the first example, we avoid trouble by biting our lip. Avoiding trouble is the reinforcer that strengthens the lip-biting behavior. In the second example, we avoid an argument or altercation by walking away. Avoiding a quarrel is the reinforcer for leaving the situation. In the third example, by preventing nail biting or picking at our faces, we avoid being reprimanded by those around us. Avoiding criticism (and the consequences of scarring our faces) is the reinforcer for restraining our hands by jamming them deep in our pockets.

Changing the Stimulus. In changing the stimulus (Skinner, 1953, pp. 233-234), we either eliminate the occasion for the punished behavior or create conditions that promote acceptable behavior. By moving a box of chocolates from view, for example, we lower the chances of seeing them and pigging out. Deleting the e-mail program off of our hard drive at work decreases goofing off online. Should increasing appropriate behavior be our aim, placing a library book against the door increases the likelihood that we will return it. In any case, the managing (controlling) response makes the managed (controlled) response more or less likely.

Depriving and Satiating. What Skinner (1953, pp. 234-235) called the concepts of *deprivation* and *satiation* fall along the same continuum. When we speak of one term, we by default also speak of the other. A little more of deprivation means a little less of satiation, and vice versa.

When we deprive ourselves of certain activities, we increase their reinforcing value. Like in the old saying "Absence makes the heart grow fonder," the longer we wait, the larger the effect of the reward. By contrast, when we saturate ourselves with a given activity, we decrease its reinforcing value, as in the old adage "Too much of a good thing is bad." Take sex as a case in point. The longer we go without it, the more we are said to "want it." On the other hand, even sex loses its appeal if we are getting it constantly. The late Marvin Gaye went so far as to write a song about this bodily condition called "Sexual Healing."

Manipulating Emotional Conditions. We manipulate emotional conditions in order to induce certain ways of responding (Skinner, 1953, pp. 235-236). For example, actors frequently dredge up painful memories to elicit tears, should the scene call for the character's sobbing. Likewise, to get us in the "mood," we might reread a personal letter so that we respond in the appropriate manner. Namely, we don't want to sound too mushy or too cold in our reply. Another example is found in treating anxiety. Breathing with the diaphragm, as opposed to breathing with the thoracic cavity or chest, reduces arousal when an individual is under a great deal of stress.

Aversive Stimulation. Aversive stimulation is used as a means of increasing or decreasing the likelihood of the targeted behavior (Skinner, 1953, pp. 236-237). As with all techniques of self-management, there is a controlling response and a controlled response. An example—unfortunately all too familiar to every reader—is using an alarm clock to get up in the morning. The controlling response is setting the alarm. The controlled response is waking up. In this instance we set the alarm clock to produce an irritating stimulus at a specific time. If we are unlucky and the power does not cut out, then we are forced out of bed to turn the damn thing off. Of course, if you are like most people, the alarm actually sets off an elaborate chain of events: hit snooze, roll over, hit snooze, roll over, hit snooze, and so forth.

Alarms of every kind work similarly when used in self-management. Kitchen timers serve as prompts so that we do not overcook our meals. Carbon monoxide detectors ensure that we leave the premises at once if ambient carbon monoxide levels become dangerously high. To move our discussion away from the home environment and into the gym, some exercise enthusiasts wear heart rate monitors that are set at upper and lower limits. Should an individual's heart rate rise above the upper limit, an alarm sounds. Consequently, the individual slows down on whatever machine is being used. Should a person's heart rate drop below the lower limit, then the alarm also sounds, and he or she picks up the pace.

Other examples of using aversive stimulation include the following. Dieters might place unflattering pictures of themselves in conspicuous places to increase the chances of exercising, all the while decreasing the probability of binge eating. In like fashion, a below-average student might post her exams in high-traffic areas so as to goad herself into studying for the next exam.

We might also subject ourselves to aversive stimulation to keep ourselves from nodding off. Students, for example, commonly splash themselves with ice-cold water to help stay alert while cramming for exams. Other techniques might be studying in an uncomfortable chair, sitting too close to the air conditioner, or leaving the window open if it's cold outside.

Drugs. Drugs are used as a control method to alter the rate of behavior (Skinner, 1953, p. 237). Stimulants and depressants are found in all industrialized societies. They play a role in everyday life for many people, from mundane events to every special occasion imaginable. Take the United States as a case in point. Few people leave the door in the morning without some kind of "pick-me-up." Some individuals drink a pot of coffee or tea. Some people have a cigarette after breakfast. Those desiring a sugar rush might have a glazed doughnut or sugar-varnished cereal. Health-conscious people might engage in rigorous exercise, unwittingly releasing massive amounts of endogenous opiates into their central nervous system ("runner's high").

As a means of coping with reality, some people turn to drink. Everyone suffers, some more than others. Those having problems coping on their own might have a glass or two of spirits at the end of the day. For others, a glass or two is not enough—ultimately, they end up drinking themselves to sleep. In extreme cases, some individuals seek out a constant state of drunkenness and in so doing lose their families and jobs. Of course, the same formula applies to all prescription and illicit drugs. That is, chemical dependency varies from person to person and from circumstance to circumstance.

Operant Conditioning and Punishment. The seventh and eighth techniques of control are operant conditioning and punishment, respectively (Skinner, 1953, pp. 237-239). We will address both of these together because they raise a sticky issue. The issue in question is whether an individual can arrange contingencies governing his or her behavior. Indeed, should we respond "Yes" to this question, then it throws Skinner's whole science of behavior into question. For if individuals are capable of providing the sole consequences for their own actions, then what role does the environment play in affecting behavior? Recall that Skinner (1953) always maintained that "the causes of behavior—are the external conditions of which behavior is a function" (p. 35) and that "these variables lie outside the organism, in its immediate environment and in its environmental history" (p. 31). In the following passage, Skinner (1953) spoke to this issue, first as regards the notion of self-reinforcement, and second, in terms of self-punishment.

> Self-reinforcement of operant behavior presupposes that an individual has it in his own power to obtain reinforcement but does so not until a particular response is emitted . . . it must be remembered that the individual may at any moment drop the work in hand and obtain the reinforcement. We have to account for his not doing so. (pp. 237-238)

To gain a better understanding of Skinner's point, think about the last time you tried to reward yourself for a given task. Say your reward is a giant chocolate chip cookie after you have completed a certain number of algebra questions. If you are like most students, you raise the bar pretty high (i.e., expecting to answer more questions than usual). Fancying yourself an expert behavior manager, you even place the cookie on the desk where you are working. This is to help motivate you, of course. You work through one question and then another. You look up at the cookie and look away, as if glancing at the sun. As you plow through each question, you catch yourself eyeing the cookie more and more. The cookie is now transforming into some kind of eye magnet. "OK," you tell yourself. "Just a little nibble for all my hard work up until now. I know I'm only a third of the way through, but I deserve it." You take a bite and set it down. Confidently you say to yourself, "Now that wasn't so bad—I can handle the temptation—Bring it on!" You continue working for five more minutes; then, much to your chagrin, your "willpower" snaps and you gobble the cookie down. Needless to say, you'll finish the remaining questions "tomorrow!"—that is, if you are lucky.

The above example might seem to be a bit of an exaggeration. However, we have all been down this road. Everyone makes commitments to him- or herself—and more often than not, everyone breaks them also, even people like Mahatma Gandhi or Mother Teresa. However, what ultimately gets people back on the straight and narrow is other people. Perhaps in the cookie example, your significant other, parent, sibling, or roommate gets on your case for blowing off your homework.

Your social network aside, eventually you have to turn in your homework or write an exam—at which point you get a "shot of reality" from your instructor. Technically speaking, you inevitably make contact with the contingencies your instructor has set for you and your class (i.e., getting a nasty grade). Of course, your "expected" grade is not really at issue. You study a given amount because of your reinforcement history with respect to your participation in the education system thus far. Remember, past consequences influence present behavior. Future consequences have no bearing on current performance (although statements about future effects may serve as discriminative stimuli. In fact, specifying connections between behavior and likely future outcomes, e.g., "smoking causes cancer" or "brushing your teeth prevents cavities," is one of the ways society teaches people to behave in ways that have no immediate benefits, only long-term ones). The future has not yet happened, and therefore it holds no influence over what goes on in the here and now.

Setting up positive reinforcement contingencies for ourselves and actually adhering to them, according to Skinner, is attributable to the behavior of others. That is, those people in our social network look out for us, so to speak. They make sure we are sticking to the plan. The same goes for self-punishment.

> Self-punishment raises the same question. An individual may stimulate himself aversively, as in self-flagellation. But punishment is not merely aversive stimulation; it is aversive stimulation which is contingent upon a given response. . . . The ultimate question of aversive self-stimulation is whether a practice of this sort shows the effect which would be generated by the same stimulation arranged by others. (Skinner, 1953, pp. 238-239)

Skinner's response is "No," as we shall soon see. With self-punishment, as in the case of self-reinforcement, there are always contingencies operating elsewhere—arranged by other people. For example, when people set up some form of response cost when they fail at something, there are always outside pressures to follow through with the punishment. If a husband forgets to take out the trash and then revokes his own television privileges, he does so mainly because he has his better half monitoring his every move (Who asked him to take out the trash in the first place?). Even in the case of self-flagellation, those devoted followers who believe they have sinned do so because of imagined consequences—purportedly set up by some divinity. To them the threat of hellfire is quite real.

> It appears, therefore, that society is responsible for the larger part of the behavior in self-control. If this is correct, little ultimate control remains with the individual. A man may spend a great deal of time designing his life—he may choose the circumstances in which he is to live with great care, and he may manipulate his daily environment on an extensive scale. Such activity appears to exemplify a higher order of self-determination. But it is also behavior, and we account for it in terms of other variables in the environment and in the history of the individual. It is these variables which provide the ultimate control. (Skinner, 1953, p. 240)

To rephrase Skinner here, self-management is environmentally determined. If you live in an environment where self-management is commonly practiced, then your chances of becoming an expert self-manager are pretty high. Conversely, should you live in a culture where such practices are nearly nonexistent, the likelihood that you would have a highly developed self-management skill set on your own would be slim to none.

From this standpoint, we gain a better understanding as to why people from different cultures have trouble assimilating into new ones. We are not overstating the case when we say that Americans are obsessed with time. When foreigners move to the United States, either they acquire self-management repertoires with respect to time quickly or they run into myriad problems personally as well as professionally. Timeliness is a virtue in the American culture—as is "workaholism" and the like.

Do Something Else. The ninth technique Skinner (1953) describes is to do something else (pp. 239-240). This applies to operant and respondent behavior. As with operant behavior, when a teenager is quietly doing her homework at the kitchen table, she is not smoking crack behind the neighborhood pool hall. Both studying and smoking crack are incompatible behaviors given this instance. For interested readers, "doing something else" is well documented in the applied behavior analytic literature. Technically speaking, depending on the circumstance, it is called *Differential Reinforcement of Appropriate Behavior, Differential Reinforcement of Incompatible Behavior,* or *Differential Reinforcement of Other Behavior* (see Foxx, 1982, for a thorough discussion on a wide array of applications of this general technique).

A similar relationship is seen among varying forms of emotional behavior. Take happiness and sorrow as a case in point. One might attempt to "put on a happy face" in order to rid oneself of the blues. And in fact, some studies show that smiling produces a slight elevation in mood. Analogously, in the clinical arena, relaxation training for anxious clients works on the same principle. That is, one cannot be relaxed and feel panicky at the same time—the two bodily states are mutually exclusive (see Wolpe, 1958, for numerous clinical examples of what he called "reciprocal inhibition").

"DISCOVERY": SKINNER'S APPROACH TO MAKING LIFE INTERESTING

Let us turn our discussion to a metaphor that was pervasive in Skinner's life: the metaphor of "discovery." As we shall soon see, Skinner made some pretty remarkable discoveries even early in his childhood. Namely, he was always building things out of discarded objects and then seeing what would happen. As Skinner would have it, these discoveries served no trivial role in shaping his behavior as a scientist. Indeed, contingencies of this sort placed his "inventive" behavior on a variable-ratio schedule of reinforcement. That is to say, sometimes his makeshift inventions worked—other times they did not. Recall that variable-ratio schedules generate a high, steady rate of responding. Variable-ratio schedules account for certain gambling addictions and addictive behavior in general, but they also account for the industriousness seen in the behavior of scientists and artists. And that particular schedule, to Skinner's good fortune, stretched into his adult life as well.

Of course, Skinner played no passive role, waiting for such schedules to kick in. Skinner actively arranged his environment such that variable-ratio schedules governing creative processes were continuously in operation. The following are Skinner's five principles of successful scientific practice—taken from his clever article "A Case History in Scientific Method" (1982).

Principle 1: "When you run onto something interesting, drop everything else and study it" (p. 78). Comment: The conditions in which ideas arise are fleeting. It is impossible to wholly re-create the circumstances in which "inspiration" occurs when one is far removed from the controlling variables.

Principle 2: "Some ways of doing research are easier than others" (p. 79). Comment: In pursuit of making matters easier, we develop new apparatuses. In so doing, we change the experimental conditions in not so trivial ways. Skinner, for example, built a device that allowed rats to deliver their own reinforcers (Skinner, 1982, p. 81). This contraption eventually led to his famous Operant Chamber, casually known as the "Skinner Box."

Principle 3: "Some people are lucky" (p. 81). Comment: Because he was a staunch determinist, it is odd that Skinner would use the term *luck.* More technically, he meant that some random variation is better than others. By following Skinner's other principles, one is sure to experience a considerable amount of this kind of luck. Skinner always seemed to somehow place himself in "the right place at the right time." You need to play to win.

Principle 4: "Apparati sometimes break down" (p. 83). Comment: When one tinkers with a lot of things—expect malfunctions. Skinner often spoke of *behavioral mutations,* borrowing this term from evolutionary biology. When working with apparatuses of all kinds, they break down and produce behavioral "mutations." When they do so, these anomalies are sometimes of use to the scientist. More often than not, however, as with biological mutations, they seldom are.

Principle 5: "Serendipity[4]—the art of finding one thing while looking for something else [*sic*]" (p. 85).* Comment: Think of the last time you took up a hobby that you really liked. How many times did you find yourself becoming consumed in the process—jumping from one thing to the next—getting something unexpected and seeing the potential in it? Science is no different. The good scientist takes advantage of unexpected events. Science ought to be fun as we discover new ways of looking at life, even though we initially set out on a different course.

Discovering What to Do With Rubbish

Let us take a brief detour into the life of young Skinner. Here we will gain a better understanding of the contingencies that shaped his industriousness, which was seen throughout the remainder of his life.

Skinner grew up embracing the Protestant pack-rat virtue of "waste not, want not." In the following passage, he revealed the origins of this:

> Another part of my early training could be summarized in "Waste not, want not." When I was perhaps twelve or thirteen I had a generator taken from an old-style telephone. I was cranking it rather aimlessly one day when my father warned me that it would wear out. I protested that it was built to last a long time, but he said, "It will only last a certain length of time, and every minute it is cranked will be subtracted from that time." I never wore it out, of course, but I no longer had much fun playing with it. (Skinner, 1976, p. 62)

Skinner never seemed to shake this habit of taking good care of his possessions and never throwing "stuff" out (for our usage of the word *stuff,* most people would substitute the word *junk*). What this amounts to is that Skinner had an ever-burgeoning collection of stuff lying around.

> The kindling wood from the grocery store included parts of boxes and crates, good for making small objects like stools I made for my brother, and we had a large supply of boards. . . . They were just right for building benches, tables, and small houses. Long oil-soaked planks from the Erie Shops, destined to be sawed into pieces for our fireplace, were ideal for slides, teeter-totters, and merry-go-rounds. . . . We made vehicles of various kinds. If we lost one roller skate, we made something of the other, possibly a scooter. For use on snowy slopes we made a kind of scooter of a large barrel stave. With the wheels and axles of discarded baby carriages we made steerable cars in which we coasted downhill in summer as on sleds in winter. . . . The stored energy of the flywheel fascinated me. I would turn my bicycle upside down and pump the back wheel to a frenetic speed, and dreamed of a car that stored energy in a flywheel as it came down one hill and used it to go up another. . . . I designed a perpetual motion machine in which water flowing from a reservoir lifted a float against a spring, the spring acquiring enough energy to pump the water back into the reservoir for a second cycle. . . . Our most ambitious piece of ordnance was a steam cannon made from a discarded hot-water boiler. (Skinner, 1976, pp. 119-121)

Skinner continued making do with what he had hanging around throughout his entire professional life, as Maggie Vaughan (1990), his friend and collaborator, recalled:

> Over the years, he designed his office—often with Rube Goldberg[5] flare—as if it were simply a problem to be solved. He remarked often that anything he needed could be bought at Sears or Radio Shack and anything could be fixed with hot glue. His office remains a labyrinth of switches, pulleys, extension cords, lights, magnifying glasses, cardboard boxes, and cubby holes connected by strings, rubber bands, masking tape, and hot glue . . . his desk, cluttered with gadgets and scraps of paper. (p. 101)[6]

Ever since Skinner was a boy, he had tinkered with things, and much to his delight, he produced clever little gadgets that stimulated his interest for hours at a time. As behaviorists would have it, in light of being exposed to variable-ratio schedules of reinforcement operating constantly, and because he always had a never-ending supply of materials close at hand, he built one apparatus after another (Epstein, 1982, p. 73). He built apparatuses unceasingly throughout his life. And over the years, he became quite skilled at developing apparatuses on the fly. He applied those skills throughout graduate school and subsequently in his professional life (Skinner, 1979). Those gadgets ranged from relatively simple pulleys to practical baby tenders (Skinner, 1945), teaching machines (Skinner, 1960), and cumulative records (Skinner, 1982), to name only a few.

Interestingly, the cumulative recorder originated out of items from a scrap heap. And in spite of its lowly origins, cumulative records turned out to be of critical importance in Skinner's scientific analysis of behavior.[7]

> The disc of wood from which I had fashioned the food magazine was taken from a storeroom of discarded apparatus. It happened to have a central spindle, which fortunately I had not bothered to cut off. One day it occurred to me if I wound a string around the spindle and allowed it to unwind as the magazine was emptied . . . I would get a different kind of record. Instead of getting a mere report of the up-and-down movement of the runway, as a series of pips as in a polygraph, I would get a *curve*. And I knew that science made great use of curves . . . as it turned out the curve revealed things in the rate of responding, and changes in that rate, which would certainly otherwise have been missed. (Skinner, 1982, pp. 81-82)

Building apparatuses out of scraps was one way Skinner modified his environment, which in turn influenced his behavior. As a boy, makeshift devices provided hours of entertainment. As a scientist, building apparatuses enabled him to discover certain lawful relations between the environment and behavior. And, as Skinner lost some of his eyesight and hearing, fashioning devices out of things lying around the house helped compensate for loss (as we shall soon see).

Discovering "What You Have to Say"

Let us turn to what Skinner (1987b) aptly called *discovering what you have to say* (i.e., the process of composition). Many people regard the creative process seen in writing as something mysterious—not Skinner.

Writing to him was no more "miraculous" than any other behavior. As such, Skinner subjected the writing process to a behavioral analysis, and throughout his life, he developed an armamentarium of self-management techniques for this purpose.

By and large, Skinner was a slow and meticulous writer[8]:

> In general I write slowly and in longhand. It took me two minutes to write each word of my thesis and that is still about my rate. From three or four hours a day I eventually salvage about one hundred publishable words. (Skinner, 1967, p. 403)

In his last year of life, that number plummeted drastically, because he was only able to "think clearly" for up to an hour daily (Wiener, 1996, p. 72).

To help offset this problem, Skinner developed what he called a *Thinking Aid* (Skinner, 1987c). A Thinking Aid is simply a device, comprising index cards and a lot of tape, that helps a writer "discover" what he or she has to say. Essentially, the manuscript is written piecemeal on index cards, and then the cards are reassembled on a plastic panel cut from a three-ring binder. Over time, through this process of writing and reassembling the cards, a paper emerges.

Where Does Inspiration Come From?

Contrary to popular notions about the nature of thought, for Skinner thinking wasn't functionally different from flexing one's biceps or dialing a telephone: "As I have argued in *Verbal Behavior,* thinking can be adequately formulated simply as behaving. A sentence is not the expression of a thought; it *is* the thought" (Skinner, 1987a, p. 87). On the same subject, he wrote,

> They [ideas] are what "occur to us" as we consider a set of circumstances. If I have forgotten the key to my house and "it occurs to me" to look under the mat, it is not an idea that has occurred to me but rather the behavior of looking, and it occurs because under similar circumstances I have found a key under the mat or have heard someone say, "The key is under the mat." What verbal responses "express" are not preverbal ideas but the past history and present circumstances of the speaker. . . . Verbal behavior, like all behavior, is not inside the speaker or writer before it appears. (Skinner, 1987b, p. 132)

Tips for Would-Be Writers

Writing for Skinner was one of the activities he enjoyed most, and, as with every other behavior, especially verbal behavior, he subjected it to a rigorous analysis (e.g., Skinner, 1957). The following is his advice to would-be writers derived from that analysis (Skinner, 1987b). We have provided subject headings for your convenience.

1. *Stay healthy and write well.* Skinner's advice: "A first step is to put yourself in the best possible condition for behaving verbally. . . . Good physical condition is relevant to all kinds of effective behavior but particularly to that subtle form we call verbal" (Skinner, 1987b, pp. 132-133).

2. *Eliminate hassle and discomfort while writing (lower response cost).* Skinner's advice:

> Equally important are the conditions in which the behavior occurs. A convenient place is important. It should have all the facilities needed for the execution of writing: pens, typewriters, recorders, files, books, a comfortable desk and chair. It should be a pleasant place and should smell good. Your clothing should be comfortable. (Skinner, 1987b, p. 133)

3. *Establish situational (stimulus) control—by location and by time.* Skinner's advice: "Since the place is to take control of a particular kind of behavior, you should do nothing else there at any time" (Skinner, 1987b, pp. 133-134). Regarding time, Skinner advised,

> It is helpful to write at the same time of day. Scheduled obligations often raise problems, but an hour or two can almost always be found in the early morning—when the telephone never rings and no one knocks at the door. (Skinner, 1987b, p. 134)

4. *In order to produce the products of behavior, one needs to BEHAVE.* Skinner's advice:

> And it is important that you write something, regardless of quantity, everyday. As the Romans put it, *Nulla dies sine linea* [pronounced "new-la day-ess sign lean-ee-ah"]—No day without a line. . . . As a result of all of this, the setting almost automatically evokes verbal behavior. . . .

A circadian rhythm (e.g., your body is used to getting up at a particular time each day) develops that is extremely powerful. (Skinner, 1987b, p. 134)

5. *Schedule in breaks—don't kill yourself working too hard and for too long.* Skinner's advice:

How should you spend the rest of the day? Usually you will have little choice, for other demands must be met. But there is usually some leisure time, and a fundamental rule is not to try more writing. You may tease out a few more words, but you will pay the price the next morning. (Skinner, 1987b, p. 134)

6. *Ideas are fleeting.* Skinner's advice:

There is an exception to the rule against writing away from your desk. Verbal behavior may occur to you at other times of the day, and it is important to put it down in lasting form. A notebook or a pocket recorder is a kind of portable study. Something you see, hear, or read sets off something relevant, and you must catch it on the wing. Jotting down a brief reminder to develop the point later is seldom enough, because the conditions under which it occurred to you are the best conditions for writing a further account. A longer note written at the time will often develop into something that would be lost if the writing were postponed. (Skinner, 1987b, pp. 134-135)

7. *Reviewing previous work keeps you on task.* Skinner's advice:

By reviewing what you have already written, going over notes, reworking a manuscript, you keep your verbal behavior fresh in your history (not in your mind!), and you are then most likely to say all you have to say with respect to a given situation or topic. (Skinner, 1987b, p. 136)

8. *What to do when you get bored.* Skinner's advice:

There is also a kind of subject-matter fatigue. One starts to write in excellent condition but eventually becomes "sick of the subject." One solution is to work on two subjects at the same time. It is easier to write short sections of two papers during a session than to spend the whole session on one. (Skinner, 1987b, p. 140)

9. *The manner of writing facilitates discovering what we have to say.* Skinner's advice:

Stay out of prose as long as possible (just write "automatically"—don't worry about grammar). The verbal behavior evoked by the setting you are writing about does not yet exist in the form of sentences,[9] much will be irrelevant to the final product. By composing too early you introduce a certain amount of trash that must later be thrown away. The important parts of what you have to say are manipulated more easily if they have not yet become parts of sentences. (Skinner, 1987b, p. 141)

10. *Organize your work.*[10] Skinner's advice:

Indicate valid relations among responses by constructing an outline. . . . Your final verbal product (sentence, paragraph, chapter, book) must be linear—with a bit of branching—but the variables contributing to your behavior are arranged in many dimensions. Numbering the parts of a composition are helpful in making cross-references and temporary indexes and in noting connections among parts. (Skinner, 1987b, p. 141)

11. *How should the first draft look?* Skinner's advice:

Construct the first draft prose without looking too closely at style. . . . When what you say about a given state of affairs exists at last in prose, rewrite as you please, removing unnecessary words, articulating sentences with better connectives, rearranging as seems necessary, and so on. (Skinner, 1987b, p. 142)

Discovery "Is the Spice of Life": Still Making Discoveries Well Into Old Age

Skinner lived a productive and happy life, right up to the eve of his death. Skinner approached old age with a sense of gusto that would have made even George Burns blush. Skinner seldom resigned himself to the "lifestyle" of most elderly people. Rather, as he was faced with an increasing number of obstacles, he confronted each challenge as though it were a problem that he would ultimately solve (Skinner & Vaughan, 1983). Furthermore, as the reader is well aware after reading the present chapter, Skinner enjoyed solving problems and coming up with practical solutions. He arranged his environment in such a way as to downplay the multiple impairments that come with age, and he played up his opportunity to explore exciting avenues. Here are some of the environmental modifications he recommended in his book *Enjoy Old Age* (Skinner & Vaughan, 1983), among many others:

Vision

A lens mounted on a floor stand will enlarge type and can be surrounded by a helpful fluorescent ring. A large hand lens can be used as you read, and a small folding lens for pocket or purse will help at other times. With a pocket or purse flashlight, you will be able to read menus in dark restaurants and get about in dark places. Your library probably has books in large type, and some periodicals have editions printed in large type. (Skinner & Vaughan, 1983, p. 39)

Hearing

Talking with other people can be made easier in various ways. Be sure it is clear to them that you do not hear well. Say so, and cup a hand behind an ear as a reminder to them. Speak loudly yourself. You probably hear yourself partly through bone conduction and therefore speak more softly than you suppose. Others then speak at the same level, which is too low for you. You will usually find, when speaking with friends, that if you suddenly speak more loudly, your friends will do the same. (Skinner & Vaughan, 1983, p. 43)

Taste and Smell

It helps to season food a bit more and sip a drink as you eat. . . . Aware of your reduced sensitivity (smell), you may want to be doubly careful about odors in your clothing and living space, which may affect your relations with other people. (Skinner & Vaughan, 1983, pp. 46-47)

Touch

Heavier plates, glasses and cups, and knives and forks, will be easier to handle. You may find it harder to turn the pages of a book, especially if the paper is thin, and if so you will miss pages. Glancing at page numbers helps and can become almost automatic. And now you have an extra reason to watch the serial numbers when you separate bills fresh from the mint. (Skinner & Vaughan, 1983, p. 47)

Balance

An easy solution is to move more slowly. In old age you at least have plenty of time. When out for a walk, you will find a cane helpful, even if you are not lame. . . . A light, attractive cane can be a pleasant aid. And you will feel safer and avoid accidents if you wear shoes with rough soles, and attach miniature crampons when you will be walking on icy surfaces. (Skinner & Vaughan, 1983, pp. 47-48)

In sum, Skinner loved to think, write, and build apparatuses. The glint in his eye from childhood never left him, even when he was crippled by the adversities seen in old age.

Notes

1. This final work is Skinner (1990).
2. T. E. Frazier is the designer of the Walden Two community and the book's protagonist.
3. Augustine Castle, a professor of philosophy, serves as T. E. Frazier's antithesis.
4. Horace Walpole, an English writer, is credited with inventing the word. His father, Sir Robert Walpole, was British prime minister during the 1800s.
5. A *Rube Goldberg* is a term for a complicated arrangement of objects. Moreover, this arrangement appears improvised to onlookers.
6. For interested readers, the B. F. Skinner Foundation has left his study as is. Eventually they plan to convert his house into a museum.
7. *Schedules of Reinforcement* (Ferster & Skinner, 1957), a seminal work in the science of behavior, contains over 900 figures demonstrating orderly processes of how contingencies of reinforcement influence behavior. Every figure is a cumulative record.
8. John Platt (1973, p. 38) makes an interesting observation. He likens Skinner's prose style to the manner in which he wrote programmed material (cf. Holland and Skinner, 1961). That is to say, every point is developed carefully, such that later points are constructed out of earlier ones.

9. See Skinner's (1957) Chapter 14 on composition.
10. Skinner (1987c) developed what he called a *Thinking Aid* as a more systematic means of working through this process.

References

Allen, H. N., & Craighead, L. W. (1999). Appetite monitoring in the treatment of binge eating disorder. *Behavior Therapy, 30,* 253-272.

Bjork, D. W. (1993). *B. F. Skinner: A life.* New York: HarperCollins.

Blanchard, E. B. (1992). Psychological treatment of benign headache disorders. *Journal of Consulting and Clinical Psychology, 60,* 537-551.

CinCiripini, P. M., CinCiripini, L. G., Wallfisch, A., Haque, W., & Vunakis, H. V. (1996). Behavior therapy and the transdermal nicotine patch: Effects on cessation outcome, affect, and coping. *Journal of Consulting and Clinical Psychology, 64,* 314-323.

Coon, C. S. (1955). *The story of man: From the first human to primitive culture and beyond.* New York: Knopf.

Cornman, J. W., & Lehrer, K. (1968). *Philosophical problems and arguments: An introduction.* New York: Macmillan.

Dixon, M. R., Hayes, L. J., Binder, L. M., Manthey, S., Sigman, C., & Zdanowski, D. M. (1998). Using a self-control training procedure to increase appropriate behavior. *Journal of Applied Behavior Analysis, 31,* 203-210.

Epstein, R. (1982). Editor's note. In *Skinner for the classroom: Selected papers* (pp. 73-74). Champaign, IL: Research Press.

Epstein, R. (1997). Skinner as self-manager. *Journal of Applied Behavior Analysis, 30,* 545-568.

Ferster, C. B., & Skinner, B. F. (1957). *Schedules of reinforcement.* New York: Appleton-Century-Crofts.

Foxx, R. M. (1982). *Decreasing behaviors of persons with severe retardation and autism.* Champaign, IL: Research Press.

Fremouw, W. J., Callahan, E. J., Zitter, R. E., & Katell, A. (1981). Stimulus control and contingency contracting for behavior change and weight loss. *Addictive Behaviors, 6,* 289-300.

Gould, R. A., Clum, G. A., & Shapiro, D. (1993). The use of bibliotherapy in the treatment of panic: A preliminary investigation. *Behavior Therapy, 24,* 241-252.

Guercio, J., Chittum, R., & McMorrow, M. (1997). Self-management in the treatment of ataxia: A case study in reducing ataxic tremor through relaxation and biofeedback. *Brain Injury, 11,* 353-362.

Heward, W. L. (1987). Self-management. In J. O. Cooper, T. E. Heron, & W. L. Heward (Eds.), *Applied behavior analysis* (pp. 515-549). Columbus, OH: Merrill.

Heward, W. L., & Cooper, J. O. (1992). Radical behaviorism: A productive and needed philosophy for education. *Journal of Behavioral Education, 2,* 345-365.

Holland, J. G., & Skinner, B. F. (1961). *The analysis of behavior.* New York: McGraw-Hill.

Jacob, R. G., Wing, R., & Shapiro, A. P. (1987). The behavioral treatment of hypertension: Long-term effects. *Behavior Therapy, 18,* 325-352.

Jaynes, J. (1976). *The origins of consciousness in the breakdown of the bicameral mind.* Boston: Houghton Mifflin.

Lacks, P., Bertelson, A. D., Gans, L., & Kunkel, J. (1983). The effectiveness of three behavioral treatments for different degrees of sleep onset insomnia. *Behavior Therapy, 14,* 593-605.

Michael, J. (1993). *Concepts and principles of behavior analysis.* Kalamazoo, MI: Association for Behavior Analysis.

Platt, J. R. (1973). The Skinnerian revolution. In H. Wheeler (Ed.), *Beyond the punitive society* (pp. 22-56). San Francisco: Freeman.

Richards, C. S. (1976). Improving study behaviors through self-control techniques. In J. D. Krumboltz & C. E. Thoresen (Eds.), *Counseling methods* (pp. 462-467). New York: Holt, Rinehart & Winston.

Skinner, B. F. (1945, October). Baby in a box (The machine age comes to the nursery! Introducing the mechanical baby-tender). *Ladies Home Journal, 62,* 30-31, 135-136, 138.

Skinner, B. F. (1948). *Walden two.* London: Macmillan.

Skinner, B. F. (1953). *Science and human behavior.* New York: Macmillan.

Skinner, B. F. (1957). *Verbal behavior.* New York: Appleton-Century-Crofts.

Skinner, B. F. (1960). Teaching machines. *Review of Economics and Statistics, 42*(Suppl.), 189-191.

Skinner, B. F. (1967). B. F. Skinner. In E. G. Boring & G. Lindzey (Eds.), *A history of psychology in autobiography: Vol. 5* (pp. 387-413). New York: Appleton-Century-Crofts.

Skinner, B. F. (1971). *Beyond freedom and dignity.* New York: Knopf.

Skinner, B. F. (1974). *About behaviorism.* New York: Knopf.

Skinner, B. F. (1976). *Particulars of my life.* New York: Knopf.

Skinner, B. F. (1979). *The shaping of a behaviorist.* New York: Knopf.

Skinner, B. F. (1980). *Notebooks: B. F. Skinner.* Englewood Cliffs, NJ: Prentice Hall.

Skinner, B. F. (1982). A case history in scientific method. In R. Epstein (Ed.), *Skinner for the classroom: Selected papers* (pp. 73-97). Champaign, IL: Research Press.

Skinner, B. F. (1987a). The evolution of verbal behavior. In *Upon further reflection* (pp. 75-92). Englewood Cliffs, NJ: Prentice Hall.

Skinner, B. F. (1987b). How to discover what you have to say: A talk to students. In R. Epstein (Ed.), *Upon further reflection* (pp. 131-143). Englewood Cliffs, NJ: Prentice Hall.

Skinner, B. F. (1987c). A thinking aid. *Journal of Applied Behavior Analysis, 20,* 379-380.

Skinner, B. F. (1990). Can psychology be a science of the mind? *American Psychologist, 45,* 1206-1210.

Skinner, B. F., & Vaughan, M. E. (1983). *Enjoy old age: A program of self-management.* New York: Norton.

Vargas, J. S. (1990). B. F. Skinner—The last few days. *Journal of Applied Behavior Analysis, 23,* 409-410.

Vaughan, M. E. (1990). Reflections on B. F. Skinner. *Behavior Analyst, 13,* 101-102.

Watson, D. L., & Tharp, R. G. (1997). *Self-directed behavior: Self-modification for personal adjustment.* Pacific Grove, CA: Brooks/Cole.

Wiener, D. N. (1996). *B. F. Skinner: Benign anarchist.* Boston: Allyn & Bacon.

Wolpe, J. (1958). *Psychotherapy by reciprocal inhibition.* Palo Alto, CA: Stanford University Press.

CHAPTER 10

Skinner's Views on Bettering Society

❖

From conception on, we are in the company of other human beings. Our mothers, of course, are the first people with whom we interact. We interact with mother long before we take our first breath (e.g., via the umbilical cord). The next person with whom we interact is usually our father (or, for a moment, an obstetrician or a nurse).

Since the dawning of the species, fathers played a significant role in ensuring the survival of their offspring. They provided shelter for the nursing mother. They brought food. And, when mother got sick, they looked after her and the baby. But early humans soon found out, as countless other species have, that this arrangement was not entirely safe. Environments back then were usually hostile (and still are)—the physical environment constantly threatened our little triad (mother—father—child) with "cold, heat, wind, rain, snow, flood, earthquake, and fire," and many predators, including other humans, loomed large (Sidman, 1989, p. 16).

THE ORIGINS OF SOCIETY

In response to danger all around, our triad joined other triads, forming larger collectivities. Eventually these collectivities banded together with other collectivities, forming bigger alliances, and so on. In time (many generations later), these alliances reached critical mass and societies were formed. A *society*

> is a group of people with a shared and somewhat distinct culture (a culture consists of customs, values, ideas, and artifacts), who live in a

defined territory, feel some unity as a group, and see themselves as distinct from other peoples. A society needs to be independent enough to avoid being swallowed up by other societies. One test of a society is whether it could survive in a form close to its present one if all other societies in the world disappeared. A society, in short, is a relatively independent collection of people who share a common heritage and common ways of interacting. (Persell, 1987, p. 48)

UTOPIANISM

As societies grew in complexity and as languages became increasingly sophisticated, citizens began musing over what they considered to be the ideal society. An ideal society is called a *utopia,* a term coined by Sir Thomas More in 1516. The term first appeared in his book *Utopia* (More, 1516/1961). The word *utopia* is derived from the Greek words *ou* and *topos* (literally, "no place"). It is envisioned as a perfect (but unlikely) society.

The earliest record of the idea of utopian societies (though not labeled as such) is found in classic Greek literature, in Plato's *Republic* (trans. 1941), written roughly 2,500 years ago (Hollis, 1998, p. xii). In brief, *The Republic* is about how to live the "good life," which Plato argued could only arise out of living in a perfect society or ideal state. The book is written in dialogue form and takes place in one room in the house of Cephalus, a wealthy old man. Through this dialogue between Socrates (the protagonist), Cephalus, and a handful of other people, Plato defines what he considers to be a perfect society. Plato constructs his "perfect society" through the words of his former teacher, Socrates.

Interestingly, there are a couple of parallels between Plato's *Republic* and Skinner's (1948) utopian novel *Walden Two.* Namely, Skinner's novel was also written in dialogue form, a dialogue between Frazier and his guests. And just as Plato speaks through Socrates, Skinner speaks through the protagonist Frazier. But more on *Walden Two* later in the chapter.

Since More, modern Utopianism has been "in and out of fashion" throughout the course of its 500-year history (Kumar, 1991, p. vii). In particular, Utopianism has gone through four distinct stages, according to Claeys and Sargent (1999):

1. The first stage was the *religious radicalism* (holding extreme religious views) of the 1500s and 1600s. This movement engendered a variety of *egalitarian* (everyone is equal) themes, in which *communal* (everyone shares in the wealth) property holding was ranked highly by society. Egalitarianism would eventually give rise to socialism in the 1800s.

2. Second, travels abroad in the 1500s on "voyages of discovery" provoked heated debates over the "virtues and vices of primitive peoples and their relation to pagan and Christian traditions of an original age of innocence" (Claeys & Sargent, 1999, p. 3). This "age of innocence" notion is common in utopian literature in which humans had simple pleasures and lived in harmony (Kumar, 1991, pp. 3 ff.).

3. Third, scientific discovery and technological advancement during the 1600s inspired hope in the "indefinite progress of the human species toward better health, longer life, and the domination of nature in the interest of humankind" (Claeys & Sargent, 1999, p. 3). People believed that science could make the world a better place. However, centuries later, this hope was to a large extent replaced with despair. Twentieth-century science fiction entered into the picture, painting a bleak future for the human species. Called *millenarians*, people with this pessimistic view believed that the "end" was near (Kumar, 1991, pp. 6 ff.).

4. Fourth, resulting from the outcome of revolutions in France and North America in the late 1700s, we see a return to egalitarianism, where "the utopian promise of a society of greater virtue, equality, and social justice [was] projected onto a national scale" (Claeys & Sargent, 1999, p. 3).

At a national level, these utopian "promises" fall somewhere between two extremes: totalitarianism and democracy (Persell, 1987, pp. 356 ff.). Totalitarian states, including Nazi Germany and the former Soviet Union, are on one extreme. Totalitarian states are usually run by a dictator (e.g., Stalin) or by a select privileged group. Citizen participation is extremely limited and often discouraged. Those in power "hold all the cards."

At the other extreme, democratic states, including the United States and Great Britain, emphasize the protection of individual rights and put political power into the hands of the people. *Democracy* literally means "government of the people." Those in power have to "share their hand," so to speak, with the rest of society.

Democracies permit some individuals to withdraw from society. Henry David Thoreau wrote about such a life in *Walden,* a book that obviously influenced Skinner's utopian novel *Walden Two.* In the following, Skinner (1978) provided a brief overview of Thoreau's captivating little book:

> Thoreau's book is profoundly anti-utopian. . . . Far from trying to escape into a "brave new world," Thoreau, the cosmic bum, set out resolutely to make the best of what he could find around home . . . Thoreau set up housekeeping by the edge of a duck pond outside of his native village. As Elliot Paul has said, he "got away from it all" by moving just a little farther from town than a good golfer could drive a ball. The lumber for Thoreau's cabin was taken from a shanty that had belonged to James Collins, an Irishman who had worked on the Fitchburg Railroad; the beans that Thoreau hoed and ate were Yankee beans, grown in recalcitrant New England soil. . . . In the world in which he lived he was not *compelled* to do much of anything. He was free to do the things he wanted to do—to be a "self-appointed spectator at a snow storm," to anticipate nature, to begin an adventure in life starting with a vacation from toil. He could do these things by walking from Concord and squatting on the shores of Walden Pond. (pp. 189-191)

Parts of this idyllic, simple life are also seen in *Walden Two.*

SKINNER ON BEHAVIORISM AND SOCIETY

Let us turn to Skinner's views on behaviorism and society. First, we will consider the "building blocks" of his analysis of society.

Skinner considered the experimental analysis of behavior a natural science, specifically, a branch of biology. From biology he took such terms as *stimulus* and *response,* and at a macrolevel he was influenced by a brand of functionalism espoused by Charles Darwin (Skinner, 1938, pp. 4, 9). Darwin, as you know, established a highly influential theory of evolution, natural selection (Gould, 1977).

Skinner picked up where Darwin left off, extending his analysis to include two additional types of variation and selection, namely, selection by consequences (operant conditioning) and cultural selection. These three types of variation and selection serve as the foundation for Skinner's views on behaviorism and society (see Figure 10.1).

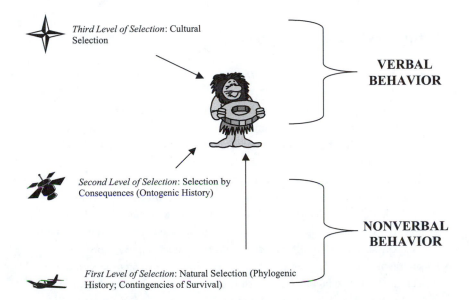

Third Level of Selection: Cultural Selection

VERBAL BEHAVIOR

Second Level of Selection: Selection by Consequences (Ontogenic History)

NONVERBAL BEHAVIOR

First Level of Selection: Natural Selection (Phylogenic History; Contingencies of Survival)

Figure 10.1. Skinner maintained that the human species underwent three levels of selection. The first level is natural selection, which accounts for our physical makeup. The second level is selection by consequences (operant behavior). Operant behavior permitted our species to quickly adapt to ever-changing environmental conditions. The third level is cultural selection. This third level is what makes us uniquely human. At this level, members of a verbal community are taught verbal behavior. And once humans are verbally able, they can efficiently transmit cultural practices from one generation to the next.

ENVIRONMENTAL SELECTIONISM

The concepts of variation and selection fall under the general heading of *environmental selectionism*, which is a critical concept in Skinner's views on the behavior of organisms. And as we shall see, Skinner's views on bettering society hinge on this concept. Selectionism is the glue that holds Skinner's analysis of culture together. Skinner (1990, p. 1206) maintained that the human organism as a whole is the product of three types of variation and selection.

Natural Selection

The first type is *natural selection:*

> The story (of human behavior) presumably began not with the big bang, but with that extraordinary moment when a molecule that had the power to reproduce itself came into existence. It was then that the selection by consequences made its appearance as a causal mode. Reproduction was itself a first consequence, and it led, through natural selection, to the evolution of cells, organs, and organisms that reproduced themselves under increasingly diverse conditions. What we call behavior evolved as a set of functions furthering the interchange between organism and environment. In a fairly stable world it could be as much a part of the genetic endowment of the species as digestion, respiration, or any other biological function. The involvement with the environment, however, imposed limitations. The behavior functioned well only under conditions fairly similar to those under which it was selected. (Skinner, 1987, pp. 51-52)

This mechanism of selection is responsible for the evolution of our species and of species-specific behavior. However, natural selection only goes so far in accounting for behavioral adaptations to an ever-changing environment—natural selection has limitations:

> All types of variation and selection have certain faults, and one of them is especially critical for natural selection: *It prepares a species only for a future that resembles the selecting past.* Species behavior is only effective in a world that fairly closely resembles the world in which the species evolved. (Skinner, 1990, p. 1206 [italics added])

This analysis provides an explanation for the extinction of species. Take dinosaurs, for example. There are those who theorize that mammals led to the dinosaurs' demise by preying on their unguarded eggs. According to this argument, the species-typical behavior of laying eggs wasn't adaptive in a new environment that now contained fuzzy little egg-eating rodents.

Selection by Consequences (Operant Conditioning)

In the following passage Skinner (1990) described how this limitation was rectified:

> That fault was corrected by the evolution of a second type of variation and selection, operant conditioning, through which variations in the behavior of the individual are selected by features of the environment that are not stable enough to play any part in evolution. In operant conditioning, behavior is reinforced, in the sense of strengthened or made more likely to occur, by certain kinds of consequences, which first acquired the power to reinforce through natural selection. (p. 1206)[1]

This mechanism enables an organism to better adapt to changes in environmental circumstances.

Advantages aside, there is also a fault in this second type of variation and selection. Namely, selection must wait for variation. And this process is slow—taking millions of years for a repertoire of behavior to be constructed during a single lifetime (Skinner, 1990, p. 1206).

Cultural Selection

This fault was corrected when individuals started taking advantage of other people's repertoires by way of imitation (Skinner, 1990, p. 1206). Imitation brings imitators into contact with the reinforcing consequences engendered by the behavior imitated. For example, when one individual cooks a food that is inedible raw so that it becomes edible, others can imitate this practice. Once imitators contact similar reinforcers, the imitated behavior is thereby strengthened.

Even though imitation expedites the development of increasingly sophisticated repertoires, the biggest evolutionary step in the history of species (as discussed in Chapter 7) took place when humans began speaking to one another:

> The human species presumably became much more social when its vocal musculature came under operant control. . . . The development of environmental control of the vocal musculature greatly extended the help one person receives from others. By behaving verbally people cooperate more successfully in common ventures. By taking advice, heeding warnings, following instructions, and observing rules, they profit from what others have already learned. Ethical practices are strengthened by being codified in laws, and special techniques of ethical and intellectual self-management are devised and taught. . . . Verbal behavior greatly increased the importance of the third kind of selection by consequences, the evolution of social environments—cultures. . . . A culture evolves when practices (acquired individually) . . . contribute to the success of the practicing group in solving its problems. It is the effect on the group, not the reinforcing consequences for individual members, that is responsible for the evolution of the culture. (Skinner, 1987, pp. 53-54)

Skinner (1971) added,

> A culture survives if those who carry it survive, and this depends in part upon certain genetic susceptibilities to reinforcement, as the result of which behavior making for survival in a given environment is shaped and maintained. Practices which induce the individual to work for the good of others presumably further the survival of others and hence the survival of the culture the others carry. (p. 135)

EVOLUTIONARY EPISTEMOLOGY[2]

Skinner's views on culture and society stem from an evolutionary epistemological perspective (Staddon, 1993, pp. 63 ff.).[3] That is to say, our present state of knowledge is the product of an evolutionary history, a history in which certain ideas are favored by way of natural and cultural selection, while other ideas become obsolete (i.e., they are not transmitted from one generation to the next). Take cultural values such as "thou shalt not steal" as a case in point. According to Skinner (1971),

> Things are good (positively reinforcing) or bad (negatively reinforcing) presumably because of the contingencies of survival under which the species evolved. . . . To make a value judgment by calling something good or bad is to classify it in terms of reinforcing effects. The classification is important . . . when reinforcers begin to be used by other people (when, for example, the verbal responses "Good!" and "Bad!" begin to function as reinforcers). (pp. 104-105)

Early in the history of the human species, sugar and fattening foods were necessary for survival—especially during famine or times of food shortages. Heightened sensitivity to sugar and fat had its advantages. The unrefined sugar found in fruits, vegetables, and starches is bound up with essential vitamins, minerals, fiber, and oils. Sugar itself is transformed into glucose, which produces immediate body energy. Heightened sensitivity to sweet tastes led those foraging for food to valuable nourishment.

Likewise, with fat, nomadic tribes required high-calorie foodstuffs in order to survive harsh climates. As it turns out, fat is an important source of energy for metabolism, and it supplies the fatty acids the body needs for vital chemical processes (e.g., manufacturing sex hormones and cell membranes). As with heightened sensitivity to sugary substances, heightened sensitivity to fatty tastes also led hunters and gatherers to survive.

The evolutionary advantages of heightened sensitivity to sugar and fat are obvious. Those members highly sensitive to these substances lived to reproduce and share their practices with their offspring. Those that did not are long gone. While alive, they may have been too diseased or too malnourished to mate, so there weren't any offspring around to "carry the torch," so to speak.

By contrast, in industrialized societies, where obesity is rampant and there is an overabundance of food, heightened sensitivity to sugary and fatty substances contributes to a shorter life. Indeed, loading up on too much sugar and fat leads to a host of health complications over extended periods of time.

What makes matters worse is that certain cultures intentionally "pump" refined sugar into our daily diet. The average American, for example, consumes more than 100 pounds of sugar annually, two thirds of which is added to food during processing (*Reader's Digest*, 1996, p. 335). Why has so much sugar been dumped into food, you might ask? Technically speaking, sugar enhances the "reinforceability" of products distributed by the food industry, thus increasing profits. Increasing the reinforcing properties of commodities increases sales, plain and simple.[4]

For a time, our culture permitted the "greedy" food industry to go unchallenged. We eventually woke up, however—one culture can be taken over by a more aggressive one when its members are too obese to fend for themselves. "When it becomes clear that a culture may . . . perish, some of its members may begin to act to promote its survival" (Skinner, 1971, p. 134). Those members are by and large scientists, and as Sir Karl Popper (1985) pointed out, science is particularly well suited to help cultures adapt to an ever-changing world:

> From a biological or evolutionary point of view, science, or progress in science, may be regarded as a means used by the human species to adapt itself to the environment: to invade new environmental niches, and even to invent new environmental niches. (Popper, 1985, p. 78)

Science assists us mainly by means of eliminating error (Popper, 1985, pp. 79 ff.). For example, after millions of Americans die off from poor diets, science can shed light on how to prevent our culture from making the same mistakes by identifying causal mechanisms.

Let us turn our discussion to Skinner's critique of our present culture. His critique sets the stage for his views on bettering society. This chapter then closes with a discussion of Skinner's utopian society.

Skinner's Unrelenting Attack on "Autonomous Man"

Skinner's views on bettering society incited an enormous backlash from critical audiences and the lay public. The controversy was so widespread that he ended up on the cover of *Time* magazine in September 1971. When was the last time you saw a psychologist's picture on the cover of one of North America's hottest news magazines?

Skinner's views ignited the press like wildfire. He appeared on dozens of talk shows and was inundated with invitations to give lectures (Bjork, 1993, pp. 191 ff.). The media had a heyday with Skinner. Unfortunately, on many occasions he became something of a "whipping boy" on behalf of every despot, real and imagined. Carl Rogers, for example, said that Skinner's utopian vision depicted in *Walden Two* and George

Orwell's nightmarish dystopian[5] society portrayed in *1984* "seemed in-distinguishable" (Skinner, 1972c, p. 37). The following excerpts, taken from the third volume of Skinner's autobiography, give the flavor of some people's reactions to Skinner's utopia:

> In a televised round-table discussion, Margaret Mead[6] responded to something I said by shouting, "I don't want to play God! I don't want to control people." . . . In another television conversation . . . Charles Hampden Turner characterized me as a power-mad scientist. (Skinner, 1983, p. 242)

Indeed, many Americans reacted to Skinner as if he had tossed his trash at the feet of the Statue of Liberty.[7]

Skinner's views on bettering society made him extremely famous, or rather, infamous. Defenders of freedom and dignity saw Skinner as a threat to humanity. He was called a totalitarian, a fascist, and the prover-bial "evil scientist." These critics feared that Skinner's "behavioral manifesto" on building experimental cultures would fall into the wrong hands and enslave millions. Taking an extreme example, a movie based on Anthony Burgess's book *A Clockwork Orange* is said to have been inspired by the darker side of Skinner's social philosophy (despite the fact that the procedures used were Pavlovian, not operant; Booker, 1994, p. 247). In *A Clockwork Orange*, behavior modification[8] was portrayed as nothing short of cold and calculated torture. Of course, anyone who knows Skinner's work well would be cognizant of the fact that there is no "dark side." Skinner never played Jekyll and Hyde.

The reason why many readers were so outraged by Skinner's social views is likely due to the fact that he challenged a value that Americans held sacred—free will (Carpenter, 1974, p. xi). For over 2,000 years, the notion of free will has remained largely untouched (e.g., Plato, trans. 1941, pp. 355 ff.). Free will is the belief that human beings have the power to choose one action over the other. To say a person has free will is to deny that "all human actions are caused" (Cornman & Lehrer, 1968, p. 131). This view holds that, although humans are influenced by outside sources (e.g., peer pressure), they ultimately are free to decide to act on those influences (or to elect not to).

Free will is the antithesis of the determinism that Skinner espoused. Recall from Chapter 9 that determinism "is the thesis of *universal causa-*

tion, the thesis that *everything is caused*" (Cornman & Lehrer, 1968, p. 120 [italics added]). From a deterministic standpoint, the person's *environment* (the history of the species and the individual's history) is what chooses one action over the other (actually the correct term is *selects*).

One of the rudimentary assumptions of natural science is determinism. Science is all about understanding, predicting, and controlling nature. We need to assume order in the universe to understand it scientifically. Chemists, for example, must assume that mixing certain elements will result in predictable outcomes. Otherwise, they would simply haphazardly mix elements and hope not to blow themselves up.

Of course, the debate over determinism and free will or self-determinism has been tossed around in philosophical circles for years, but few have seriously considered practical implications of choosing one or the other—certainly not at a global level.

Within the past 500 years, Western civilization has undergone drastic changes. Most notably, secularism (i.e., indifference to religion) has spread rampant throughout the western hemisphere. At one time, not long ago in our history, state and church were inseparable. This is certainly not the case in modern times, when the chasm between church and state increasingly widens.

The Fall of Man as Demigod

In Western societies, before science was developed, human beings were said to harbor miraculous forces. Humans were seen as demigods, created in the image of their divine Maker. However, as men practicing science grew in number and as science became increasingly organized, scientists began casting a different light on our understanding of humans; humans were presented, not as demigods, but as biological organisms, albeit complex ones.

Two of the biggest intellectual movements that challenged the "man created in God's own image" notion began with Copernicus and Darwin. Let us briefly consider these in the order in which they "rocked Noah's boat," so to speak. After that, we will discuss Skinner's advance of yet another intellectual movement. This movement is the usurping of "autonomous man"—that is, the idea of a human making free choices. As we shall soon see, the demise of autonomous man marks the complete transformation of man from demigod to lowly beast, as some would have it. What else is there?

Before Skinner, Copernicus was one of the first to transform the traditional conception of our place in the universe (Kuhn, 1957, p. 1). In other words, he threw the notion "man as demigod" into question. As it turned out, humans were not at the center of the universe after all (i.e., Copernicus refuted the geocentric theory of the universe).

At that point humans were bumped down a notch in the pecking order. Humans became less sublime and more mundane. Humans achieved a new status, not as demigod, but more like spectators in a colosseum that seats billions.

Copernicus delayed printing his great work *De Revolutionibus Orbium Coelestium* (1543) until he lay in his deathbed. Publishing it earlier would have placed him in front of the Church's tribunal. He would have been excommunicated from the Church or, worse, executed for being a heretic.

In spite of what Copernicus thought, few paid attention to his ideas for decades following his death, and even fewer read his book (Goodstein & Goodstein, 1996, p. 23). The Roman Catholic Church was more concerned with Martin Luther and his crusade at the time. However, Copernicus's beliefs were eventually adopted by society (particularly through the work of Tycho Brahe, Johannes Kepler, and Galileo Galilei).

There are few in modern times who still embrace geocentric beliefs. They join the ranks of those who still think the earth is flat and that fire is forged out of magic.

Several hundred years later, Darwin (1859) gave humankind another advance in understanding with his book *The Origin of Species*. After sailing around the small Galapagos Archipelago[9] in the *Beagle* collecting evidence, Darwin mounted a convincing argument that humanity shares common ancestry with the animal kingdom generally and in particular with primates.[10] Initially, Darwin incited public outcry. However, eventually much of society has adopted Darwin's evolutionary thesis—most patently shown in genetic research.

Roughly 100 years after Darwin comes Skinner, whose views again fly in the face of this man-as-demigod notion. Like his predecessors, Skinner has rocked the boat. He said that not only have humans descended from other animals but they also have no free will. And like Darwin, after gathering enough evidence, he mounted a persuasive argument that

behavior is not governed by capricious forces. All behavior, from sneez-
ing to snoring, snubbing, and snuggling, is determined. Everything we
do, say, and feel is caused not by something within us but by factors that
lie outside our bodies. In other words, the environment is responsible for
our accomplishments as well as for every wrongdoing. Skinner slew autonomous man and buried him along with the magical forces that had
kept him alive for over 2,000 years. And if the environment is indeed
responsible for our accomplishments as well as for every wrongdoing,
then to improve society we need to redesign the environment. That is
exactly what Skinner proposes.

We turn now to Skinner's views on bettering society. In discussing
utopian literature, one must first describe the context in which it was
written for it to make sense. Utopias are envisioned as perfect societies.
They are inspired by cultures that are far from perfect. Utopian literature
is born out of human suffering caused by people's ill deeds.

For these reasons, we will first set the stage for Skinner's social plan
by illustrating what he felt was wrong with his own world. Skinner believed that the world was going "to hell in a handbag" (not surprising,
considering the fact that Skinner lived through two world wars). And,
according to Skinner, doubtless the chief means of averting disaster was
developing an effective technology of behavior.

According to Skinner, only a technology of behavior can rescue humankind. Because social ills are caused by behavior, it follows, therefore,
that the cure is found somewhere in the variables of which behavior is a
function.

Society's Ills Are Based on Behavior

To reduce overcrowding, disease, pollution, starvation, obesity, and
the threat of nuclear war, among myriad other social ills, one needs to
make vital changes in human behavior (Skinner, 1971, p. 4). Even
though science in general has made rapid strides in developing effective birth control, in improving agricultural technology, and in designing
more efficient ways to consume natural resources, getting people to
adopt such strategies falls within the province of behavior science. And
unless society develops an effective technology of behavior, according

to Skinner, humanity will eventually extinguish itself through its own ignorance.

In spite of Skinner's warning, it has been estimated by the United Nations (1995) that the world population will be 9.8 billion in 2050, up from 5.8 billion today, which is an increase of about 2 billion since *Beyond Freedom and Dignity* (Skinner, 1971) was published roughly three decades ago. What this means is that in about half a century, there will be almost twice as many people around to produce twice the waste. Nearly twice the population will further overcrowding. Overcrowding will increase the prevalence of communicable diseases because of a rise in unsanitary living conditions. There will be almost twice the population to further milk already scarce natural resources. And to make room for future generations, urban communities will usurp viable farmland. Much of what is left will be wiped away by global warming. In light of this laundry list of problems, perhaps the world is in fact going to hell in a handbag as Skinner predicted. Only time will tell.

In *Walden Two* and *Beyond Freedom and Dignity,* Skinner proposed a solution in response to the social ills that plague contemporary society. Whereas *Walden Two* is seen more as fictional writing, *Beyond Freedom and Dignity* is a call to action. It is a treatise on why society needs to develop a solid behavioral technology before it is too late.

Most critically, according to Skinner (1971, pp. 7 ff.), we need to abandon the notion that human behavior is caused by magical forces— just as physics abandoned invented explanations to account for momentum centuries ago. Science must shift its emphasis away from the miraculous autonomous man and place both responsibility and achievement in the environment (Skinner, 1971, p. 25). Responsibility and achievement are synonymous with the notions of freedom and dignity, to which we now turn.

Freedom

According to Skinner (1971, pp. 26 ff.), the term *freedom* is usually used to describe escape or avoidance. *Escape* is doing whatever it takes to remove contact with an aversive stimulus that is already present (Skinner, 1953, p. 171). This involves either removing, stopping, or reducing the intensity of the stimulus, or simply moving out of harm's way. Similarly, *avoidance* is doing whatever it takes to prevent contact with the aversive stimulus not yet present (Skinner, 1953, p. 176). With prevention, there must be some reason to believe that that "something" has a pretty good chance of returning. Therefore, an additional requirement for avoidance is some kind of warning signal.

Technically speaking, we call this warning signal a *conditioned aversive stimulus*. Conditioned aversive stimuli acquire their functions by being frequently paired with unconditioned aversive stimuli or other conditioned stimuli that have already acquired certain punishing functions. Seeing funnel clouds whirling about overhead indicates danger. Funnel clouds that haven't touched down are conditioned aversive stimuli that have been paired with tornadoes (unconditioned aversive stimuli). You see a funnel cloud—you run and hide. In so doing, you avoid contact with an unconditioned aversive stimulus and you escape from the warning signal that is scaring the hell out of you.

Most animals will make every effort to free themselves from aversive circumstances. Deer will scurry out of harm's way upon catching wind of potential predators skulking in the underbrush. Fish will violently resist the hook until they break free. Foxes will struggle to the point of exhaustion when caught in a trap, sometimes gnawing off their own limbs. Examples of this kind of freedom abound in nature. And as Skinner (1971, p. 26) pointed out, one does not say that animals struggle because of their love of freedom. Rather, behavior of this sort arises in most species because of its survival value. Such behavior is merely a concatenation of reflexes and operants. Humans elicit this same concatenation of reflexes when they free themselves from ingested toxins by vomiting, when they sneeze to free their nasal passages from irritants, and when they struggle to break free from a snag.

Defenders of freedom would likely agree with Skinner's analysis. And by and large they do not concern themselves with situations of this sort. Skinner broke with the defenders of freedom with his analysis of aversive contingencies put in place by humans. Using Skinner's terms, the so-called contingency managers are labeled *controllers*, and those individuals who are being controlled are called *controllees*. Such is the condition that has engendered a proliferation of literature by the champions of freedom.

The literature of freedom has been highly successful in identifying apparent aversive practices and suggesting ways in which controllees ought to defend themselves. Skinner would agree that the literature of freedom has afforded us with valuable information on what to do when we "feel bad" about how we are being treated.

However, to Skinner, the literature of freedom falls short of protecting citizens from potential harm in modern times. The reason why the literature of freedom is defective, Skinner (1971, p. 32) maintained, is because it focuses on feelings and states of mind. The causal variables are said to reside in the individual.

Focusing on feelings and states of mind becomes a problem, particularly when would-be controllers switch to alternative strategies (Skinner, 1971, pp. 32 ff.). Namely, individuals can be exploited when controllers switch from aversive to nonaversive control. Even though nonaversive control seems fine at first, it often has deferred aversive consequences.

Take writing a bad check as a case in point. The person receiving the bad check initially feels pretty good. And that feeling typically lasts a while longer than the time it takes for the felon to turn tail and run. If we were focusing only on feelings and states of mind, then we would have never seen it coming, because the feelings associated with receiving a good and bad check are identical. To prevent exploitative relationships, one needs to gain a better understanding of the conditions in which they occur.

In contrast to the literature of freedom, Skinner parsed out feelings from the circumstances in which they arise. According to Skinner (1971, p. 36), the literature of freedom has never provided effective countercontrol strategies for techniques of control that do not generate escape or counterattack. Their system would not allow it, because they deal with the problem of control in terms of slippery feelings and states of mind. In turning the analysis away from internal states to the environment, we pave the way for establishing effective countercontrol. Before proceeding further, we would like to clarify what Skinner meant by *control* and *countercontrol*.

Control

Skinner's use of the term *control* has provoked countless attacks from defenders of autonomous man—especially when used in the same context with words like *freedom, dignity, culture,* and *society.* These defenders of

autonomous man claim that human beings are inherently free to do whatever they want (i.e., self-determinism). Any attempt at trying to control
behavior is seen as an infringement on personal liberty. It should come as
no surprise that behavioral engineering would be seen as something to
fear by those who misunderstand what Skinner is really saying. They see
a dichotomy between freedom and oppression (control). As we shall see
in a moment, Skinner saw this dichotomy as artificial. According to Skinner, all behavior is controlled all of the time. Ignoring this fact only harms
us in the long run. This is why we have made little progress in developing
behavioral technology over the centuries (Skinner, 1971, pp. 5 ff.).

As Skinner (1974, p. 83) pointed out, these critics' concern for autonomous man or free will narrows their behavioral technology to only
ineffective techniques (permissiveness, pp. 83-84; "the controller as mid-
wife," pp. 84-87; guidance, pp. 87-88; "building dependence on things,"
pp. 89-91; changing minds, pp. 91 ff.). Space will not allow us to discuss
these techniques in detail; however, all of these can be summed up in the
following passage:

> Like permissiveness, maieutics (the therapist or educator as midwife),
> guidance, and building a dependence on things, changing a mind is con-
> doned by defenders of freedom and dignity because it is an ineffective
> way of changing behavior, and the changer of minds can therefore es-
> cape from the charge that he is controlling people. He is exonerated
> when things go wrong. Autonomous man survives to be credited with
> his achievements and blamed for his mistakes. . . . The apparent free-
> dom respected by weak measures is merely inconspicuous control. When
> we seem to turn control over to a person himself, we simply shift from
> one mode of control to another. . . . The fundamental mistake made by
> all those who choose weak methods of control is to assume that the
> balance of control is left to the individual, when in fact it is left to other
> conditions. The other conditions are often hard to see, but to continue to
> neglect them and attribute their effects to autonomous man is to court
> disaster. When practices are concealed or disguised, countercontrol is
> made difficult; it is not clear from whom one is to escape or whom one is
> to attack. . . . A scientific analysis of behavior must, I believe, assume
> that a person's behavior is controlled by his genetic and environmental
> histories rather than by the person himself as an initiating, creative agent.
> . . . We cannot prove, of course, that human behavior as a whole is fully

determined, but the proposition becomes more plausible as facts ac-
cumulate, and I believe that a point has been reached at which its
implications must be seriously considered. . . . *We cannot choose a way
of life in which there is no control. We can only change the controlling
conditions.* (Skinner, 1974, pp. 97, 99, 194-195 [italics added])

As will be described later on in greater detail, Skinner's views on
bettering society are all about changing the *controlling conditions* in which
people live. To make a long story short, these conditions boil down to
positive reinforcement—with an eye on immediate and deferred consequences. This is Skinner's utopian vision in a nutshell. However, let's not
prematurely jump ahead in our discussion. Let us get back on track by
turning now to Skinner's analysis of countercontrol.

Countercontrol

As Skinner (1974, p. 195) pointed out, organized control is often
arranged in a manner that most effectively reinforces the behavior of the
controller at the controllee's expense. What this typically means for
controllees is either immediate aversive consequences or exploitation over
time (i.e., deferred aversive consequences).

Immediate aversive consequences might be in the form of cracking a
whip or rapping a child's knuckles with a birch rod. The effect of employing aversives is usually immediate compliance. Technically speaking,
using an aversive stimulus (contingent on the controllee's behavior) negatively reinforces the behavior of, say, the slave or child (they escape or
avoid a further lashing), and the punishee's behavior (compliance) in turn
positively reinforces the punisher's use of that aversive technique (see
Figure 10.2).

From reading previous chapters, you may recall that immediate reinforcers work better than delayed ones. In light of the speed with which
controllers achieve compliance in their controllees, it is no wonder that
aversive control is so widely used in every institution imaginable. Of
course, aversive control works only in environments where controllees
are incapable of exerting strong countercontrol.

With exploitation, controllees feel free because they are immediately
provided with small reinforcers (therefore, the literature of freedom is of

Figure 10.2. An exchange illustrating aversive control (modeled after Baum, 1994, p. 153). The interrogator (controller) threatens the suspect (controllee) with serving time if he doesn't "squeal" on his partners in crime. To escape the threat the suspect divulges his accomplices' names. In so doing the suspect positively reinforces the interrogator's verbal threat.

little to no use here). Only in the long run do controllees receive aversive consequences. A historical example illustrates this point well. Prior to labor laws (countercontrol), factory workers were once paid in piecemeal (small immediate reinforcers). This translates into the following simple equation: the more one produced, the greater the reward (1 widget = $1, 10 widgets = $10, 100 widgets = $100, etc.). Workers shifted production into high gear, at which point employers upped the ratio required for the same amount of pay. The ratios got so high that workers became exhausted working for a living wage, and some employees literally worked themselves to death.

Recall from previous chapters that schedules of this sort are called *fixed-ratio schedules of reinforcement*. Fixed-ratio schedules produce a high and steady rate of behavior. With just the right ratio, slowly increasing ratios, most organisms will work themselves to the point of exhaustion.

Should they continue on such schedules, many eventually die before "giving up."

People being controlled under either of the above circumstances are miserable. Everyone hates being whipped, and no one welcomes illness, as in the case of the perpetually exhausted factory worker. And as Skinner (1974) pointed out in the following passage, they eventually escape from or retaliate against the powers that be (e.g., eventually they form labor unions or abolitionists form rallies):

> They escape from the controller—moving out of range if he is an individual, or defecting from the government, becoming an apostate from a religion, resigning, or playing truant—or they may attack in order to weaken or destroy the controlling power, as in a revolution, a reformation, a strike, or a student protest. In other words, *they oppose control with countercontrol.* (Skinner, 1974, p. 195 [italics added])

As governments and religious institutions become increasingly sophisticated in using nonaversive techniques, along with other conventional strategies of social control, society in general must also become increasingly sophisticated in order to preempt certain forms of exploitation. When governments, for example, shift from generating revenue by way of taxation to legalized gambling (i.e., intermittent-ratio schedules), community advocacy groups should see that regulations (countercontrol) are put firmly in place to reduce the risk of exploiting citizens. In the absence of such countercontrol measures, we would almost certainly see more people living on the streets after gambling away their savings.[11]

No other discipline in the physical or social sciences can help us develop as effective a technology of countercontrol as the analysis of behavior can. Indeed, we first have to buy into the notion that our behavior is always under control before we can even advance highly sophisticated countercontrol efforts (see Skinner, *Science and Human Behavior,* 1953, Sections IV, V, and VI for a thorough analysis of controlling agencies). Otherwise, we tend to blame people for their own misfortunes. The alcoholic is seen as "weak-minded." The homeless are said to be "lazy." Prostitutes and their pimps are considered "bad seeds." The drug peddler suffers from a lack of "conscience," and the jewel thief is "criminally minded." Skinner would look at the circumstances that produced these behaviors to help all segments of society improve.

Dignity

On the opposite side of the coin we have dignity. The terms used are different. Instead of *blame* and *culpability,* we now have terms like *credit* and *merit*. However, in principle the idea is still the same. Just as autonomous man takes blame for his wrongdoings, autonomous man also receives credit for his accomplishments.

Most Americans take great pride in what they do. Special holidays are observed in honor of those who fought bravely for our freedom from tyranny, when they could have deserted. Ceremonies are held in honor of those who contribute to science or literature in the face of competing rewards, such as the possibility of selling out. Scholarships are conferred on those who attain high academic standards or who promote the welfare of society. Individuals are considered particularly heroic when they do so in spite of disability or disease. In short, there are awards, accolades, and citations for almost every conceivable activity wedded to the notion of dignity. Because this notion is so ingrained in our culture, when dignity is in danger of being squelched, not surprisingly people react violently.

As Skinner (1971, pp. 45 ff.) pointed out, dignity is related to the conspicuousness of the controlling variables of which behavior is a function. In other words, credit is apportioned commensurably with the visibility of the causes of behavior (Skinner, 1971, calls this "good husbandry" [p. 51]). If people make a hefty contribution to charity with a gun held to their heads (conspicuous control), then these individuals would not receive much credit (seen as generosity or lack thereof). Of course, they lose credit only if observers know about the circumstances in which such "donations" are made. Under slightly different circumstances— namely, the observer is unaware of the situation in which the money is handed over—in all likelihood those making the donation would be given full credit for their supposed "generosity."

Have you ever wondered why talk show hosts use cue cards? It's all about preserving their dignity. Face it, we are far more impressed when we think they are "winging it" than if they are obviously following cue cards. Talking "off the cuff" receives more credit than reading off of "cheat sheets" written on the back of one's hand.

The same can be said about athletic events. In hockey, for example, an unassisted goal (a "breakaway") is given far more credit (less conspicuous control) than an assisted one. In pursuit of full credit, some players take gambles by taking "wild" shots from far away. If they make it, they have much to gain, but if they miss, their shots go largely unnoticed.

What happens to this notion of dignity when the environment makes it easier on a person? Celibacy, for example, seems far easier when a guy is stranded on a deserted island than when lodging at a brothel or touring the country with Hawaiian Tropic bikini girls. Credit is clearly dispensed based on the conspicuousness of control. Taking the example of the man on the Hawaiian Tropic tour, if it is found out that he is of a same-sex sexual orientation, would we still give him credit? Certainly not. The control (i.e., the reinforcement obtained from the intimate company of other men) is obvious.

As we will see in a moment, Skinner endorses the notion that all credit and blame is found in the environment. This makes perfect sense in light of the fact that, from his philosophical standpoint, our behavior is determined. According to Skinner, it is just a matter of time before we make all control conspicuous by way of a science of behavior.

This does not do away with feeling "good" about one's accomplishments. "Accomplishments" so conceived are amply reinforced, and positively reinforced behavior almost always feels good any way you look at it. From Skinner's standpoint, dispensing with notions such as dignity and credit and turning to the controlling variables of which accomplishments are a function enables us to become more effective at what we do. In so doing, we access more reinforcement and in turn "feel" better than we have ever felt.

Discovering Controlling Variables: Building Experimental Communities

According to Skinner (1971), cultures and experimentation are alike:

A culture is very much like the experimental space used in the analysis of behavior. Both are sets of contingencies of reinforcement. A child is born into a culture as an organism is placed in an experimental space. Designing a culture is like designing an experiment; contingencies are arranged and effects noted. In an experiment we are interested in what happens, in designing a culture with whether it will work. (p. 153)

Of course one cannot expect to change a culture overnight. One needs to break the task down:

> Perhaps we cannot now design a successful culture as a whole, but we can design better practices in a piecemeal fashion. The behavioral processes in the world at large are the same as those in a utopian community, and practices have the same effects for the same reasons. (Skinner, 1971, p. 156)

Would Building Experimental Communities Work?

The *Walden Two* community, as indicated in Skinner's (1948) book by this name, consists of 1,000 citizens. People wear comfortable utilitarian dress. Citizens are paid with labor credits for completing a number of tasks, and they work for roughly four hours a day. Children are raised and taught by the "community," and there is very little need for "law and order," because behavior is controlled socially through positive reinforcement.

Walden Two (Skinner, 1948) sparked a number of communal societies. The two best known are Twin Oaks in Virginia and East Wind in Missouri. Both are still around, though they have since abandoned many details of Skinner's model. Los Horcones, a small communal society in Mexico, states in its literature that it is based upon Walden Two.

CONCLUDING REMARKS

In closing, our culture would be foolhardy to reject Skinner's thesis on behaviorism and society. He definitely has a plan for building a better world in which people would indeed be happier. He has given us the tools to build his utopian society. Perhaps in time, behavior scientists will pick up where he left off—perhaps not. Skinner had a pragmatic answer to "tame" antisocial behaviors (pollution, overpopulation, war).

His pragmatic answer is using the science of human behavior to promote our society's survival. It is hard to say whether our world is in fact going to "hell in a handbag" like countless societies before us (e.g., the Roman Empire, Nazi Germany, Communist Russia, the Shakers). In the spirit of a deterministic attitude, only our future "knows" the answer to this question.

We would now like to close with Skinner's "Ten Commandments" for building a better world:

(1) No way of life is inevitable. Examine your own closely. (2) If you do not like it, change it. (3) But do not try to change it through political action. Even if you succeed in gaining power, you will not be able to use it any more wisely than your predecessors. (4) Ask only to be left alone to solve your problems in your own way. (5) Simplify your needs. Learn how to be happy with fewer possessions. . . . (6) Build a way of life in which people live together without quarreling, in a social climate of trust rather than suspicion, of love rather than jealousy, of cooperation rather than competition. (7) Maintain that world with gentle but pervasive ethical sanctions rather than a police or military force. (8) Transmit the culture effectively to new members through expert child care and a powerful educational technology. (9) Reduce compulsive labor to a minimum by arranging the kinds of incentives under which people enjoy working. (10) Regard no practice as immutable. Change and be ready to change again. Accept no eternal verity. Experiment. (Skinner, 1948, pp. vii-viii)

Notes

1. Elsewhere, Skinner (1987) described another behavioral process critical in responding to moment-to-moment changes in environmental circumstances, which is respondent conditioning: "Through respondent (Pavlovian) conditioning, responses prepared in advance by natural selection could come under the control of new stimuli" (p. 52).
2. The philosophical study of the nature and limitations of knowledge.
3. One could also call them *natural epistemological* (see Segel, 1996, for a discussion of this topic).
4. Of the two thirds that have been added during food processing, for example, the soft drink industry contributes 23% of that value, and an additional 14% goes into your sugar-varnished cereal, triple-chocolate fudge brownie, triple sugar in your coffee,

and into everything else your dentist warns you about (Reader's Digest, 1996, p. 335).

5. For readers unfamiliar with the term *dystopia,* dystopian literature situates itself opposite to utopian thought (Booker, 1994, p. 3). By contrast with utopian novels, dystopian literature warns against a punitive society in which people are treated as automatons as those in power milk them for all they are worth.

6. A famous anthropologist who wrote *Coming of Age in Samoa* (1953).

7. At one point the Kennedy family took a liking to Skinner. In fact, they invited him to Hyannis Port, Massachusetts. Once he published *Beyond Freedom and Dignity* (1971), however, they dropped him like a hot potato (B. F. Skinner, personal communication, February 1981).

8. Skinner never liked the term *behavior modification;* he preferred *applied behavior analysis.*

9. The Galapagos Archipelago lies between 500 and 600 miles off the shores of South America.

10. According to the zoologist Desmond Morris (1967, p. 9), there are 193 living species of monkeys and apes. Of the 193, only one is hairless. To our knowledge, it is the only primate that has a name for itself: It calls itself *Homo sapiens.*

11. Throughout his writings, Skinner also described ways in which society can prevent abuse and neglect for those who can't exert countercontrol on their own (e.g., the aged, people with intellectual impairment, the very young, people with mental disorders, those who are incarcerated; see Skinner, 1972a, for an in-depth discussion of this topic).

References

Baum, W. M. (1994). *Understanding behaviorism: Science, behavior, and culture.* New York: HarperCollins.

Bjork, D. W. (1993). *B. F. Skinner: A life.* New York: HarperCollins.

Booker, M. K. (1994). *Dystopian literature: A theory and research guide.* Westport, CT: Greenwood.

Carpenter, F. (1974). *The Skinner primer: Behind freedom and dignity.* New York: Free Press.

Claeys, G., & Sargent, L. T. (Eds.). (1999). *The utopian reader.* New York: New York University Press.

Cornman, J. W., & Lehrer, K. (1968). *Philosophical problems and arguments: An introduction.* New York: Macmillan.

Darwin, C. (1859). *The origin of species by means of natural selection.* London: John Murray.

Goodstein, D. L., & Goodstein, J. R. (1996). *Feynman's lost lecture: The motion of planets around the sun.* New York: Norton.

Gould, S. J. (1977). *Ever since Darwin: Reflections in natural history.* New York: Norton.

Hollis, D. W., III. (1998). *The ABC-CLIO world history companion to utopian movements.* Santa Barbara, CA: ABC-CLIO.

Kuhn, T. S. (1957). *The Copernican revolution.* New York: Vintage.

Kumar, K. (1991). *Utopianism.* Minneapolis: University of Minnesota Press.

Mead, M. (1953). *Coming of age in Samoa: A psychological study of primitive youth for Western civilization.* New York: Modern Library.

More, T. (1961). *Utopia.* New York: Penguin. (Original work published 1516)

Morris, D. (1967). *The naked ape: A zoologist's study of the human animal.* New York: McGraw-Hill.

Persell, C. H. (1987). *Understanding society: An introduction to society.* New York: Harper & Row.

Plato. (1941). *The Republic of Plato.* (F. M. Cornford, Trans.). Oxford, UK: Oxford University Press.

Popper, K. R. (1985). Evolutionary epistemology. In D. Miller (Ed.), *Popper selections* (pp. 78-86). Princeton, NJ: Princeton University Press.

Reader's Digest. (1996). *Foods that harm, foods that heal: An A-Z guide to safe and healthy eating.* Pleasantville, NY: Reader's Digest.

Segel, H. (1996). *Naturalism and the abandonment of normality.* In W. O'Donohue & R. F. Kitchener (Eds.), *The philosophy of psychology* (pp. 4-18). London: Sage.

Sidman, M. (1989). *Coercion and its fallout.* Boston: Authors Cooperative.

Skinner, B. F. (1938). *The behavior of organisms.* New York: Appleton-Century-Crofts.

Skinner, B. F. (1948). *Walden two.* London: Macmillan.

Skinner, B. F. (1953). *Science and human behavior.* New York: Macmillan.

Skinner, B. F. (1971). *Beyond freedom and dignity.* New York: Knopf.

Skinner, B. F. (1972a). Compassion and ethics in the care of the retardate. In *Cumulative record* (3rd ed., pp. 283-291). New York: Appleton-Century-Crofts.

Skinner, B. F. (1972b). The design of cultures. In B. F. Skinner (Ed.), *Cumulative record* (3rd ed., pp. 39-50). New York: Appleton-Century-Crofts.

Skinner, B. F. (1972c). Some issues concerning the control of human behavior. In *Cumulative record* (3rd ed., pp. 25-38). New York: Appleton-Century-Crofts.

Skinner, B. F. (1974). *About behaviorism.* New York: Knopf.

Skinner, B. F. (1978). Walden (one) and Walden two. In B. F. Skinner (Ed.), *Reflections on behaviorism and society* (pp. 188-194). Englewood Cliffs, NJ: Prentice Hall.

Skinner, B. F. (1983). *A matter of consequences.* New York: New York University Press.

Skinner, B. F. (1987). Selection by consequences. In R. Epstein (Ed.), *Upon further reflection* (pp. 51-63). Englewood Cliffs, NJ: Prentice Hall.

Skinner, B. F. (1990). Can psychology be a science of the mind? *American Psychologist, 45,* 1206-1210.

Staddon, J. E. R. (1993). *Behaviorism.* London: Duckworth.

United Nations. (1995). *World population prospects: The 1994 revision.* New York: Author.

CHAPTER 11

Criticisms of Skinner

❖

The former British Prime Minister Benjamin Disraeli (1804-1881) once said before the House of Commons, "It is much easier to be critical than correct." If the Honorable Disraeli were a behavior analyst, these words would have been directed at the many invalid criticisms of Skinner's work—invalid criticisms based on bad exegesis. By *bad exegesis,* we mean reading something out of context or misunderstanding it, and then criticizing it based on inaccurate interpretation of the text. Bad exegesis is simply poor scholarship.

Unfortunately, many in the field of psychology have little more than a cursory understanding of radical behaviorism and the science of behavior (see Todd & Morris, 1983). That is to say, many psychologists can accurately provide definitions of basic principles and concepts of behavior analysis. But beyond that, they are unfamiliar with advanced issues such as selectionism, the concept of stimulus control, verbal behavior, and the like. Inadequate knowledge makes it difficult to tell the difference between good and bad exegesis, between valid and invalid criticisms of behavior analysis.

To make matters worse, based on commonsense theories of behavior called *folk psychology,* students of psychology are more likely to reject Skinner's work at the outset than to give it a chance (O'Donohue, Callaghan, & Ruckstuhl, 1998). Skinner's ideas don't mesh well with "folk wisdom." Many people, for example, are convinced that human beings have nonphysical "minds" that govern their actions. Skinner didn't deny the existence of the mind in a physical sense (e.g., the brain or its behavior); he did, however, deny the existence of a nonphysical mind. He

221

said that much of what we do, even complex behavior, is attributable to what goes on around us. By eschewing mind-body dualism (the idea that the mind governs our bodies) and espousing environmental determinism (the idea that the environment governs our bodies), Skinner placed himself poles apart from folk wisdom and much of contemporary psychology.

We hope that by addressing what we believe to be invalid criticisms in the first part of the chapter, we might help set the record straight. And, of course, part of setting the record straight is also discussing valid criticisms that are based on good exegesis. Valid criticisms will be considered next. Finally, we close the chapter by discussing the problem of appealing to Skinner as an authority (which some behavior analysts do). Appealing to authority uncritically is arguably no better than bad exegesis. Both are equally problematic in science, and, of course, Skinner would have agreed with this statement.

BAD EXEGESIS AND INVALID CRITICISMS[1]

Invalid Criticism #1: The science of behavior does not deal with "consciousness, cognitive processes, feelings, and states of mind" (Skinner, 1974, p. 2). Comment: Skinner did in fact deal with these phenomena. Skinner referred to these as *private events* (see Chapters 6 and 7). Private events, according to Skinner, take place within our bodies and can be studied as a natural science.

Invalid Criticism #2: The science of behavior ignores innate endowment and maintains that all behavior is learned within a lifetime. Comment: Recall from previous chapters that Skinner maintained that *all* behavior is the product of three types of variation and selection; one of these refers to innate endowment (i.e., contingencies of survival responsible for natural selection). However, as we shall see later, in the section on valid criticisms, Skinner only "scratched the surface" in dealing with innate characteristics of behaving organisms.

Invalid Criticism #3: The science of behavior ignores intention and purpose. Comment: Intention and purpose, for Skinner, is what operant behavior is all about. According to Skinner (1974, pp. 56 ff.), intention and purpose are found in the contingencies of reinforcement (the present circumstances and past consequences), not inside the person. For example, an individual goes to the grocery store not because he or she *wants* bread (wanting takes place within a person). Technically speaking, the individual goes to the store because the receipt of bread has *reinforced* the behavior of going to the store for bread in the past.

Invalid Criticism #4: The science of behavior does not deal with "a self or sense of self, or personality" (Skinner, 1974, p. 2). Comment: In *About Behaviorism* (1974), Skinner dedicated an entire chapter (Chapter 11) to a behavioral interpretation of *self* and *personality.* A self or personality, according to Skinner (1974), is

> a *locus,* a point at which many genetic and environmental conditions come together in a joint effect. As such, he remains unquestionably unique. No one else (unless he has an identical twin) has his genetic endowment, and without exception no one else has his personal history. Hence no one else will behave in precisely the same way. We refer to the fact that there is no one like him as a person when we speak of his identity. (p. 172)

Invalid Criticism #5: Experimental results under carefully controlled environments cannot be replicated in daily life. Comment: There is an overwhelming body of evidence in applied behavior analysis that refutes this claim. The principles discovered in the laboratory do extend into the activities of daily life. For example, consider the behavior of an addicted gambler and that of an experimental nonhuman subject on a variable-ratio schedule of reinforcement. Both show almost identical patterns of "lever-pulling" behavior—even though only one of them can tell you that he or she is "having a good time." These schedule-induced patterns of behavior (i.e., high, steady rates) are also seen in the "dedicated" work of scientists, artists, and "industrious" students and in "difficult" children who have frequent temper tantrums. Most remarkably, behavior analysts have been able to predict and modify (if necessary) these "everyday" patterns of responding for well over half a century.

Invalid Criticism #6: The techniques derived from the science of behavior could have arisen out of common sense. Comment: Consider Skinner's work on intermittent reinforcement as a case in point. Common sense tells us that reinforcing only some actions would make a person behave less frequently. Skinner even believed this at one time, before his experiments. However, as it turns out, behavior on intermittent schedules of reinforcement produce the exact opposite (i.e., high, steady rates of responding).

Invalid Criticism #7: The science of behavior considers abstract ideas "such as morality or justice as fictions" (Skinner, 1974, p. 3). Comment: Skinner did in fact deal with "values" of this sort (see Chapter 10). Recall what Skinner (1971) had to say on this topic: "To make a value judgment by calling something good or bad is to classify it in terms of its reinforcing effects" (p. 105). And things are considered "good" or "bad," according to Skinner (1971), "presumably because of the contingencies of survival under which the species evolved" (p. 104). So we see that Skinner didn't regard these notions as fictions.

Invalid Criticism #8: Skinner's analysis of culture is necessarily anti-democratic, because the relationship between the experimenter and subject is manipulative. Comment: At a superficial level, one must agree with this statement. The experimenter clearly attempts to manipulate the behavior of his or her subject. This is the whole point of experimentation: Move the independent variables (causes) around—and see systematic changes in the dependent variables (i.e., the subject's behavior). This arrangement is undeniably manipulative. But at a deeper level, there is much more in this relationship than meets the eye.

The direction of control *never* goes in one way only. The subject controls the behavior of the experimenter as much as the experimenter controls the behavior of the subject. First, the subject can control the experimenter's behavior by cooperating. Technically speaking, the subject *reinforces* the behavior of the experimenter by participating freely. Second, the subject might also refuse to participate or perhaps leave. In this case, the subject can also exert *countercontrol* over the behavior of the experimenter (e.g., "If you keep this up, I'll leave!").

Thus, as the experimenter manipulates the behavior of the subject, so too does the subject manipulate the behavior of the experimenter. Both control and countercontrol are supposedly *always* present in every experiment; both of these are presumably *always* present in all forms of government as well. A science of behavior doesn't threaten democracy because it talks about control. It maintains that control is already there. The science of behavior helps to clarify this relationship between the government and the rest of society.

An Exercise in Bad Exegesis: Chomsky's Review of *Verbal Behavior*

We conclude the first part of the chapter by turning to the influential Massachusetts Institute of Technology linguistic theorist Noam Chomsky's (1959) infamous review of Skinner's (1957) book *Verbal Behavior* (see Chapter 7). This review exemplifies bad exegesis of Skinner's work. Unfortunately, as mentioned, many in psychology are ignorant of Skinner's work. Therefore, many have accepted Chomsky's criticisms as valid. Worse yet, Chomsky's scathing review had a greater impact on psychology and linguistics (the study of language) than the book itself did (Baars, 1986, p. 187). The following is an excerpt to give you the flavor of Chomsky's influential paper:

> Careful study of this book (and the research on which it draws) reveals, however, that these astonishing claims are far from justified. It indicates, furthermore, that the insights that have been achieved in the laboratories of the reinforcement theorist, though quite genuine, can be applied to complex human behavior only in the most gross and superficial way, and that speculative attempts to discuss linguistic behavior in these terms alone omit from consideration factors of fundamental importance. (Chomsky, 1959, p. 28)

Chomsky's criticisms can be broken down into three general points, as outlined by MacCorquodale (1970).

Criticism 1: Verbal behavior is an untested hypothesis which has, therefore, no claim upon credibility (MacCorquodale, 1970, pp. 84-88). This first criticism can easily be dismissed. If Chomsky would have thoroughly read Skinner's other books (e.g., *The Behavior of Organisms,* 1938, and *Science and Human Behavior,* 1953), he would have likely come to the realization that Skinner's analysis of verbal behavior is an extension of his previous work—wholly consistent with Skinner's analysis of and experimentation on nonverbal behavior. Nonverbal and verbal behavior, according to Skinner, are both natural phenomena and are in principle governed by the same natural laws. It makes sense, therefore, that Skinner would use his analysis of nonverbal behavior in his analysis of verbal behavior, given that both manners of responding boil down to simply "behavior." For example, asking for a glass of water is functionally similar to getting it ourselves. In the latter case, the environment mediates reinforcement. That is, we act on the environment, and it "gives us water," so to speak. In the former case, someone else mediates reinforcement by getting the water for us.

Criticism 2: Skinner's technical terms are mere paraphrases for more traditional treatments of verbal behavior (MacCorquodale, 1970, pp. 88-90). Like the first criticism, the second can also be dismissed. MacCorquodale (1970) shot this second criticism down nicely in the following passage:

> Skinner's analysis is far more objective and less vague than the traditional one and therefore scientifically preferable. Every term in Skinner's account names some real thing which must be physically involved and locatable in any verbal event for which it is evoked. *That* is objectivity. If in his hypothesis Skinner invokes a particular stimulus to account for the occurrence of a response, he is saying that at least *some* of the occurrences of the response are due to the physical presence of that particular stimulus. . . . To make a similar claim for the objectivity of such terms as "reference" (and "wishing," "wanting," "liking," and so forth) would presuppose first defining them in terms of some physical dimensions. But that would at once be another "mere paraphrase" of these terms in which, if we follow Chomsky, instead of the mentalism's gaining in objectivity, the defining physical dimensions are doomed, by some logical alchemy, to lose their objectivity. (pp. 89-90)

In other words, Skinner's terms aren't mere paraphrases of more traditional terms such as *referring to, wanting, liking,* and so on; instead, they refer to real objects in the environment. As MacCorquodale (1970) pointed out, "All of the events, processes, and mechanisms invoked [in Skinner's analysis of verbal behavior] are themselves empirical, and therefore the hypothesis containing them is in principle fully testable and possibly disconfirmable" (p. 85). The same can't be said of traditional terms. Traditional terms are defined using other traditional terms, not in reference to physical objects. *To want,* for example, is to "feel or suffer the need for." And *to need* is defined as "being in want." If these terms actually referred to something physical, then where does "wanting" or "needing" take place?

Criticism 3: Speech is complex behavior whose understanding and explanation require a complex, mediational, neurological-genetic theory (MacCorquodale, 1970, pp. 90-98). This criticism is also invalid. Chomsky misinterpreted Skinner. Skinner's analysis is, in fact, capable of dealing with complex behavior. If Chomsky would have read the entire book thoroughly, he would have likely come to the conclusion that Skinner considered much of verbal behavior to be multiply determined—not made up of simple stimulus-response relationships (see Chapters 9 through 11 in *Verbal Behavior*). For example, Skinner never said that the response *red* is triggered much the same way as a patellar (i.e., knee) reflex is triggered (i.e., a simple stimulus-response relationship). Rather, we respond "red" for different reasons at different times. Skinner called this *stimulus control*. For example, we might say "red" when someone asks us our favorite color. We might also say "red" when ordering a bottle of wine, or in completing the following: "_____, white, and blue." The point to notice here is that the response *red* is multiply determined. In Skinner's (1957) own words,

> TWO FACTS EMERGE from our survey of the basic functional relations in verbal behavior: (1) the strength of a single response may be, and usually is, a function of more than one variable and (2) a single variable usually affects more than one response. (p. 227)

These countless permutations and combinations of variables can account for a host of complex phenomena. Moreover, there is a critical flaw in invoking mediational theories in dealing with behavioral phenomena. Physiological explanations tell us about physiology, not about behavior. Therefore, the utility of physiological and neurological-genetic explanations is thrown into question.

> Unless one is a neurophysiologist it is not necessary in the least to know *how* the internal structure goes about doing so nor which structures are involved. The psychologist's knowing how it does so would not improve the precision of predicting behavior from knowledge of the speaker's circumstances, nor would this knowledge make existing functional laws of behavior any more true, nor could it show them to be untrue. . . . Where interest in the mediating structures survives, it is behavioral data which illuminate them, not the other way around. (MacCorquodale, 1970, p. 91)

Unfortunately for the science of behavior, more people read the review than the book and, based on this inaccurate interpretation of the text, dismissed Skinner's (1957) *Verbal Behavior* (all 478 pages) without further consideration. This outcome is testament to the potential dangers of bad exegesis. Because of what Chomsky (1959) said, many psychologists abandoned an otherwise potentially fruitful line of inquiry.

Before concluding this section, here is an interesting fact for the reader to consider. Since *Verbal Behavior* (Skinner, 1957) was published, hundreds of studies, most conducted by behavior analysts, have suggested that Skinner's analysis is valid (see the behavioral journal *The Analysis of Verbal Behavior* for examples). Since Chomsky's review was published, neither Chomsky nor his colleagues have provided a shred of empirical evidence to support Chomsky's position that Skinner was wrong.

GOOD EXEGESIS AND VALID CRITICISMS

Because there are potential holes in every theory in science, including Skinner's, new findings often overturn older ones. Based on careful inspection of Skinner's work, such holes have been identified by his colleagues. In this section, we will discuss these valid criticisms. Of course, as with the invalid criticisms, including all or most of them is beyond the scope of this book. Instead, we will just touch on a few high points.

Valid Criticism #1: The science of behavior is S-R psychology, and thus a person becomes an "automaton, robot, puppet, or machine" (Skinner, 1974, p. 2). Comment: Even though Skinner (1974) denied this claim, this criticism is largely true (less so the S-R psychology part). If one embraces the notion of *environmental determinism,* we are by definition automatons—though automatons whose responses alter the environment in ways that in turn alter our own behavior. To argue otherwise would endorse the notion of free will.

Valid Criticism #2: The science of behavior cannot deal with creative behavior, as seen in "music, literature, and science" (Skinner, 1974, p. 3). Comment: Skinner (1974) denied this criticism as well, although it is true. First let us consider Skinner's discussion of creativity. After that we will consider flaws as identified by one of Skinner's former students, Robert Epstein, flaws that lend support to this criticism.

According to Skinner (1974),

> creative thinking is largely concerned with the productions of "mutations" . . . mutations are familiar to writers, artists, composers, mathematicians, scientists, and inventors. Either the setting or the topography of behavior may be deliberately varied. The painter varies his colors, brushes, and surfaces to produce new textures and forms. The composer generates new rhythms, scales, melodies, and harmonic sequences, sometimes through the systematic permutation of older forms, possible with the help of mathematical or mechanical devices. The mathematician explores the results of changing a set of axioms. (p. 118)

This notion of *mutation* is derived from evolutionary theory. Namely, genetic mutations account for differences observed within and between species. To use a common example, the "freaks" seen in giraffes—those with the longest necks—tended to survive because they were able to reach scarce nourishment. Those with shorter necks tended to die off from malnourishment. Similarly, according to Skinner, novel behavioral patterns emerge in much the same way. Through deliberate variations in the setting or behavior, some of this novel behavior is selected by the environment, while others are selected out. In other words, as "the environment changes, old forms disappear, while new consequences build new forms" (Skinner, 1957, p. 1).

Take the style of Spanish painter Salvador Dali as a case in point. Early in his career, his work was similar to that of his contemporaries, including such works as *Self-Portrait: Cadaques* (1922). If he had never varied his style, he probably would have remained unknown. By degrees, however, a more bizarre style emerged. It likely emerged because of increased reinforcement from his audience. With passing years, Dali's work continued to "mutate." His style culminated in such outlandish works as *The Weaning of Furniture-Nutrition* (1934), *The Disintegration of the Persistence of Memory* (1952-1954), and *The Hallucinogenic Toreador* (1970)—a far cry from his earlier, more mundane pieces.

At first blush, Skinner's analysis of creative behavior makes sense and is compatible with his analysis of behavior seen elsewhere. However, there is a problem in his analysis. Insofar as there is a mechanism of variation in natural selection (i.e., errors in gene replication), there isn't a comparable mechanism in operant conditioning. Consider Epstein's (1991) argument:

> *Skinner's work focuses on the effects of various* interventions *on ongoing behavior; it says little about where that behavior comes from in the first place.* . . . Selection alone doesn't produce anything new in evolution. Mechanisms of variation are also necessary. Selection merely limits the range of variation that occurs in the next generation. Similarly, reinforcement doesn't produce any of the particular behavior variants from which it may select (except to the extent that it is acting as an eliciting or discriminative stimulus, but these cases are not pertinent to Skinner's position). Before behavior can be selected in ontogeny, it must somehow be *generated* (cf. Segal, 1972). Mechanisms of variability must exist, some relatively trivial, perhaps, and some profound. To rely on so-called "random" variation is by no means enough to account for the dramatic and complex instances of novelty we often observe in behavior; *Beyond Freedom and Dignity* (Skinner, 1971) was not the product of random variations of spoken or written English. To put it another way, Skinner's deterministic dyad always needed another factor: Behavior is determined by genes, environmental history, and certain *mechanisms of variability.* (pp. 362-363)

In other words, environmental selection as identified by Skinner merely sets parameters on the range of responding—it does not tell us where novel behavior originates (Epstein, 1991, p. 364). Moreover, selection by consequences fails to account for why a "great deal of irrelevant behavior always captured by reinforcement" is not strengthened along with relevant behavior (Epstein, 1991, p. 363). In theory, reinforcement strengthens all behavior—not just the behavior we have targeted for change.

Valid Criticism #3: Skinner's analysis of punishment is at best only partially true (Carpenter, 1974, pp. 56 ff.). Skinner dedicated many pages to warning society about the ill effects of using punishment. However, Skinner never provided enough empirical evidence to support abandoning punishment entirely (although he did claim that one should not abandon punishment until alternative positive controls are in place). Moreover, he never described what a society would look like without aversive control. What about violent criminals—what happens to them?

Punishment, when used judiciously, is in some cases the most effective and least restrictive treatment option available. Consider the high rate of severe self-injurious behavior seen in certain special populations. Using positive reinforcement to attempt to shape nonviolent expressions of behavior takes too long—if it turns out to be effective at all. Using positive techniques places the client, the client's caregivers, and other clients at considerable risk because problem behavior is not directly dealt with. By contrast, using punishment effectively, therapists can quickly suppress problem behavior long enough to teach the client how to behave well. To make punishment most effective, therapists have to abruptly introduce punishment at a high intensity immediately following the response on a schedule that delivers the punishing stimulus after every response. The client should not be overly motivated to respond and should be given several nonpunishable alternatives (Pierce & Epling, 1995, pp. 209-213).

Valid Criticism #4: Skinner's experimental analysis of behavior has limited relevance to complex human behavior (Carpenter, 1974, pp. 53 ff.). There are numerous examples where Skinner's analysis doesn't apply to complex human phenomena. As Carpenter (1974) pointed out,

> it is difficult if not impossible to fit *all* human learning in the operant pattern. For example, a child hears his teacher say that the moon is about 24,000 miles from the earth. He has never heard nor read that

fact before, and shows no particular evidence that he has retained it until it is asked for on a test, whereupon he answers the item correctly. In this case, it is not likely that operant conditioning can be demonstrated. There is no repetition of the response. The fact was simply heard once and later given in response to a test item. (p. 54 [italics added])

In this case, the intermediary steps between behavioral acquisition and responding escape Skinner's experimental analysis. Operant conditioning can't provide a reasonable explanation for why the information is retained. What happened in the meantime, given the fact that there is often a delay of several weeks or months between classroom learning and the time of the examination? It's not as if the student sat quietly in the corner twiddling his or her thumbs until the exam. Why did the student retain that particular bit of information—all the while engaging in a multitude of competing activities? Why wasn't it wiped away by the hundreds or thousands of new facts that the child experienced in the interim?

Carpenter (1974) added another good point:

> Why do many people retain a miscellaneous assortment of trivia? I can recall all sorts of things experienced in the distant and near past, things that occurred only once and which were quite unimportant . . . Skinner says that forgetting occurs as a function of time. A response simply fades away unless given occasional reinforcement. If that were true, I should have long ago been relieved of a useless assortment of trivia . . . I see no way of demonstrating by means of the operant system how such responses resist forgetting. (p. 55)

Again, operant conditioning doesn't provide a reasonable explanation for the phenomenon of forgetting either.

Valid Criticism #5: The science of behavior cannot adequately understand, predict, or control the behavior of any species "without knowledge of its instinctive patterns, evolutionary history, and ecological niche" (Breland & Breland, 1961, p. 684). A couple of Skinner's students, Keller and Marian Breland (Breland & Breland, 1961), who went into the commercial animal training business, uncovered an unusual behavioral phenomenon they called "instinctive drift" (p. 684). According to these authors and others (e.g., Herrnstein, 1977), Skinner's science of behavior is incapable of accurately predicting and controlling the behavior of any species unless it also takes into account instinctive behavior. Incidentally, behaviorists typically discard "instinctive" accounts of behavior. In the following, Breland and Breland describe the phenomenon of instinctive drift.

> The response concerned the manipulation of money by the raccoon . . . the contingency for reinforcement was picking up the coins and depositing them in a 5-inch metal box. . . . Raccoons condition readily, have good appetites, and this one was quite tame and an eager subject. We anticipated no trouble. Conditioning him to pick up the first coin was simple. We started out by reinforcing him for picking up a single coin. Then the metal container was introduced, with the requirement that he drop the coin into the container. Here we ran into the first bit of difficulty: he seemed to have a great deal of trouble letting go of the coin. He would rub it up against the inside of the container, pull it back out, and clutch it firmly for several seconds. However, he would finally turn it loose and receive his food reinforcement. Then the final contingency: we put him on a ratio of 2, requiring that he pick up both coins and put them in the container. . . . Now the raccoon really had problems (and so did we). Not only could he not let go of the coins, but he spent seconds, even minutes, rubbing them together (in a most miserly fashion), and dipping them into the container. He carried on this behavior to such an extent that the practical application we had in mind—a display featuring a raccoon putting money in a piggy bank—simply was not feasible. The rubbing behavior became worse and worse as time went on, in spite of nonreinforcement. (p. 682)

Indeed, the science of behavior can't account for so-called instinctive drift. Obviously the raccoon was becoming increasingly hungry as a result of nonreinforcement, so, according to operant theory, there should have been an increase in operant responding—not a decrease. The superfluous behavior (e.g., rubbing the coins together) had nothing to do with the reinforcement contingency put in place by the raccoon's trainers. Hence, in this circumstance, an operant analysis doesn't do us any good in understanding what is going on behaviorally.

Elsewhere, other instinctive behavior has been well documented—behavior not accounted for by the science of behavior:

> Threatened with shock, for example, rats find running a more congenial avoidance response than turning around (Bolles, 1970), although turning around appears easier for them than key pecking does for the pigeons under comparable conditions (Rachlin & Hineline, 1967). Though key pecking is highly resistant to becoming a shock-avoidance response, it is relatively easy to condition as an instrumental response for food reinforcement. . . . Rats, for example, learn to associate tastes with sickness but lights and sounds with electric shock (Garcia & Koelling, 1966), although quail, being visual creatures, fail to show this shift in salience (Wilcoxon, Dragoin, & Kral, 1971). (Herrnstein, 1977, pp. 594-595)

If the goals of behavior science are prediction and control, as Skinner asserted everywhere in his writings, then perhaps one ought to pay careful attention to instinctive explanations of behavior as well. As in the raccoon example, only by understanding something about the instinctive behavior of this rodent could one better predict and possibly control its behavior.

Skinner as Authority

Let us close this chapter with a brief discussion of the problem of seeing Skinner as an authority. Recall from the first part of the chapter that dismissing valid ideas because of misunderstanding is bad exegesis. But equally problematic in science is blindly accepting ideas based solely on authority. By *authority,* we mean believing in something on the basis of what one individual said—and accepting these ideas uncritically. For example, religions have sacred texts that are believed to represent certain "facts." These facts come from an authority (e.g., Jesus, Buddha, Muhammad) and are considered indisputable and final.

Knowledge based only on authority is problematic because we have no way of knowing whether or not the information is accurate. Take witch hunts as a case in point. During the mid-1400s, Pope Innocent VIII sent inquisitors throughout Europe in search of what he believed to be witches. To help guide inquisitors on their perverse quest, they used a textbook called *Malleus Maleficarum* ("witches' hammer"; Davison & Neale, 1996, pp. 11 ff.). This theological and legal document identified signs of what to look for in determining whether someone was a witch (*authoritative* knowledge). Part of the identification process was locating strange marks and insensitive regions on the skin. We must point out that none of these criteria was based on objective evidence. As it turned out, before such authority was challenged and overthrown, hundreds of thousands of innocent men, women, and children were tortured and burned at the stake.

Some behavior analysts appeal to Skinner as an authority. They say that because Skinner said x, then without question it is an indisputable fact, indisputable and final. Of course, you see the problem here, especially in science. Skinner's opinion on certain matters might be more correct than that of others, given his many successes. But these successes do not justify ignoring evidence that is relevant to the matter at hand. In fact, believing that something is true because Skinner said so would be inconsistent with Skinner's own philosophy of science. Remember that because of the influence of Bacon on Skinner, he refused to accept uncritically what people said; rather, Skinner, like Bacon, read the book of nature, not the book of authority.

What if Skinner was wrong? If we appeal to authority in this way, we might be doing something wrong without knowing it. Skinner, for example, strongly encouraged us not to use punishment. And because Skinner said this, some behavior analysts don't use punishment—even in situations where punishment is the most "humane" treatment alternative available.

Criticisms Since Skinner

We close this chapter by considering a major criticism of the field of behavior analysis in general. Many critics of contemporary behavior analysis say that the field has become too technical and is drifting away from its "roots"—a concern for "fundamental principles of behavior" (Pierce & Epling, 1980, p. 1). In the following passage Steve Hayes (1991) reflected on this shift in emphasis:

Applied behavior analysts and behavior therapists have long prided themselves on their technological precision and methodological sophistication. Some even go so far as to *define* the field on the basis of its commitment to the "specification of treatment in operational . . . terms" (Kazdin & Hersen, 1980, p. 287). This emphasis is a proud component of the behavioral tradition, but along with it has come a deemphasis of theoretical and philosophical concerns. (p. 417)

This theoretical drought could have arisen for several reasons. One, the field has discovered all the fundamental principles of behavior. Thus, there is no need for further exploration. This is possible but unlikely. The basic principles already in place have not been adequately elaborated on since Skinner's seminal work—in some areas, yes, but in all areas, no. Two, the field is waiting for another genius to come along. This is possible; however, it is hard to imagine just where he or she would fit in. What could possibly be left to discover following the Skinnerian tradition? Three, the reason is sociological. Namely, most funding for research has shifted from basic to applied work. Of all these possibilities, this last point seems the most logical.

CONCLUSION

We hope that we have achieved what we set out to accomplish in this chapter. First, we wanted to set the record straight by bringing to light common criticisms of Skinner's work that are based on inaccurate information. Of course, our effort is just a dollop in the bucket, given the fact that most textbooks provide a distorted image of Skinner's work (often in a negative light)—ours is just one book among countless others (see Todd & Morris, 1983). Second, we did not want you walking away thinking that Skinner was always right—he certainly was not. Therefore, we discussed valid criticisms of his work to balance things out. We would also like you to take note that all areas in science are severely criticized. So do not be misled into thinking that the valid criticisms of behavior analysis killed the field. They did not. Many of Skinner's students and their students have come up with solutions to these problems in the interim. Despite what many people say, the field of behavior analysis is expanding. Publications and growing membership numbers attest to this fact (see Friman, Allen, Kerwin, & Larzelere, 1993). Third, we briefly talked about some of the problems of appealing to Skinner as an authority (which certain behavior analysts do)—a problem that is a concern in all areas of science. We mentioned this to illustrate that even scientists show bias at times.

Note

1. These criticisms were taken from the opening chapter of Skinner's (1974) *About Behaviorism.*

References

Baars, B. J. (1986). *The cognitive revolution in psychology.* New York: Guilford.

Bolles, R. C. (1970). Species-specific defense reactions and avoidance learning. *Psychological Review, 77,* 32-48.

Breland, K., & Breland, M. (1961). The misbehavior of organisms. *American Psychologist, 16,* 681-1012.

Carpenter, F. (1974). *The Skinner primer: Behind freedom and dignity.* New York: Free Press.

Chomsky, N. (1959). Review of B. F. Skinner's *Verbal behavior. Language, 35,* 26-58.

Davison, G. C., & Neale, J. M. (1996). *Abnormal psychology* (Rev. 6th ed.). New York: John Wiley.

Epstein, R. (1991). Skinner, creativity, and the problem of spontaneous behavior. *Psychological Science, 6,* 363-370.

Friman, P. C., Allen, K. D., Kerwin, M. L. E., & Larzelere, R. (1993). Changes in modern psychology: A citation analysis of the Kuhnian displacement thesis. *American Psychologist, 48,* 658-664.

Garcia, J., & Koelling, R. A. (1966). Relation of cue to consequence in avoidance learning. *Psychonomic Science, 4,* 123-124.

Hayes, S. C. (1991). The limits of technological talk. *Journal of Applied Behavior Analysis, 24,* 417-420.

Herrnstein, R. J. (1977). The evolution of behaviorism. *American Psychologist, 32,* 593-603.

Kazdin, A. E., & Hersen, M. (1980). The current status of behavior therapy. *Behavior Modification, 4,* 283-302.

MacCorquodale, K. (1970). On Chomsky's review of Skinner's *Verbal behavior. Journal of the Experimental Analysis of Behavior, 13,* 83-99.

O'Donohue, W. T., Callaghan, G. M., & Ruckstuhl, L. E. (1998). Epistemological barriers to radical behaviorism. *Behavior Analyst, 21,* 307-320.

Pierce, W. D., & Epling, W. F. (1980). What happened to analysis in applied behavior analysis? *Behavior Analyst, 3,* 1-9.

Pierce, W. D., & Epling, W. F. (1995). *Behavior analysis and learning.* Englewood Cliffs, NJ: Prentice Hall.

Rachlin, H., & Hineline, P. N. (1967). Training and maintenance of keypecking in the pigeon by negative reinforcement. *Science, 157,* 954-955.

Segal, E. F. (1972). Induction and the province of operants. In R. M. Gilbert & J. R. Millenson (Eds.), *Reinforcement: Behavioral analyses* (pp. 14-27). New York: Academic Press.

Skinner, B. F. (1938). *The behavior of organisms: An experimental analysis.* New York: Appleton-Century.

Skinner, B. F. (1953). *Science and human behavior.* New York: Macmillan.

Skinner, B. F. (1957). *Verbal behavior.* New York: Appleton-Century-Crofts.

Skinner, B. F. (1971). *Beyond freedom and dignity.* New York: Knopf.

Skinner, B. F. (1974). *About behaviorism.* New York: Knopf.

Todd, J. T., & Morris, E. K. (1983). Misconception and miseducation: Presentations of radical behaviorism in psychology textbooks. *Behavior Analyst, 6,* 153-160.

Wilcoxon, H. C., Dragoin, W. B., & Kral, P. A. (1971). Illness-induced aversions in rat and quail: Relative salience of visual and gustatory cues. *Science, 171,* 826-828.

CHAPTER 12

Skinner's Legacy

❖

By this point the reader should have some appreciation for the breadth of Skinner's ideas and for the indelible impression he left on psychology. We could have written several volumes exploring every avenue of his influence. However, because of page limitations we can touch on only a few of the high points.

In what follows, we provide illustrations of Skinner's legacy. In the first part of the chapter, we outline his major contributions to psychology. In the second, we explore several extensions of his basic operant work in greater detail—particularly his treatment of reinforcement. From the time of his earliest work (e.g., Skinner, 1938), the concept of *reinforcement* played a central role in Skinner's psychology. We can therefore justify giving it special attention. Let us turn to Skinner's legacy.

At the outset, be forewarned that the first part of the chapter jumps around. Skinner's psychology branched out in many directions, and because of this these areas are at most only trivially related. To tie these points together thematically for our present purpose would take yet another book. To help move things along, we present them in point form.

PART I. SKINNER'S MAJOR INFLUENCES ON PSYCHOLOGY

1. *Skinner advanced a branch of philosophy of the science of psychology known as* radical behaviorism. To this day, those who call themselves *behavior analysts* almost exclusively lean toward this philosophical

orientation. His philosophical writings also inspired the journal *Behaviorism* (established in 1972 and now called *Behavior and Philosophy*).

2. *Skinner's psychology is solidly based on hard facts.* The science of behavior has more empirical evidence supporting its claims than any other area in psychology. Take *Schedules of Reinforcement* (Ferster & Skinner, 1957/1997) as one example. The data depicted in over 900 figures are derived from roughly a quarter of a billion responses (Cheney, 1957/1997). And these data do not constitute "background noise" either. Almost all of these responses combine into one of 15 schedule-induced patterns of behavior. Most remarkably, Skinner could turn these patterns on and off at will (mainly with nonverbal organisms).

3. *Skinner's psychology is practical.* The science of behavior is relevant to daily life. Positive reinforcement, for example, can be and has been used in the classroom, at home, in the office, when house-training a pet, in advertising, on the court, in hospitals, in factories, and on and on. On the contrary, other areas of psychology concern themselves with immovable personality constructs, abstract information-processing models, and highly complicated neuronetwork representations of cognitive processes—all of which have limited practical utility. Theories about information processing (e.g., how quickly the "mind-brain" is said to process incoming information), for example, shed no light on how individuals might improve the speed or accuracy with which they solve problems. But this is not any cause for alarm, because these theorists' scientific goals aren't pragmatic. Their goals are to better understand cognitive phenomena— "behavior" is merely an expression of underlying cognitive processes.

4. *Skinner warned about "invented" explanations in lieu of functional analyses (explanatory fictions).* Skinner dedicated much of his writing to debunking "myths" in psychology, that is, *explanatory fictions*. Scientists can waste time and resources pursuing a dead end.

Skinner's critique of what he considered prescientific explanatory systems shaped the current of psychology. Although Skinner's criticisms meant that his adversaries were under fire, the criticisms forced them into seriously considering the strengths and weaknesses of their own viewpoints before mounting counterarguments (see *Behaviorism and*

Phenomenology, Wann, 1964, for a lively debate between Skinner and eminent humanistic psychologists such as Sigmund Koch and Carl Rogers). As a result, considerable conceptual "fat" was cut from both sides of the debate. Negative feedback helped eliminate inconsistencies in their logic (Popper, 1985, p. 80). Taken as a whole, psychology became more cautionary in its interpretation of behavioral phenomena.

5. *Skinner provided a parsimonious account of psychological phenomena.* In Skinner's psychology there are three causes of behavior: natural selection, selection by consequences, and cultural selection. There are no references to unresolved conflicts in early childhood. There aren't any complicated mathematical formulas (premature use of mathematics can give the illusion of precision). Finally, concepts don't extend beyond events that cannot be observed (even private events can be observed by the behaving individual—cognitive events are fair game in behavior analysis).

6. *He built apparatuses that enabled scientists to predict and control the behavior of nonhuman subjects.* As you know, the bulk of the science of behavior hinges on experimental work with nonhumans. Even our analysis of human behavior is largely forged out of basic operant work with nonhumans.

7. *He promoted a single-subject methodology that revealed powerful lawful relations between environmental contingencies and behavior* (as opposed to weak statistical significance, e.g., 4.2 is statistically significantly different from 4.4). At the present moment, the enthusiasm for single-subject methodology hasn't waned, especially in applied areas in behavior analysis.

8. *Skinner wrote about utopianism.* Although his ideas did not catch on in the society at large, one could say that Skinner's science of behavior built a utopian society for special populations all over the world. No other area in psychology has ever come as close as Skinner's to helping people with disabilities maximize their full potential.

9. *He wrote about cognition.* His analysis of so-called private events has become the cornerstone of a subarea of behavior analysis called *clinical*

behavior analysis. In this area, therapists focus as much on the private events of their clients as on their publicly observable behavior.

10. *Skinner wrote about language.* Despite a popular belief that Skinner's analysis of verbal behavior is dead (a belief largely caused by Chomsky's, 1959, scathing review, no doubt), it is still very much alive. For example, between 1975 and 1991, 772 sessions at the annual meeting of the Association for Behavior Analysis (ABA; established 1974) dealt with verbal behavior (Eshleman, 1991, p. 64). At the time this book was written, the ABA 2000 Convention program had 51 items under the subject heading Verbal Behavior. And last, we would be remiss in not mentioning that a journal titled *The Analysis of Verbal Behavior* (originally called *Verbal Behavior News,* established 1982) spun out from Skinner's work in this area.

11. *Skinner wrote about self-control.* Skinner's seminal work in self-control evolved into what is now called *self-management.* Self-management has far-reaching implications in almost every applied area you can think of.

PART II. EXTENSIONS OF HIS WORK

In Chapter 3 we discussed the notion of a *scientific revolution*. Recall that Kuhn (1996) advanced the idea that when revolutions occur, scientists are sure to adopt the successful definition of the field, the problems it raises, and its newly defined puzzle-solving methodology. Scientists then use the puzzle-solving methods and concepts as a *paradigm* for solving other scientific problems. Kuhn called this process *normal science*. In Chapter 5, we argued that Skinner's research in operant conditioning did, in fact, solve a problem and therefore developed a paradigm. However, as Kuhn pointed out, "In a science . . . a paradigm is *rarely an object for replication.* Instead, like an accepted judicial decision in the common law, it is an object for *further articulation* and *specification* under *new* and *more stringent* conditions" (Kuhn, 1996, p. 23 [italics added]). Kuhn called this *mopping-up* and claimed that it engages "most scientists throughout their careers" (Kuhn, 1996, p. 24). Because of weaknesses as a puzzle-solving method, a mopping-up occurred with Skinner's concept of reinforcement.

Herrnstein (1977) best articulated the inadequacies with Skinner's reinforcement theory:

> The list of drives in a behavioral theory based on reinforcement should be crucial to behavioral engineers. Ever since drive-reduction theory slid into history, we have tended to forget that, in fact, **most reinforcing stimuli either reduce drives or are closely associated with subsequent physiological events that reduce them.** Given evolution, it is not surprising that the class of reinforcers forming a drive includes stimuli that weaken the drive, as food does hunger and water does thirst, but there is no necessity in the connection. The down-fall of drive-reduction theory can be blamed on its insistence that reinforcement was *necessarily* drive reducing, instead of only *probably* so. **Behavior seems adaptive when it fends off objective threats to the organism or otherwise promotes well-being. The adaptiveness is often mediated by the creature's drives.** For example, there is a correspondence, though not an equivalence, between the psychological state called hunger, which specifies a class of behaviors and reinforcers, and an underlying set of nutritional needs. The behaviors and reinforcers tend to reduce the drive and, in so doing, to fulfill the needs. But other drives might be harder to justify as adaptive and may, indeed, be counteradaptive, as for example, with too great a fondness for sweets or sex . . . **each additional drive on the list of human drives is likely to mean another category of more or less independently varying primary reinforcers and more or less independently varying classes of behavior.** As the length of the list of drives grows, so does the complexity of the task confronting the behavioral engineer. **The level of each drive at each moment sets the probabilities for a class of behaviors and the strengths of a class of reinforcers.** To the extent that the behavioral engineer lacks this knowledge in advance, **his programmed contingencies of reinforcement will fail to account for the behavior he actually observes.** (pp. 597-598 [boldface added])

To summarize this passage, Skinner failed to clearly specify how so-called drives, such as deprivation, are related to reinforcement. Contemporary analyses provide a more complete picture (or mopping-up, to use Kuhn's phrase).

Timberlake and Farmer-Dougan (1991) suggested three criteria for an adequate reinforcement analysis:

(a) Identification of reinforcement circumstances should involve a small number of simple, nonintrusive, and widely applicable procedures. . . . (b) Identification of reinforcement circumstances should be accurate and complete. Not only should the circumstances produce reinforcement but the critical determinants (such as when reinforcement effects cease) should be identified. . . . (c) The resultant circumstances of reinforcement should be adaptable to a variety of situations rather than limited to a small number of stimuli, responses or settings. (p. 380)

Other desirable features of a reinforcement identification procedure include (a) escaping the well-known circularity complaint about the law of effect (Meehl, 1950; O'Donohue & Krasner, 1988); (b) contributing to the theoretical base of the nature of reinforcement; (c) developing a practical procedure that could identify reinforcers for persons for whom finding reinforcers is difficult (e.g., some persons with severe retardation or autism); and (d) specifying all the effects of reinforcers (e.g., effects on other behaviors not part of the contingency).

The Empirical Law of Effect

Although a *reinforcer* was originally defined as a response-contingent stimulus that increases the rate of that response (e.g., Ferster & Skinner, 1957/1997), the prediction of which stimuli will actually function as reinforcers can be difficult. Reinforcing conditions that work at one time do not work at another time (perhaps because of satiation effects or counterpreparedness). Moreover, Meehl's (1950) transsituational hypothesis (i.e., a stimulus that reinforces one response will reinforce all other responses) has been shown to be false (Premack, 1962). Therefore, the identification of the conditions of reinforcement can be difficult because these can change over time (e.g., as the student becomes sated); they can change as a function of the behavior to be modified (Garcia, Ervin, & Koelling, 1966; Premack, 1962); and they can be somewhat idiographic and thus can change across individuals.

In practice, the most common method of identifying reinforcers has been an informal approach in which practitioners use their intuition, previous experience, and trial and error to identify potentially reinforcing stimuli (Konarski, Johnson, Crowell, & Whitman, 1981; O'Brien & Repp, 1990; Timberlake & Farmer-Dougan, 1991). In this approach, the clinician asks the question "Given what I know about this individual and the behavior to be modified, what stimuli will function as reinforcers?" Thus, the clinician in this approach does not initially assess the circumstances of reinforcement empirically, but rather makes some antecedent conjectures regarding these circumstances. In this approach to reinforcement identification, the major reason baseline data are collected is to identify the pretreatment rate of responding, which will serve as a standard by which posttreatment effects can be evaluated.

The advantage of this approach is that it requires little time and effort and is thus fairly inexpensive. The disadvantages of this approach are (a) it is an unsystematic method, and thus the reliability of this method is unknown (i.e., it is unclear to what extent two different practitioners would identify the same reinforcing circumstances); (b) this approach is often based on depriving access to a stimulus in the long term, raising ethical concerns; (c) although deprivation seems to be an important initial condition in this method, the method provides no detail regarding the specifics of deprivation (e.g., how much deprivation is necessary?); (d) it provides no information about how to set *contingency values* (i.e., how much reinforcement should be contingent upon how much responding); and, most important, (e) the validity of this approach is questionable. There have been only a few studies that have investigated the ability of persons using this informal method to correctly identify reinforcing circumstances. All have found staff to be poor at selecting reinforcers (Green et al., 1988; Pace, Ivancic, Edwards, Iwata, & Page, 1985). For example, O'Brien and Repp (1990), in a review of reinforcement-based reductive procedures, found that reinforcement selection was seldom systematic and that social reinforcement was often relied upon, although the outcome data indicated it was the least effective type of consequence.

We believe that this informal, unsystematic procedure for identifying reinforcers has been the Achilles' heel in the practice of behavior therapy and behavior analysis. The success of the intervention depends upon the quality of the identification of the circumstances of reinforcement. We shall show later in this chapter that developments in reinforcement analysis obviate the need for practitioners to continue to rely on this hit-or-miss, informal approach of unknown reliability and validity.

Premack's Probability-Differential Model of Reinforcement

In recent years, there has been a movement to develop more empirical and systematic methods of reinforcement identification (Konarski et al., 1981; Premack, 1962; Timberlake & Farmer-Dougan, 1991). Premack's probability-differential model, for example, is a significant improvement over Meehl's (1950) approach, which assumes that reinforcers and punishers form mutually exclusive classes. Premack showed that the same activity could function as a reinforcer for some responses and as a punisher for other responses. Premack also showed that access to certain responses would reinforce some responses but not others. Also, applied researchers have reported that reinforcers are not transsituational and may in other circumstances function as punishers (e.g., Konarski, Crowell, & Duggan, 1985).

Premack's (1962) probability-differential model asserts that a schedule in which a higher-probability response is contingent upon a lower-probability response will produce reinforcement of the lower-probability behavior (and that a reversal of this contingency will produce punishment). For example, when given a free choice, most children will watch TV more frequently than they will read. Thus, when watching TV is contingent on reading, reading should increase; conversely, when there is forced access to reading following a period of watching TV, watching TV should decrease.

Premack's (1962) model begins to be informative about the underlying nature of reinforcement (i.e., the criterion of how to set contingency values). The therapist-driven empirical model as well as the self-report model seems to be arbitrary: A list can be developed that contains some stimuli that function as reinforcers and some that do not. But two important questions remain: Why do these particular stimuli function as reinforcers? Is there some common attribute underlying them, or is there no explanation for these results? Premack's analysis suggests that this list is not arbitrary, but, rather, that a common property of these stimuli is that they are relatively preferred and therefore relatively more frequent activities. The necessary and sufficient condition for reinforcement, according to this model, is the opportunity to exchange a less valued activity for a more valued one.

Premack's (1962) analysis produces an important conceptual shift regarding reinforcement: Reinforcement is construed as access to a response rather than as a response-contingent stimulus. Reinforcement is not an absolute property of some stimulus but rather a relation between a more preferred and a less preferred activity. Moreover, another notable difference is that in Premack's analysis, reinforcement is something within the behavioral system rather than a stimulus coming from outside the system. In this approach, baseline data are gathered not only to measure the pretreatment level of the dependent variable, but also to directly assess possible reinforcers. In fact, a stronger statement needs to be made: A free-operant baseline is necessary in order to identify reinforcing relations.

According to this model, the reinforcing value of an activity is revealed in the probability that a child will actually engage in the activity in a situation in which the child is free to do anything he or she wants (i.e., a free-operant baseline). Thus, in this analysis of reinforcement, baseline data must also be collected to assess two frequencies: the frequency of the targeted behavior and the frequency of the reinforcing behavior. In the most general terms, baseline assessment that measures the child's behavioral allocation under unconstrained conditions reveals a hierarchy of behavioral preferences. Punishment occurs when any lower-preference behavior is made contingent upon any higher-preference behavior. Reinforcement occurs when this contingency is reversed. Thus, a value of this approach is that it empirically reveals multiple potential reinforcers or punishers.

The probability-differential model has been applied to children with considerable success. Lattal (1969) required preadolescent boys to brush their teeth (lower-probability behavior during baseline free-operant period) before they could swim (higher-probability behavior) and observed an increase in tooth brushing. Hopkins, Schutte, and Garton (1971) made access to a playroom contingent upon the quality of printing and writing and observed an improvement in the latter. Mithaug and Mar (1980) used a variation of this process to assess the effects between choice behaviors and responses required to complete two tasks. They found that when a person's choice of an object with which to work resulted in work that had been previously assessed as less preferred, subsequent choices of that object decreased. Conversely, when selections resulted in work on tasks previously assessed as more preferred, subsequent choices increased.

Premack's (1962) analysis is more accurate in identifying the circumstances of reinforcement than the transsituational approach is; however, his approach still suffers from numerous problems. First, it fails to set values for the contingency. Premack tended to use a 1:1 ratio between amount of the target response required and amount of contingent access granted. However, there is clear evidence that this constant ratio does not always produce reinforcement (Timberlake & Allison, 1974). Second and, as we shall see later in the chapter, quite important, Premack's model fails to produce reinforcement when the ratios between the higher-probability behavior and the lower-probability behavior are identical or greater than the free-operant-baseline ratios. In addition, the set of reinforcers is constrained, in that a reinforcer must always be a higher-probability response. However, it has been shown that lower-probability behaviors can be arranged to reinforce higher-probability behavior (Timberlake & Farmer-Dougan, 1991).

Baseline Assessment. In following the Premack (1962) model, we would observe behaviors in baseline according to their naturally occurring rate. Data would then be ordered hierarchically in terms of duration of responding, and the clinician would choose the contingency depending upon whether the objective were to increase or to decrease responding. If the objective were to increase the target behavior, then one would make access to a behavior higher on the hierarchy, contingent on the emission of the target behavior.

Response Deprivation Model of Reinforcement

Timberlake and Allison (1974) have developed and tested a different model of reinforcement, the *response deprivation model.* This approach is concerned with the relationship between naturally occurring rates of behavior and constraints on naturally occurring behavior such as reinforcement contingencies. In this model, people are viewed as engaging in various response rates in a manner that is optimal for them. This model assumes that the person will try to maintain an optimal response level when it is disrupted by constraints placed on the opportunity to respond (Staddon, 1982). These constraints occur when contingencies are placed on behavior, that is, when individuals are not allowed access to a particular response unless they first perform some other response.

In education classes, this would mean, for example, that a student would try to engage in a behavior during a teaching period for the same proportion of the time that he or she would have engaged in the behavior if free to do so. For example, if the student engaged in stereotypy for 10 minutes of a 20-minute free time, he or she would try to engage in stereotypy for 10 minutes during a 20-minute teaching period. Thus, the principal role of reinforcement schedules in this model is not to present external reinforcement like praise, but rather to arrange contingencies among the existing behaviors of the individual.

Like Premack's (1962) model, this model requires observation during periods in which the person is free to behave in any manner (i.e., free-operant baselines). In education classes, this would mean that we should observe the target behavior (e.g., social interactions) and the contingent behavior (e.g., stereotypy) during a period in which they both are free to occur. We would then record the amount of time the student engaged in both behaviors.

For example, if we measured the operant level of the target behavior (O_T) and the operant level of the contingent behavior (O_C) during a 20-minute free time and found that the target behavior occurred for 1 minute and the contingent behavior for 10 minutes, we would have Equation 1:

(1) O_T/O_C (1 min/10 min)

If we further assume that the target behavior (O_T) was social interaction and the contingent behavior (O_C) was stereotypy, and if we then developed a contingency in which the student was deprived of the opportunity to engage in stereotypy as much as he or she did in the free-time baseline (as we do when we teach), we would have Equation 2, where the relative value of the target behavior (I_T) to the contingent behavior (I_C) is established. Equation 2 presents an example of this relationship, in which we allow the child to engage in two minutes of stereotypy (I_C) if one minute of social interaction (I_T) occurs:

(2) I_T/I_C = 1 min/2 min (i.e., student is allowed to engage in 2 minutes of stereotypy if 1 minute of social interaction occurs)

The deprivation condition occurs whenever Equation 2 is greater than Equation 1, as shown in Equation 3. Response deprivation exists if

(3) $I_T/I_C > O_T/O_C$

In the case of our example, the values are as follows, and a deprivation condition occurs:

1/2 > 1/10
0.5 > 0.2

Although we generally deprive the student of competing behaviors during teaching periods because we want the child to attend to the task, traditionally, behavioral practitioners do not then use the deprived response as a reinforcing contingency for the target response. The point of response deprivation theory is that we can use the deprived response as a reinforcer for the target response. Further, because the reinforcer is behavior rather than an external stimulus (e.g., an M&M), the student brings the potential reinforcer to all teaching situations if we can establish a contingency that disrupts the free-baseline ratio, as we did in Equation 3. The implications of this procedure for difficult-to-motivate students with disabilities, students for whom staff say they cannot find reinforcers, are enormous.

Another example will show how the contingencies can be reversed. If a child in free time works on coloring 10 minutes for each minute that he or she works on arithmetic problems, contingencies can be arranged from this ratio according to Equation 3 in the following manners:

1. Coloring as a reinforcer for math behavior. If an increase in work on math problems is desired, then math becomes the target response (O_T), coloring becomes the reinforcing response (O_C), and the terms of the contingency are set so that coloring (I_C) becomes deprived relative to math (I_T). More technically, according to Equation 3, the following contingency would produce an increase in working arithmetic problems:

   $I_T/I_C > O_T/O_C$

That is,

> 1 min of math/5 min of coloring (intervention) > 1 min of math/10 min of coloring (baseline)

2. Contingency producing no change. Moreover, a contingency of 30 seconds of math for five minutes of coloring would produce no change in behavior (because it preserves the free-baseline ratio of 1:10).
3. Coloring as a punisher for math behavior. Third, a contingency of 1 minute of math for 20 minutes of coloring would punish math behavior, because the contingency would disrupt the free-operant relationship of math to coloring of 1:10. This, of course, is a situation we would want to avoid in special education classrooms.
4. Math reinforcing (or punishing) coloring. Finally, an important implication of this approach is that classes of reinforcers or punishers are not mutually exclusive. Thus, math can become the reinforcing response and coloring the target response. To increase the level of coloring, Equation 3 again needs to be satisfied. Thus, the following equation would increase coloring:

> 20 min of coloring/1 min of math (intervention) > 10 min of coloring/1 min of math (baseline)

Empirically, this model has been tested and supported by research with animals and humans. Changing the terms of the schedule according to Equation 3 has been shown to reverse the target and reinforcing response in rats (Heth & Warren, 1978; Timberlake & Allison, 1974; Timberlake & Wozny, 1979). Fortunately, the effects have been replicated with humans. Konarski, Johnson, and Whitman (1980) measured the free baseline of coloring and working math problems in grade school children. A contingency was then set so that there was a relative deficit in working on math problems (i.e., working on math problems was the reinforcer and coloring was the target response!). The children then increased the rate of coloring (I_T) to gain access to working on math problems (I_C). In another study of a special education population, Konarski et al. (1985) assessed the free-baseline rates of working on math problems and writing. In this study, the authors directly tested predictions from Premack's (1962) model with a response deprivation model and found that Premack's model did not accurately identify the circumstance of reinforcement, whereas the response deprivation model did. Specifically, higher-probability responses served as reinforcers only when there was a condition of relative deficit in the higher-probability response. Also, inconsistent with Premack's model, the lower-probability response functioned as a reinforcer when the schedule specified a relative deficit of this response. Thus, these authors also demonstrated that reinforcement effects could be reversed.

Several features of this model should be noted. First, the units for measuring responding are not fixed. The only requirement is that the same units be used in baseline (free time) and in contingency (teaching period). Second, temporal contiguity is not a necessary feature of reinforcement; rather, the necessary feature is a disruption in baseline-response relations. Third, long-term deprivation is not necessary to produce a reinforcement effect. Fourth, the circumstances for producing reinforcement and punishment are quite flexible in this model; any response, when constrained, can function as a reinforcer.

The response deprivation model, although a considerable improvement over Premack's (1962) analysis, still has several problems: (a) The model provides no information about the magnitude of changes from baseline behavior that will occur when a contingency is implemented. It simply indicates the direction of change, that is, the conditions under which the behavior will increase, decrease, or remain unchanged. (b) It fails to provide any information about what effects the contingency will have on other activities. (c) It fails to provide information about how free-operant baselines can be reliably and validly assessed.

Baseline Assessment. The assessment for the response deprivation model is the same as that for the Premack (1962) model; the difference in the model is the way baseline data on free-operant rates are arranged in order to predict the circumstances of reinforcement. Instead of arranging 1:1 relationships of target-to-contingent behavior during intervention, specific reinforcement schedules are arranged based on the baseline ratios.

Choice: The Matching Law

The matching law (Herrnstein, 1961) describes the allocation of behavior within a choice paradigm. It is a mathematical statement of the relationship between frequencies of responding and frequencies of reinforcers in a two-choice concurrent schedule. A concurrent schedule presents at least two choices at the same time. For example, on a two-choice concurrent schedule, a pigeon might be given two translucent disks to choose from. Once it begins pecking on one of them, the pigeon is put on a specific schedule of reinforcement (e.g., a fixed or variable amount of responding is required). When the pigeon makes its choice, the other disk becomes inoperative until the pigeon has met the reinforcement requirement. Although most matching research has been conducted with nonhuman species, the relevance of the matching law for understanding the behavior of humans has also been investigated through basic (see Davison & McCarthy, 1988, and DeVilliers, 1977, for reviews) and applied research (Mace, McCurdy, & Quigley, 1990; Martens & Houk, 1989; Martens, Lochner, & Kelly, 1992; McDowell, 1981; Neef, Mace, Shea, & Shade, 1992).

According to the matching law (Herrnstein, 1970), all behavior involves choice and is governed by reinforcement in the following manner: (a) response rate varies with reinforcement in a systematic fashion, and (b) responding on a particular task is governed not only by reinforcement obtained for responding on that task but also by reinforcement obtained from all other concurrent sources. Suppose, for example, that you like chocolate and vanilla ice cream equally well. How much money you choose to spend on one or the other (choice) is determined by their reinforcing value at a given time. If you have been eating chocolate for the last three days in a row, its reinforcement value diminishes because of satiation. As chocolate decreases in reinforcement value, vanilla increases. Chances are the next time you go to the store, you are more likely to choose vanilla over chocolate.

This law is described in the following equation:

(4) $R_A/R_B = r_A/r_B$

where R is the rate of responding for a behavior and r is the rate of reinforcement obtained for that responding. This equation can also accommodate time spent responding on each of the alternatives by directly substituting appropriate values in place of rates of responses.

Several authors (e.g., Epling & Pierce, 1990; McDowell, 1982, 1988; Myerson & Hale, 1984) have argued that conceptualizing reinforcement and behavior in terms provided by the matching equation may lead to more efficient treatment strategies. They have asserted that the ubiquitous presence of concurrent schedules in the natural environment points to the greater generalizability of interventions that consider target behaviors as choice behaviors that are not independent of other behaviors under the control of competing sources of reinforcement.

According to McDowell (1982), implementing intense reinforcement procedures may not be necessary in lean environments where the rate of alternative reinforcement is low. In these environments, minimal rates of reinforcement can support large rates of behavior. Further, when environments are rich in reinforcement, reinforcement procedures may be unsuccessful, because responding approaches its maximum only at very high reinforcement rates. For example, the behavior of billionaires would be almost impossible to reinforce with $5 bills. They are from environments rich (no pun intended) with this reinforcer.

Several studies have investigated the applicability of the matching law for describing and predicting clinically relevant behavior of humans in the natural environment. McDowell (1981) demonstrated that the self-injurious behavior of an 11-year-old boy was reinforced by reprimands from family members, and the relationship between the behavior and reinforcement fit the matching equation. Martens and Houk (1989) found that the relationship between duration of disruptive behavior and teacher attention also fit the matching equation. In an experimental study, Mace et al. (1990) evaluated the relationship between concurrent schedules of reinforcement for completion of academic and vocational tasks. Although response topographies and reinforcer qualities differed across the schedule components, rates of task completion approximated the relative amount of reinforcement programmed for each alternative. In a more recent study, Neef et al. (1992) examined the role of reinforcer quality in the matching relation by examining how three special education students allocated responding across similar response choices (math problems) for which reinforcer quality or rate was varied systematically. Neef et al.

found that sensitivity to reinforcer schedule developed only after reinforcement intervals were signaled via a timing device. With this condition, time allocation to response alternatives approximated reinforcement rates as predicted by the matching law when the quality of the reinforcer was the same for each response alternative. The matching relationship was disrupted when the quality of the reinforcers varied across the response alternatives.

Although the practical implications of the matching law have been discussed in several sources (e.g., McDowell, 1988; Myerson & Hale, 1984) and have been empirically demonstrated (e.g., Mace et al., 1990; McDowell, 1982; Neef et al., 1992), arguments delineating its limited applicability for describing and predicting behavior in the natural environment have also been presented (e.g., Fuqua, 1984). These limitations involve difficulties in extrapolating from the laboratory to the natural environment. Problems include the identification and measurement of qualitatively different and potentially incompatible reinforcers and response alternatives and the role of the changeover delay.

Baseline Assessment. Within matching theory, baseline assessment involves measuring response rates or time spent responding for the target behavior and the competing response alternative or alternatives. Identification of the reinforcement schedule is typically based on an estimation of the actual number of reinforcers obtained. Prediction of intervention effects involves estimating the obtained reinforcers for each of the response alternatives, that is, the target behavior and the competing response alternatives, which technically include all nontarget behaviors. The mathematical expression of the relationship between a single-response alternative reinforcement schedule and extraneous reinforcement is described in Equation 5:

(5) $R = kr/r + r_e$

This form is referred to as the *quantitative law of effect* (Herrnstein, 1970) and describes the rate of responding (R) as a hyperbolic function of scheduled reinforcement (r) and extraneous sources of reinforcement (r_e); k is a constant.

CONCLUSION

In this chapter, some of the more important methods and principles of the experimental analysis of behavior have been described. The reader can see that the methodology is consistent with Skinner's philosophy of science discussed in the previous chapters. Moreover, it should be clear that this philosophy and this methodology have been quite successful in discovering orderly relations in behavior. Finally, although Skinner is credited with many important discoveries, it is a sign of a healthy research program that his findings have been extended and elaborated on by other scientists.

References

Cheney, C. D. (1997). Foreword I. In C. B. Ferster & B. F. Skinner (Eds.), *Schedules of reinforcement* (pp. vii-xii). Acton, MA: Copley. (Original work published 1957)

Chomsky, N. (1959). Review of B. F. Skinner's *Verbal behavior. Language, 35,* 26-58.

Davison, M., & McCarthy, D. (1988). *The matching law: A research review.* Hillsdale, NJ: Lawrence Erlbaum.

DeVilliers, P. (1977). Choice in concurrent schedules and a quantitative formulation of the law of effect. In W. K. Honig & J. E. R. Staddon (Eds.), *Handbook of operant behavior* (pp. 233-287). Englewood Cliffs, NJ: Prentice Hall.

Epling, W. F., & Pierce, W. D. (1990). Laboratory to application: An experimental analysis of severe problem behaviors. In A. C. Repp & N. N. Singh (Eds.), *Perspectives on the use of nonaversive and aversive interventions for persons with developmental disabilities* (pp. 451-464). Sycamore, IL: Sycamore Publishing.

Eshleman, J. W. (1991). Quantified trends in the history of verbal behavior research. *Analysis of Verbal Behavior, 9,* 61-80.

Ferster, C. B., & Skinner, B. F. (Eds.). (1997). *Schedules of reinforcement.* Acton, MA: Copley. (Original work published 1957)

Fuqua, R. W. (1984). Comments on the applied relevance of the matching law. *Journal of Applied Behavior Analysis, 17,* 381-386.

Garcia, J., Ervin, F. R., & Koelling, R. A. (1966). Learning with prolonged delay of reinforcement. *Psychonomic-Science, 5*(3), 121-122.

Green, C. W., Reid, D. H., White, L. K., Halford, R. C., Brittain, D. P., & Gardner, S. M. (1988). Identifying reinforcers with profound handicaps: Staff opinion versus systematic assessment of preferences. *Journal of Applied Behavior Analysis, 21,* 31-43.

Herrnstein, R. J. (1961). Relative and absolute strengths of responses as a function of frequency of reinforcement. *Journal of the Experimental Analysis of Behavior, 4,* 267-272.

Herrnstein, R. J. (1970). On the law of effect. *Journal of the Experimental Analysis of Behavior, 13,* 243-266.

Herrnstein, R. J. (1977). The evolution of behaviorism. *American Psychologist, 32,* 593-603.

Heth, C. D., & Warren, A. G. (1978). Response deprivation and response satiation as determinants of instrumental performance: Some data and theory. *Animal Learning and Behavior, 6,* 294-300.

Hopkins, B. L., Schutte, R. C., & Garton, K. L. (1971). The effects of access to a playroom on the rate and quality of printing and writing of first and second grade students. *Journal of Applied Behavior Analysis, 4,* 77-87.

Konarski, E. A., Jr., Crowell, C. R., & Duggan, L. M. (1985). The use of response deprivation to increase the academic performance of EMR students. *Applied Research in Mental Retardation, 6,* 15-31.

Konarski, E. A., Johnson, M. R., Crowell, C. R., & Whitman, T. L. (1981). An alternative approach to reinforcement for applied researchers: Response deprivation. *Behavior Therapy, 12,* 653-666.

Konarski, E. A., Jr., Johnson, M. R., & Whitman, T. L. (1980). A systematic investigation of resident participation in a nursing home activities program. *Journal of Behavior Therapy and Experimental Psychiatry, 11,* 249-257.

Kuhn, T. S. (1996). *The structure of scientific revolutions* (3rd ed.). Chicago: University of Chicago Press.

Lattal, K. A. (1969). Contingency management of toothbrushing behavior in a summer camp for children. *Journal of Applied Behavior Analysis, 2,* 195-198.

Mace, F. C., McCurdy, B., & Quigley, E. A. (1990). A collateral effect of reward predicted by matching theory. *Journal of Applied Behavior Analysis, 23,* 197-205.

Martens, B. K., & Houk, J. L. (1989). The application of Herrnstein's law of effect to disruptive and on-task behavior of a retarded adolescent girl. *Journal of the Experimental Analysis of Behavior, 51,* 17-27.

Martens, B. K., Lochner, D. G., & Kelly, S. Q. (1992). The effects of variable-interval reinforcement on academic engagement: A demonstration of matching theory. *Journal of Applied Behavior Analysis, 25,* 143-151.

McDowell, J. J. (1981). Wilkinson's method of estimating the parameters of Herrnstein's hyperbola. *Journal of the Experimental Analysis of Behavior, 35,* 413-414.

McDowell, J. J. (1982). The importance of Herrnstein's mathematical statement of the law of effect for behavior therapy. *American Psychologist, 37,* 771-779.

McDowell, J. J. (1988). Matching theory in natural human environments. *Behavior Analyst, 11,* 95-109.

Meehl, P. E. (1950). On the circularity on the law of effect. *Psychological Bulletin, 47,* 52-75.

Mithaug, D. E., & Mar, D. K. (1980). The relation between choosing and working prevocational tasks in two severely retarded young adults. *Journal of Applied Behavior Analysis, 13,* 177-182.

Myerson, J., & Hale, S. (1984). Practical implications of the matching law. *Journal of Applied Behavior Analysis, 17,* 367-380.

Neef, N. A., Mace, F. C., Shea, M. C., & Shade, D. (1992). Effects of reinforcer rate and reinforcer quality on time allocation: Extensions of matching theory to educational settings. *Journal of Applied Behavior Analysis, 25,* 691-699.

O'Brien, S., & Repp, A. C. (1990). Reinforcement-based reductive procedures: A review of 20 years of their use with persons with severe or profound retardation. *Journal of the Association for Persons With Severe Handicaps, 15*(3), 148-159.

O'Donohue, W., & Krasner, L. (1988). The logic of research and the scientific status of the law of effect. *Psychological Record, 35,* 157-174.

Pace, G. M., Ivancic, M. T., Edwards, G. L., Iwata, B. A., & Page, T. J. (1985). Assessment of stimulus preference and reinforcer value with profoundly retarded individuals. *Journal of Applied Behavior Analysis, 18,* 249-255.

Popper, K. R. (1985). Evolutionary epistemology. In *Popper selections* (pp. 78-86). Princeton, NJ: Princeton University Press.

Premack, D. (1962). Reversibility of the reinforcement relation. *Science, 136,* 235-237.

Skinner, B. F. (1938). *The behavior of organisms: An experimental analysis.* New York: Appleton-Century-Crofts.

Staddon, J. E. (1982). On the dangers of demand curves: A comment on Lea and Tarpy. *Behaviour Analysis Letters, 2,* 321-325.

Timberlake, W., & Allison, J. (1974). Response deprivation: An empirical approach to instrumental performance. *Psychological Review, 81,* 146-164.

Timberlake, W., & Farmer-Dougan, V. A. (1991). Reinforcement in applied settings: Figuring out ahead of time what will work. *Psychological Bulletin, 110,* 379-391.

Timberlake, W., & Wozny, M. (1979). Reversibility of reinforcement between eating and running by schedule changes: A comparison of hypotheses and models. *Animal Learning and Behavior, 7,* 461-469.

Wann, T. W. (Ed.). (1964). *Behaviorism and phenomenology: Contrasting bases for modern psychology.* Chicago: University of Chicago Press.

CHAPTER 13

B. F. Skinner's Published Works

❖

1930

On the conditions of elicitation of certain eating reflexes. *Proceedings of the National Academy of Sciences, 16*, 433-438.
On the inheritance of maze behavior. *Journal of General Psychology, 4*, 342-346.
The progressive increase in the geotropic response of the ant Aphaenogaster. *Journal of General Psychology, 4*, 102-112.

1931

The concept of the reflex in the description of behavior. *Journal of General Psychology, 5*, 427-458.
Review of the book *Reflex action, a study in the history of physiological psychology. Journal of General Psychology, 5*, 125-129. (With W. J. Crozier [2])

1932

Drive and reflex strength. *Journal of General Psychology, 6*, 22-37.
Drive and reflex strength: II. *Journal of General Psychology, 6*, 38-48.
On the rate of formation of a conditioned reflex. *Journal of General Psychology, 7*, 274-286.
A paradoxical color effect. *Journal of General Psychology, 7*, 481-482.

1933

The abolishment of a discrimination. *Proceedings of the National Academy of Sciences, 19*, 825-828.

AUTHORS' NOTE: For coauthored works, a bracketed number following the coauthor's name indicates order of authorship; that is, [1] indicates the primary author, [2] the secondary author, and so forth.

The measurement of "spontaneous activity." *Journal of General Psychology, 9,* 3-23.
On the rate of extinction of a conditioned reflex. *Journal of General Psychology, 8,* 114-129.
The rate of establishment of a discrimination. *Journal of General Psychology, 9,* 302-350.
"Resistance to extinction" in the process of conditioning. *Journal of General Psychology, 9,* 420-429.
Some conditions affecting intensity and duration thresholds in motor nerve, with reference to chronaxie of subordination. *American Journal of Physiology, 106,* 721-737. (With E. F. Lambert [1] & A. Forbes [3])

1934

A discrimination without previous conditioning. *Proceedings of the National Academy of Sciences, 20,* 532-536.
The extinction of chained reflexes. *Proceedings of the National Academy of Sciences, 20,* 234-237.
Has Gertrude Stein a secret? *Atlantic Monthly, 153,* January, 50-57.

1935

A discrimination based upon a change in the properties of a stimulus. *Journal of General Psychology, 12,* 313-336.
The generic nature of the concepts of stimulus and response. *Journal of General Psychology, 12,* 40-65.
Two types of conditioned reflex and pseudo type. *Journal of General Psychology, 12,* 66-77.

1936

Conditioning and extinction and their relation to drive. *Journal of General Psychology, 14,* 296-317.
The effect on the amount of conditioning of an interval of time before reinforcement. *Journal of General Psychology, 14,* 279-295.
A failure to obtain "disinhibition." *Journal of General Psychology, 14,* 127-135.
The reinforcing effect of a differentiating stimulus. *Journal of General Psychology, 14,* 263-278.
Thirst as an arbitrary drive. *Journal of General Psychology, 15,* 205-210.
The verbal summator and a method for the study of latent speech. *Journal of General Psychology, 2,* 71-107.

1937

Changes in hunger during starvation. *Psychological Record, 1,* 51-60. (With W. T. Heron [1])
The distribution of associated words. *Psychological Record, 1,* 71-76.
Effects of caffeine and benzedrine upon conditioning and extinction. *Psychological Record, 1,* 340-346. (With W. T. Heron [2])

Is sense necessary? [Review of the book *New frontiers of the mind*]. *Saturday Review of Literature, 16*, October 9, 5-6.
Two types of conditioned reflex: A reply to Konorski and Miller. *Journal of General Psychology, 16*, 272-279.

1938

The behavior of organisms: An experimental analysis. New York: Appleton-Century.

1939

The alliteration in Shakespeare's sonnets: A study in literary behavior. *Psychological Record, 3*, 186-192.
An apparatus for the study of animal behavior. *Psychological Record, 3*, 166-176. (With W. T. Heron [1])
Some factors influencing the distribution of associated words. *Psychological Record, 3*, 178-184. (With S. W. Cook [1])

1940

A method of maintaining an arbitrary degree of hunger. *Journal of Comparative Psychology, 30*, 139-145.
The nature of the operant reserve [Abstract]. *Psychological Bulletin, 37*, 423.
The rate of extinction in maze-bright and maze-dull rats. *Psychological Record, 4*, 11-18. (With W. T. Heron [1])

1941

The psychology of design. In *Art education today* (pp. 1-6). New York: Bureau of Publications, Teachers College, Columbia University.
A quantitative estimate of certain types of sound-patterning in poetry. *American Journal of Psychology, 54*, 64-79.
Some quantitative properties of anxiety. *Journal of Experimental Psychology, 29*, 390-400. (With W. K. Estes [1])

1942

The processes involved in the repeated guessing of alternatives. *Journal of Experimental Psychology, 30*, 495-503.

1943

Reply to Dr. Yacorzynski. *Journal of Experimental Psychology, 32*, 93-94.

1944

[Review of the book *Principles of behavior*]. *American Journal of Psychology, 57*, 276-281.

1945

Baby in a box. *Ladies' Home Journal, 62*, October, 30-31, 135-136, 138.
The operational analysis of psychological terms. *Psychological Review, 52*, 270-277, 291-294.

1946

Differential reinforcement with respect to time [Abstract]. *American Psychologist, 1*, 274-275.

1947

An automatic shocking-grid apparatus for continuous use. *Journal of Comparative and Physiological Psychology, 40*, 305-307. (With S. L. Campbell [2])
Experimental psychology. In W. Dennis (Ed.), *Current trends in psychology* (pp. 16-49). Pittsburgh, PA: University of Pittsburgh Press.
"Psi" and its manifestations [Review of the book *The reach of the mind*]. *New York Times Book Review*, November 2, 34.

1948

Card-guessing experiments. *American Scientist, 36*, 456, 458.
"Superstition" in the pigeon. *Journal of Experimental Psychology, 38*, 168-172.
Walden two. New York: Macmillan.

1950

Are theories of learning necessary? *Psychological Review, 57*, 193-216.

1951

The experimental analysis of behavior. *Proceedings and Papers of the 13th International Congress of Psychology*, 62-91.
How to teach animals. *Scientific American, 185*(12), 26-29.
[Review of the book *The human use of human beings*]. *Psychological Bulletin, 48*, 367-368.

1953

Science and human behavior. New York: Macmillan.
Some contributions of an experimental analysis of behavior to psychology as a whole. *American Psychologist, 8*, 69-78.

1954

A critique of psychoanalytic concepts and theories. *Scientific Monthly, 79*, 300-305.

A new method for the experimental analysis of the behavior of psychotic patients [Abstract and discussion]. *Journal of Nervous and Mental Disease, 120,* 403-406. (With H. C. Solomon [2] & O. R. Lindsley [3])

The science of learning and the art of teaching. *Harvard Educational Review, 24,* 86-97.

1955

The control of human behavior. *Transactions of the New York Academy of Sciences, 17,* 547-551.

Freedom and the control of men. *American Scholar, 25,* Winter, 47-65.

1956

A case history in scientific method. *American Psychologist, 11,* 221-233.

[Review of the book *Stochastic models for learning*]. *Contemporary Psychology, 1,* 101-103.

Some issues concerning the control of human behavior: A symposium. *Science, 124,* 1057-1066. (With C. R. Rogers [1])

What is psychotic behavior? In F. Gildea (Ed.), *Theory and treatment of the psychoses: Some newer aspects* (pp. 77-99). St. Louis, MO: Committee on Publications, Washington University.

1957

Concurrent activity under fixed-interval reinforcement. *Journal of Comparative and Physiological Psychology, 50,* 279-281. (With W. H. Morse [2])

The experimental analysis of behavior. *American Scientist, 45,* 343-371.

The psychological point of view. In H. D. Kruse (Ed.), *Integrating the approaches to mental disease* (pp. 130-133). New York: Hoeber-Harper.

Schedules of reinforcement. New York: Appleton-Century-Crofts. (With C. B. Ferster [1])

A second type of superstition in the pigeon. *American Journal of Psychology, 70,* 308-311. (With W. H. Morse [1])

Verbal behavior. New York: Appleton-Century-Crofts.

1958

Diagramming schedules of reinforcement. *Journal of the Experimental Analysis of Behavior, 1,* 67-68.

Fixed-interval reinforcement of running in a wheel. *Journal of the Experimental Analysis of Behavior, 1,* 371-379. (With W. H. Morse [2])

Reinforcement today. *American Psychologist, 13,* 94-99.

Some factors involved in the stimulus control of operant behavior. *Journal of the Experimental Analysis of Behavior, 1,* 103-107. (With W. H. Morse [1])

Sustained performance during the very long experimental sessions. *Journal of the Experimental Analysis of Behavior, 1,* 235-244. (With W. H. Morse [2])

Teaching machines. *Science, 128,* 969-977.

1959

Animal research in the pharmacotherapy of mental disease. In J. Cole & R. Gerard (Eds.), *Psychopharmacology: Problems in evaluation* (pp. 224-228). Washington, DC: National Academy of Sciences, National Research Council.

Cumulative record. New York: Appleton-Century-Crofts.

An experimental analysis of certain emotions [Abstract]. *Journal of the Experimental Analysis of Behavior, 2,* 264.

The flight from the laboratory. In B. F. Skinner, *Cumulative record* (pp. 242-257). New York: Appleton-Century-Crofts.

John Broadus Watson, behaviorist. *Science, 129,* 197-198.

The programming of verbal knowledge. In E. Galanter (Ed.), *Automatic teaching: The state of the art* (pp. 63-68). New York: John Wiley.

1960

Concept formation in philosophy and psychology. In S. Hook (Ed.), *Dimensions of mind: A symposium* (pp. 226-230). New York: New York University Press.

May we have a positive contribution? [Review of the book *The child buyer*]. *New Republic, 143,* October 10, 22.

Modern learning theory and some new approaches to teaching. In J. W. Gustad (Ed.), *Faculty utilization and retention* (pp. 64-72). Winchester, MA: New England Board of Higher Education.

Pigeons in a pelican. *American Psychologist, 15,* 28-37.

Special problems in programming language instruction for teaching machines. In F. J. Oinas (Ed.), *Language teaching today* (pp. 167-174). Bloomington: Indiana University Research Center in Anthropology, Folklore, and Linguistics.

Teaching machines. *Review of Economics and Statistics, 42*(Suppl.), August, 189-191.

The use of teaching machines in college instruction (Parts II-IV). In A. A. Lumsdaine & R. Glaser (Eds.), *Teaching machines and programmed learning: A source book* (pp. 159-172). Washington, DC: Department of Audio-Visual Instruction, National Education Association. (With J. G. Holland [2])

1961

The analysis of behavior: A program for self-instruction. New York: McGraw-Hill. (With J. G. Holland [1])

Cumulative record (Enlarged ed.). New York: Appleton-Century-Crofts.

The design of cultures. *Daedalus, 90,* 534-546.

Learning theory and future research. In J. Lysaught (Ed.), *Programmed learning: Evolving principles and industrial applications* (pp. 59-66). Ann Arbor, MI: Foundation for Research on Human Behaviors.

Teaching machines. *Scientific American, 205*(11), 90-102.

The theory behind teaching machines. *Journal of the American Society of Training Directors, 15,* July 15, 27-29.

Why we need teaching machines. *Harvard Educational Review, 31,* 377-398.

1962

Operandum. *Journal of the Experimental Analysis of Behavior, 5,* 224.
Squirrel in the yard: Certain sciurine experiences of B. F. Skinner. *Harvard Alumni Bulletin, 64,* 642-645.
Technique for reinforcing either of two organisms with a single food magazine. *Journal of the Experimental Analysis of Behavior, 5,* 58. (With G. S. Reynolds [1])
Two "synthetic social relations." *Journal of the Experimental Analysis of Behavior, 5,* 531-533.
Verbal behavior. *Encounter,* November, 42-44. (With I. A. Richards [1])

1963

Behaviorism at fifty. *Science, 140,* 951-958.
A Christmas caramel, or, a plum from the hasty pudding. *Worm Runner's Digest, 5*(2), 42-46.
Conditioned and unconditioned aggression in pigeons. *Journal of the Experimental Analysis of Behavior, 6,* 73-74. (With G. S. Reynolds [1] & A. C. Catania [2])
L'avenir des machines à enseigner. *Psychologie Française, 8,* 170-180.
Operant behavior. *American Psychologist, 18,* 503-515.
Reflections on a decade of teaching machines. *Teachers College Record, 65,* 168-177.
Reply to Thouless. *Australian Journal of Psychology, 15,* 92-93.

1964

Man. *Proceedings of the American Philosophical Society, 108,* 482-485.
New methods and new aims in teaching. *New Scientist, 122,* 483-484.
On the relation between mathematical and statistical competence and significant scientific productivity. *Worm Runner's Digest, 6*(1), 15-17. (Published under the pseudonym F. Galtron Pennywhistle)
On theory [Letter to the editor]. *Science, 145,* 1385, 1387.

1965

Stimulus generalization in an operant: A historical note. In D. I. Mostofsky (Ed.), *Stimulus generalization* (pp. 193-209). Palo Alto, CA: Stanford University Press.
The technology of teaching. *Proceedings of the Royal Society, Series B, 162,* 427-443.
Why teachers fail. *Saturday Review, 48,* October 16, 80-81, 98-102.

1966

The behavior of organisms: An experimental analysis. New York: Appleton-Century-Crofts.
Conditioning responses by reward and punishment. *Proceedings of the Royal Institution of Great Britain, 41,* 48-51.
Contingencies of reinforcement in the design of a culture. *Behavioral Science, 11,* 159-166.

An operant analysis of problem solving. In B. Kleinmuntz (Ed.), *Problem solving: Research, method, and theory* (pp. 225-257). New York: John Wiley.
Operant behavior. In W. K. Honig (Ed.), *Operant behavior: Areas of research and application* (pp. 12-32). New York: Appleton-Century-Crofts.
The phylogeny and ontogeny of behavior. *Science, 153,* 1205-1213.
Some responses to the stimulus "Pavlov." *Conditional Reflex, 1,* 74-78.
What is the experimental analysis of behavior? *Journal of the Experimental Analysis of Behavior, 9,* 213-218.

1967

An autobiography. In E. G. Boring & G. Lindzey (Eds.), *A history of psychology in autobiography: Vol. 5* (pp. 387-413). New York: Appleton-Century-Crofts.
The problem of consciousness—A debate. *Philosophy and Phenomenological Research, 27,* 317-337. (With B. Blanshard [1])
Utopia through the control of human behavior. *The Listener, 77,* January 12, 55-56.
Visions of utopia. *The Listener, 77,* January 5, 22-23.

1968

The design of experimental communities. In D. L. Sills (Ed.), *International encyclopedia of the social sciences: Vol. 16* (pp. 271-275). New York: Macmillan.
Handwriting with write and see. Chicago: Lyons & Carnahan. (With S. Krakower [2])
The science of human behavior. In *Twenty-five years at RCA laboratories 1942-1967* (pp. 92-102). Princeton, NJ: RCA Laboratories.
Teaching science in high school—What is wrong? *Science, 159,* 704-710.
The technology of teaching. New York: Appleton-Century-Crofts.

1969

Contingencies of reinforcement: A theoretical analysis. New York: Appleton-Century-Crofts.
Contingency management in the classroom. *Education, 90,* 93-100.
Edwin Garrigues Boring. In *The American Philosophical Society: Yearbook 1968* (pp. 111-115). Philadelphia: American Philosophical Society.
The machine that is man. *Psychology Today, 2,* April, 20-25, 60-63.
Operant reinforcement of prayer (An excerpt from the writings of Benjamin Franklin). *Journal of Applied Behavior Analysis, 2,* 247.

1970

Creating the creative artist. In A. J. Toynbee (Ed.), *On the future of art* (pp. 61-75). New York: Viking.

1971

Autoshaping. *Science, 173,* 752.

A behavioral analysis of value judgments. In E. Tobach, L. R. Aronson, & E. Shaw (Eds.), *The biopsychology of development* (pp. 543-551). New York: Academic Press.

Beyond freedom and dignity. New York: Knopf.

B. F. Skinner says what's wrong with the social sciences. *The Listener, 86,* September 30, 429-431.

Humanistic behaviorism. *The Humanist, 31,* May/June, 35.

Operant conditioning. In *The encyclopedia of education: Vol. 7* (pp. 29-33). New York: Macmillan and Free Press.

1972

Compassion and ethics in the care of the retardate. In B. F. Skinner, *Cumulative record* (3rd ed., pp. 283-291). New York: Appleton-Century-Crofts.

Cumulative record (3rd ed.). New York: Appleton-Century-Crofts.

Freedom and dignity revisited. *New York Times,* August 11, p. 29.

Humanism and behaviorism. *The Humanist, 32,* July/August, 18-20.

A lecture on "having a poem." In B. F. Skinner, *Cumulative record* (3rd ed., pp. 345-355). New York: Appleton-Century-Crofts.

Some relations between behavior modification and basic research. In B. F. Skinner, *Cumulative record* (3rd ed., pp. 276-282). New York: Appleton-Century-Crofts.

1973

Answers for my critics. In H. Wheeler (Ed.), *Beyond the punitive society* (pp. 256-266). San Francisco: Freeman.

Are we free to have a future? *Impact, 3*(1), 5-12.

The free and happy student. *New York University Education Quarterly, 4*(2), 2-6.

The freedom to have a future [The 1972 Sol Feinstone Lecture]. Syracuse, NY: Syracuse University.

Reflections on meaning and structure. In R. Brower, H. Vendler, & J. Hollander (Eds.), *I. A. Richards: Essays in his honor* (pp. 199-209). New York: Oxford University Press.

Some implications of making education more efficient. In C. E. Thoresen (Ed.), *Behavior modification in education* (pp. 446-456). Chicago: National Society for the Study of Education.

Walden (one) and Walden Two. *Thoreau Society Bulletin, 122,* Winter, 1-3.

1974

About behaviorism. New York: Knopf.

Designing higher education. *Daedalus, 103,* 196-202.

1975

Comments on Watt's "B. F. Skinner and the technological control of social behavior." *American Political Science Review, 69,* 228-229.

The ethics of helping people. *Criminal Law Bulletin, 11,* 623-636.

The shaping of phylogenic behavior. *Acta Neurobiologiae Experimentalis, 35,* 409-415.
The steep and thorny way to a science of behaviour. In R. Harre (Ed.), *Problems of scientific revolution: Progress and obstacles to progress in the sciences* (pp. 58-71). Oxford, UK: Clarendon.

1976

Farewell, my LOVELY! *Journal of the Experimental Analysis of Behavior, 25,* 218.
Particulars of my life. New York: Knopf.
Walden two revisited. In B. F. Skinner, *Walden two* (Paperback ed., pp. v-xvi). New York: Macmillan.

1977

Between freedom and despotism. *Psychology Today, 11,* September, 80-82, 84, 86, 90-91.
The experimental analysis of operant behavior. In R. W. Rieber & K. Salzinger (Eds.), *The roots of American psychology: Historical influences and implications for the future* (*Annals of the New York Academy of Sciences,* Vol. 291, pp. 374-385). New York: New York Academy of Sciences.
The force of coincidence. In B. C. Etzel, J. M. LeBlanc, & D. M. Baer (Eds.), *New developments in behavioral psychology: Theory, method, and application* (pp. 3-6). Hillsdale, NJ: Lawrence Erlbaum.
Freedom, at last, from the burden of taxation. *New York Times,* July 26, p. 29.
Herrnstein and the evolution of behaviorism. *American Psychologist, 32,* 1006-1012.
Why I am not a cognitive psychologist. *Behaviorism, 5,* 1-10.

1978

A happening at the annual dinner of the Association for Behavioral Analysis, Chicago, May 15. *Behavior Analyst, 2*(1), 30-33. (Published anonymously)
Reflections on behaviorism and society. Englewood Cliffs, NJ: Prentice Hall.
Why don't we use the behavioral sciences? *Human Nature, 1,* 86-92.

1979

Le renforcateur arrange (R. Beausoleil, Trans.). *Revue de modification du comportement, 9,* 59-69.
My experience with the baby-tender [An expanded excerpt from *The shaping of a behaviorist* (1979)]. *Psychology Today,* March, 28-31, 34, 37-38, 40.
The shaping of a behaviorist: Part two of an autobiography. New York: Knopf.

1980

Notebooks. Englewood Cliffs, NJ: Prentice Hall. (Ed. R. Epstein)
Resurgence of responding after the cessation of response-independent reinforcement. *Proceedings of the National Academy of Sciences, 77,* 6251-6253. (With R. Epstein [1])

The species-specific behavior of ethologists. *Behavior Analyst, 3*(1), 51.
Symbolic communication between two pigeons (*Columba livia* domestics). *Science, 207,* 543-545. (With R. Epstein [1] & R. P. Lanza [2])

1981

Charles B. Ferster—A personal memoir. *Journal of the Experimental Analysis of Behavior, 35,* 259-261.
How to discover what you have to say—A talk to students. *Behavior Analyst, 4*(1), 1-7.
Pavlov's influence on psychology in America. *Journal of the History of the Behavioral Sciences, 17,* 242-245.
Selection by consequences. *Science, 213,* 501-504.
"Self-awareness" in the pigeon. *Science, 212,* 695-696. (With R. Epstein [1] & R. P. Lanza [2])
The spontaneous use of memoranda by pigeons. *Behaviour Analysis Letters, 1,* 241-246. (With R. Epstein [1])

1982

Contrived reinforcement. *Behavior Analyst, 5*(1), 3-8.
"I am most concerned. . . ." *Psychology Today,* May, 48-49. (Part of "Understanding Psychological Man: A State-of-the-Science Report," pp. 40-59)
"Lying" in the pigeon. *Journal of the Experimental Analysis of Behavior, 38,* 201-203. (With R. P. Lanza [1] & J. Starr [2])
Skinner for the classroom. Champaign, IL: Research Press. (Ed. R. Epstein)

1983

A better way to deal with selection. *Behavioral and Brain Sciences, 3,* 377-378.
Can the experimental analysis of behavior rescue psychology? *Behavior Analyst, 6*(1), 9-17.
Enjoy old age: A program of self management. New York: Norton. (With M. E. Vaughan [2])
Intellectual self-management in old age. *American Psychologist, 38,* 239-244.
A matter of consequences: Part three of an autobiography. New York: Knopf.

1984

Canonical papers of B. F. Skinner. *Behavioral and Brain Sciences, 7,* 473-724. (Eds. A. C. Catania & S. Harnad, among many other commentators; reprinted in 1988 as *The selection of consequences: The operant behaviorism of B. F. Skinner: Comments and consequences* [New York: Cambridge University Press])
The evolution of behavior. *Journal of the Experimental Analysis of Behavior, 41,* 217-221.
The shame of American education. *American Psychologist, 39,* 947-954.

1985

Cognitive science and behaviourism. *British Journal of Psychology, 76,* 291-301.

News from nowhere, 1984. *Behavior Analyst, 8*(1), 5-14.

Reply to Place: "Three senses of the word 'tact.'" *Behaviorism, 13,* 75-76.

Toward the cause of peace: What can psychology contribute? In S. Oskamp (Ed.), *International conflict and national public policy issues (Applied Social Psychology Annual,* Vol. 6, pp. 21-25). Beverly Hills, CA: Sage.

1986

B. F. Skinner ["The books that have been most important . . ."]. In C. M. Devine, C. M. Dissel, & K. D. Parrish (Eds.), *The Harvard guide to influential books: 113 distinguished Harvard professors discuss the books that have helped to shape their thinking* (pp. 233-234). New York: Harper & Row.

The evolution of verbal behavior. *Journal of the Experimental Analysis of Behavior, 45,* 115-122.

Programmed instruction revisited. *Phi Delta Kappan, 68,* 103-110.

Sleeping in peace. *Free Inquiry, 6,* Summer, 57.

Some thoughts about the future. *Journal of the Experimental Analysis of Behavior, 45,* 229-235.

What is wrong with daily life in the western world? *American Psychologist, 41,* 568-574.

1987

A humanist alternative to A. A.'s Twelve Steps. *The Humanist, 47,* July/August, 5.

Outlining a science of feeling. *Times Literary Supplement,* May 8, 490, 501-502.

A thinking aid. *Journal of Applied Behavior Analysis, 20,* 379-380.

Upon further reflection. Englewood Cliffs, NJ: Prentice Hall.

What religion means to me. *Free Inquiry, 7,* Spring, 12-13.

Whatever happened to psychology as the science of behavior? *American Psychologist, 42,* 780-786.

1988

A fable. *Analysis of Verbal Behavior, 6,* 1-2.

Genes and behavior. In G. Greenberg & E. Tobach (Eds.), *Evolution of social behavior and integrative levels* (pp. 77-83). Hillsdale, NJ: Lawrence Erlbaum.

The operant side of behavior therapy. *Journal of Behavior Therapy and Experimental Psychiatry, 19,* 171-179.

Signs and countersigns. *Behavioral and Brain Sciences, 11,* 466-467.

A statement on punishment. *APA Monitor,* June, 22.

War, peace, and behavior analysis: Some comments. *Behavior Analysis and Social Action, 6,* 57-58.

1989

The behavior of the listener. In S. C. Hayes (Ed.), *Rule-governed behavior: Cognition, contingencies, and instructional control* (pp. 85-96). New York: Plenum.

The behavior of organisms at fifty. In B. F. Skinner, *Recent issues in the analysis of behavior* (pp. 121-135). Columbus, OH: Merrill.

The initiating self. In B. F. Skinner, *Recent issues in the analysis of behavior* (pp. 27-33). Columbus, OH: Merrill.

The origins of cognitive thought. *American Psychologist, 44,* 13-18.

Recent issues in the analysis of behavior. Columbus, OH: Merrill.

The school of the future. In B. F. Skinner, *Recent issues in the analysis of behavior* (pp. 85-96). Columbus, OH: Merrill.

1990

Can psychology be a science of mind? *American Psychologist, 45,* 1206-1210.

The non-punitive society. *Japanese Journal of Behavior Analysis, 5,* 98-106.

Some issues concerning the control of human behavior. *TACD Journal, 18,* 79-102. (With C. R. Rogers [1])

To know the future. *Behavior Analyst, 1990,* 103-106. (Published concurrently in C. Fadiman [Ed.], *Living philosophies: The reflections of some eminent men and women of our time* (pp. 193-199). New York: Doubleday)

1992

Superstition in the pigeon. *American Psychologist,* 272-274. (Reprint of original 1948 article appearing in *Journal of Experimental Psychology, 38,* 168-172)

1993

A world of our own. *Behaviorology, 1,* 3-5.

Index

❖

About the Authors

❖

WILLIAM T. O'DONOHUE is Nicholas Cummings Professor of Organized Behavioral Health Care at the University of Nevada, Reno. He received a doctorate in clinical psychology from the State University of New York at Stony Brook and a master's degree in philosophy from Indiana University. He is editor and coeditor of a number of books, including *Handbook of Behaviorism, Learning and Behavior Therapy, Management and Administration Skills for the Mental Health Professional* (with Jane Fisher), *The Philosophy of Psychology* (with Richard Kitchener), *Theories of Behavior Therapy,* and *Handbook of Psychological Skills Training* (both with Leonard Krasner).

KYLE E. FERGUSON is a graduate student in psychology at the University of Nevada, Reno. He received a master's degree in behavior analysis from Southern Illinois University and a bachelor's degree from the University of Alberta. He has coauthored a book, *Working Through Anger* (with Lawrence Williams) and two manuals, *Working Through Anger: Therapist's Manual* (with John Guercio and Lawrence Williams) and *A Practitioner's Guide to Behavior Medicine* (with John Guercio).